Working Musicians

Labor and Creativity in Film and Television Production

TIMOTHY D. TAYLOR

T0244555

Duke University Press / Durham and London / 2023

© 2023 DUKE UNIVERSITY PRESS
All rights reserved
Printed in the United States of America on
acid-free paper ∞
Project Editor: Lisa Lawley
Designed by Matthew Tauch
Typeset in Alegreya and Trade Gothic by
Westchester Publishing Services

Library of Congress Cataloging-in-Publication Data
Names: Taylor, Timothy Dean, author.
Title: Working musicians : labor and creativity in film and televi-
sion production / Timothy D. Taylor.
Description: Durham : Duke University Press, 2023. | Includes
bibliographical references and index.
Identifiers: LCCN 2022043771 (print)
LCCN 2022043772 (ebook)
ISBN 9781478019879 (paperback)
ISBN 9781478017172 (hardcover)
ISBN 9781478024446 (ebook)
Subjects: LCSH: Motion picture music—Production and direction. |
Motion picture music—Economic aspects—United States. | Film
composers—Economic conditions. | Music—Labor productivity—
History. | Motion picture industry—Economic aspects—United
States. | Television Music—Production and direction. | BISAC:
MUSIC / Business Aspects | PERFORMING ARTS / Film / General
Classification: LCC ML2075 .T43 2023 (print) | LCC ML2075 (ebook) |
DDC 781.5/42—dc23/eng/20230216
LC record available at https://lccn.loc.gov/2022043771
LC ebook record available at https://lccn.loc.gov/2022043772

Cover art: Hand adjusting a mixing board. Photo by Corbis/
VCG. Courtesy of Getty Images.

For Sherry, as always,
and in memory of my mother,
Jane Lundeen Taylor

Everyone on a studio lot has two jobs: their own, and music.
—ALFRED NEWMAN (from Robert Kraft)

It's a director's medium. If a director tells you to use a kazoo
and a washboard to do a love scene, you have to do it, you
know; there's nothing you can do.
—RANDY NEWMAN, *The Frame*, KPCC, August 9, 2018

CONTENTS

First, thanks must go to everyone who gave up their time in order to share with me their insights into their work. They are all referenced in the text, but I would like to acknowledge them here, above the line: Bruce Broughton, Jeff Bunnell, Tom Calderaro, Kevin Crehan, Ben Decter, Anne-Kathrin Dern, Alan Elliott, Sharon Farber, Kurt Farquhar, Alex Hackford, Oren Hadar, Lee Holdridge, Matt Hutchinson, Carol Kaye, Penka Kouneva, Robert Kraft, David Krystal, Andrés Locsey, Deborah Lurie, Miriam Mayer, Phil McGowan, Alan Meyerson, Harvey Myman, Joey Newman, John Nordstrom, Cindy O'Connor, Kamran Pasha, Craig Pettigrew, Stu Phillips, Mike Post, Trent Reznor, Zach Robinson, Dan Savant, Lalo Schifrin, David Schwartz, Nan Schwartz, Ryan Shore, Michael Stern, Jan Stevens, Edward Trybek, Terry Wollman, and Christopher Wong.

Some interviewees helped me identify more: Alan Elliott, Joey Newman, Zach Robinson, Jan Stevens, and Christopher Wong. I must also thank some family, friends, colleagues, and students for their references to interviewees: Chuck Ortner, Eric Ortner, Denise Mann, and Dexter Story. All interviews were approved under UCLA's IRB#11–002035. Virtually all interviewees were able to review and edit their words printed here; those who didn't avail themselves of the opportunity, or who didn't want a quote attributed to them, have been anonymized.

Several UCLA students transcribed the interviews over the years of this project, and I am deeply grateful to them: Shelina Brown, Erin Estrada, Maya Gutierrez, and Will Matczynski.

Funding for this study was provided by grants from the UCLA Academic Senate and the dean's office in the UCLA Herb Alpert School of Music.

It is always a delightful and humbling experience to thank many friends and colleagues for their assistance, both formal and informal: Hannah Appel, Andrew Apter, Aomar Boum, Tara Browner, Jessica Cattelino, Norma Mendoza-Denton, Robin Derby, Hauke Dorsch, Sandro Duranti, Steve Feld, Bob Fink, Kimberly Fox, Shannon Garland, Jocelyne Guilbault, Akhil Gupta, Laurie Hart, Gail Kligman, Tamara Levitz, Purnima Mankekar, Louise Meintjes, Dan Neuman, Ana María Ochoa, Elinor Ochs,

Ron Radano, Helen Rees, Tim Rice, Tony Seeger, Shana Redmond, Shu-mei Shi, Markus Verne, and Deborah Wong. A couple of colleagues graciously read the manuscript and offered comments, so I am deeply grateful to them: Philippe Bourgois and Anna Morcom. I would also like to thank the anonymous reviewers of the manuscript.

I would like to thank everyone at Duke University Press who helped bring this book into the world: senior executive editor Ken Wissoker, whose enthusiasm and support I appreciate very much; Lisa Lawley, Alejandra Mejía, Joshua Tranen, and indexer Diana Witt.

It seems I have reached the age when cherished people are dying; several departed the earth while I was writing this book. My mother, Jane L. Taylor, died after a rich, long life. She was a force of nature if ever there was one. It was from her that I learned, among other things, intellectual ambition and curiosity, which, combined with my father Lee Taylor's desire to figure out how things work, have helped make me the scholar I am. I have also learned a lot about plants.

Others passed away in the course of writing this book. My cousin-in-law Richard Ortner became more than a cousin-in-law. We shared, among other things, a love of cooking and growing the vegetables with which to cook. And we shared an appreciation for piano music; Richard pointed me in the direction of great musicians whose work I didn't know and whose performances will always remind me of him.

My editor Doug Mitchell at the University of Chicago Press also died while I was writing this book. While shepherding a couple of my books, Doug became a friend, someone I could always rely on for sound advice, support of my work, ferocious intelligence, and infallible musical taste. He was an early supporter of this book.

Finally, and as always, I thank Sherry B. Ortner, my partner and toughest critic, who has provided endless support, encouragement, and insights over nearly thirty years of marriage.

WORKING MUSICIANS

This book is an ethnographic study of music workers involved in film, television, video games, and streaming programs—not stars, but people who work every day to bring us the music we hear every day. Theirs is largely a precarious existence in a cutthroat industry. What everyone talked about was getting work, doing the work, and getting paid, endeavoring to acquire or increase or improve the social and symbolic capital they possessed that they hoped would lead to more jobs, better social and symbolic capital, and more economic capital.

Music (and other) workers don't simply labor and make a living (or attempt to), however—they work in capitalist businesses. Studies of cultural organizations as capitalist industries began, famously, with Max Horkheimer and Theodor Adorno's consideration of "the culture industry" in the mid-twentieth century (2002). For them, the culture industry wasn't just a capitalist industry that produced commodities; these businesses warranted scrutiny because doing so helped shed light on a new stage of capitalism that these authors referred to as "late capitalism," a capitalism in which use-value had been eclipsed by exchange-value, in which cultural commodities had become commodities like any other: mass-produced, standardized, serving to reinforce the dominant culture rather than critique it.[1]

There is, however, only so much one can learn about capitalism by attending solely to commodities. Capitalism or any mode of production is more than some sort of giant spaceship hovering over earth determining everything, or, to employ to classic Marxian language, it is more than a base that determines a superstructure, creating commodities in its own image. Capitalism is a social form, it is people, social beings who are entangled in their own cultures, racial groups, ethnicities, class positionalities, sexual identities, generations—people who also possess different amounts of various forms of capital, pursuing different projects (Ortner 1996; Taylor 2007). If we are to understand capitalism, we need to study not only its products but its producers, its agents, its managers and workers, as many studies after Horkheimer and Adorno have done.

But Horkheimer and Adorno and many others after them do not rely on ethnographic studies of what people actually do, so the orientation here is more informed by Pierre Bourdieu. My ethnographic data reveal that workers in these fields are very much positioned by the amounts of the various forms of capital they possess. And since composers are at the beginning of the music supply chain in these fields, many other music workers who populate this study view their job as protecting the composer's time and helping them realize their vision. But it is composers who embody the most conflicted and contradictory aspects of these fields. They speak sometimes bluntly, sometimes bitterly, about how they have tried to negotiate creative decisions with those above them in the hierarchy. As one said, sometimes "you have to check your purely artistic self at the door."[2] Surrendering one's creative desires to those of people in charge is part of the job, as I will discuss. But what composers are most concerned with, as are all the music workers, is getting hired and getting paid.

The ethnographic data also show that while economic precarity may be an effect of neoliberal capitalism in many areas of today's economy, it is not new to the cultural businesses, though it is becoming a more chronic condition.[3] However, some workers, particularly composers, actively choose their precarity, which is their privilege, as it was for the nineteenth-century bohemians studied by Bourdieu (1993). The workers in the cultural businesses who populate this study are no different, frequently coming from middle-class backgrounds (especially those at the top of the heap, composers). Composers, more than the other workers in this study, have made a choice to knowingly pursue a precarious career and they possess the cultural capital, and often the economic capital from their parents, to engage in this pursuit. Because of the middle-class makeup of the majority of the music workers and the importance of social capital, the world of the production of music for film and television production is largely a closed system, which makes it difficult for everyone to break in, but especially women and ethnic minorities. Black, Indigenous, and people of color (BIPOC) music workers are perhaps even more underrepresented than those who work in other areas of film and television production (see

Darnell Hunt and Ana-Christina Ramón's annual *Hollywood Diversity Report 2021* for data on above-the-line workers).

By examining the production of cultural goods in today's cultural businesses (I prefer this term to "cultural industries" or "creative industries," as I detail later), we can learn not just about today's capitalism (generally called neoliberal), but how capitalism more broadly understood is intermingled in complex ways with other forms of the production of value, including earlier capitalist forms. Capitalism not only adapts to the present; it finds ways to appropriate the past—the idea of creativity, for example, has been with us since the nineteenth century—but capitalism freshens it up, finds new uses for it. Capitalism is enormously adaptive, infiltrative; it doesn't just devour or displace noncapitalist modes of the production of value; it can incorporate them or work alongside them without necessarily destroying or displacing them (see Meillassoux 1981; Taylor 2020; and Tsing 2015). It can coexist for years with other forms of the production of value, then some small trigger or change, such as a technological shift, can alter the relationship of the various modes of the production of value. Such sparks can come from anywhere; it is important to bear in mind John T. Caldwell's exhortation that the organization of production in the cultural businesses can take different forms and is dependent on legal, economic, union, historical, and institutional factors, not just internal organizational dynamics or interpersonal relationships (Caldwell et al. 2013, 398; see also the introduction to Mayer, Banks, and Caldwell 2009). *Working Musicians* shows how neoliberal capitalism has sped up production, increased income inequality between music workers and their bosses, and introduced greater demands for managerialization so that composers are as much entrepreneur-managers as musicians.

The production of music for a film, episode, or video game is a complicated process that becomes more complex as budgets go up and more workers are involved. All this coordinated labor consists of many different supply chains, which, taken together, result in an intellectual property commodity. These supply chains work only because of the exercise of power in these fields, which compels workers to discipline themselves, to do as they're told or get out. Capitalist management techniques have infiltrated these supply chains, sometimes quite recently. Harry Braverman's famous argument about labor processes under monopoly capitalism carries over into the realm of cultural production, where so-called creative workers must do what they are told by producers and directors, the division of labor such that *"the unity of conception and execution may be dissolved,"* the director (in film) and the showrunner (in television) possessing the right to conceive, leaving everyone else to execute: "the idea as conceived by *one* may be executed by *another*" (1998, 35; although, see Ryan 1992). Except in rare and well-known cases of established relationships of producers or directors with particular composers, most music workers—including composers—are viewed as interchangeable and disposable; there are countless stories in the business of a producer or director or someone else with authority deciding they don't like the score a composer delivered and ordering another one at the last minute, like replacing a defective part.[4] Most composers are providers of abstract labor in Marx's terms, people who are hired simply for their capacity to work, doing what they are told.

These sorts of issues are usually spoken of in terms of the well-known antipathy between "art and commerce," but it's clear that, at least for bigger-budget films and virtually all games and streaming programs, these are businesses whose bosses' main concern is profit.[5] This is the clash of two different conceptions of value, of course—aesthetic or artistic, and capitalist. In such conflicts, forms of economic value usually prevail, which is why Bourdieu's conception of social hierarchies places those with greater economic capital (and lesser cultural capital) in the group he calls the "dominant dominant," while those with more cultural capital (but less economic capital) constitute the group he calls the "dominated dominant" (1984). But supply chains in fields of cultural production do not "translate" noncapitalist into capitalist forms of value (or effect some other sort of "translation"; see Taylor n.d.a); artistic or aesthetic values are subordinated to bosses' conceptions of hoped-for capitalist value.

Threats to the acquisition of capitalist value must be controlled and tamped down at every turn. Bosses in all businesses need to monitor their employees to ensure that they are contributing to the bottom line, but in the cultural businesses, the mystique and allure of the idea of creativity is so powerful (both as a governing ideology and as a sales mechanism) that it continually threatens to escape the control of bosses. Only certain figures are authorized to have access to what I discuss in chapter 2 as the "creative function" (drawing on Michel Foucault's concept of the author function). In a way, these privileged figures—"above-the-line" workers, such as directors, producers, actors, and writers—constitute the managers on the creative side of these businesses, who enjoy (or suffer) various degrees of autonomy from the business side.

The cultural businesses aren't just capitalist, they are patriarchal, not simply because they are dominated by white men (at least on the creative side, my concern here); they are also patriarchal in how they conceptualize and manage creative freedom and the agency of workers (Hesmondhalgh [2019] also emphasizes the importance of creative autonomy). Since the nineteenth century, creativity has been constructed and continually reconstructed as a male faculty, though these constructions have been based on metaphors likening male creativity to nature, or even to women's ability to procreate. The creative personality has been insightfully characterized by Rozsika Parker and Griselda Pollock (2013) as a quality coded as feminine—strange, different, exotic. The supply chain that produces the use-value of music desired by bosses patriarchalizes creativity by removing the last vestige of whatever was thought to be feminine in the origins of creativity through various labor processes of purification and rationalization. And these businesses are also patriarchal in their reliance on unpaid women's labor—managing the household, caring for children—since men in these businesses frequently work very long hours, though this is starting to change. Finally, these businesses are patriarchal in their dependence on complex digital technologies, which are associated with male expertise and responsibilities.

I address these and other issues in *Working Musicians* by drawing on extensive conversations and interactions with various workers in the fields that produce music for film, television, streaming programs, and video games. This project takes inspiration from Studs Terkel's classic *Working* (1974) to participate in a recent trend of ethnographic studies of the cultural businesses and cultural production (e.g., Born 2005b; Caldwell 2008; Hesmondhalgh and Baker 2011; Mayer, Banks, and Caldwell 2009; Ortner 2013) more than it is a study of the music itself.[6]

This book is most closely indebted to American scholars who work in what has become known as "production studies" (Caldwell 2008; Mayer 2011; Ortner 2013) but is influenced also by British studies of the cultural industries, most associated with the voluminous work of David Hesmondhalgh (2019 especially). But *Working Musicians* differs from the British creative industries literature and political economy approaches in that it is much more *cultural* in the American anthropological sense of attempting to learn what is meaningful to the social actors one studies and how conceptions of meanings are organized and systematized among them. I identify and analyze these systems of meanings by using a Bourdieusian practice theory framework.

Working Musicians also departs somewhat from the political economy approaches to the cultural businesses (or media more generally), and while this book could, I suppose, be considered to be adopting a similar approach, it nonetheless is different from these works in its focus on supply chains and the creation or refinement of value. Capitalism (especially neoliberal capitalism) is no less a central focus in *Working Musicians* than it is in those writings on the political economy of media (e.g., Maxwell 2001; Wasko 2003; Wasko, Murdock, and Sousa 2011), but this book is just as inspired by recent writings on anthropological value theory, especially by Anna Tsing, which consider ways that value can be created or transformed through processes that are not strictly capitalist, even as they exist in capitalism.

Horkheimer and Adorno's argument, that the use-value of a cultural good had been eclipsed in favor of exchange-value under late capitalism, suffers from the rather Romantic idea that the autonomous conditions under which artists created their works afforded them unique positions from which to critique society. For them, the use-value of cultural commodities was the social critiques made audible and legible to consumers; the two authors set aside the sorts of use-value of cultural goods whose consumption marks their consumers' distinction (explored most thoroughly, of course, in Bourdieu 1984). But as we know from Marx, exchange-value can't be realized unless a commodity is believed by a potential purchaser to possess use-values that the potential purchaser desires: that is, one form of value doesn't exist without the other.

It is use-values that interest me in these pages (though not those of the consumer—this is not a reception study). The aim of *Working Musicians* is to examine the complex ways that music traverses a supply chain on a path from what is seen as raw material generated by a composer to its ultimate employment as use-value in a film, episode, or game. Composers produce use-values for their bosses (directors and producers) as part of a music supply chain that is embedded in a complex of supply chains, all of which are coordinated to result in a commodity with use-value for consumers.

There is a small corner of the literature on the cultural businesses that considers the production of cultural goods through assembly lines (e.g., Caves 2000) or value chains (Rainbird 2004; Keeble and Cavanagh 2008) or "value-creating ecologies" (Hearn, Roodhouse, and Blakey 2007); the point seems to be the elucidation of the structure of these businesses (Fitzgerald 2012 and 2015) through the construction of models and typologies. My focus here is different. I am not concerned with devising models or typologies of how economic value is accumulated or maximized along the way. My approach, unlike that of others in the cultural businesses literature, is (Anna) Tsingian—examining how supply chains create value not

just through the expenditure of labor, but through the refinement or purification of the products of people's labor; in other words, how use-value is
created—use-value that leads to butts in seats (or faces in front of screens),
which leads (producers and studios hope) to profits (Tsing 2009, 2013, 2015).
In the end, *Working Musicians*, following Horkheimer and Adorno, is less
about these cultural businesses themselves and more a study of how we
can better understand neoliberal capitalism through an examination of the
cultural businesses today.

This book builds on my previous books about capitalism (Taylor 2012,
2016) to a certain extent in that it is concerned with what we can learn about
today's capitalism by looking at those who toil in it as music and other sorts
of cultural production workers, but it is more focused in its interest in the
question of value, which has been a recent preoccupation (most writings are
collected in Taylor n.d.a). How is value created and refined as it traverses a
supply chain in a field of cultural production in neoliberal capitalism? It is
in addressing this question that Tsing's work has been inspirational, helping me understand that value is generated outside of capitalist structures
but can be "translated" into them, or ignored until a capitalist devises a
way to effect a translation, if that ever occurs. To the extent I am employing
Foucault on the question of the subject, I am also more concerned in this
book with the forms of self-discipline and self-exploitation (drawing on
Byung-Chul Han [2017]) that are evident from the ethnography, effects of
capitalism I did not explore in these earlier works.

The form of cultural production studied here isn't new because the cultural businesses have relied on different sorts of supply chains since they
became businesses. There was a major shift in this form of cultural production starting in the 1970s, however. An ensemble of changes that mark the
shift to neoliberalization is a good point of demarcation, though all of these
changes were slow. First: the rise of electronic technologies in the 1970s,
followed by digital technologies, a slow transformation that took over a decade. When I asked people who had entered the business in the 1970s or
1980s about the biggest shift they encountered, all said that it was the rise
of these technologies, which, among other things, have left composers even
less time to do their work and have unemployed many live musicians since
their playing can be generated by software. Older composers also discussed
another major change, the demise of their union, the Composers and Lyricists Guild of America, a dissolution that began with a lawsuit by the Guild
against the major studios in 1972, which ended up by destroying the union
in 1982. This book begins after these momentous changes, though I will

mention them when necessary for the historical narratives that follow (the earlier period I consider in another book, Taylor n.d.b).

Another major shift has occurred in episodic television. The old system of three major television networks has expanded greatly, first with cable starting in the 1980s and now with a growing number of streaming services, such as Netflix, Hulu, Amazon Prime Video, Apple TV+, and others. Bruce Broughton, one of the most successful composers I interviewed, with film credits such as *Silverado*, told me that there are now more composers working in film and television than at any time in the past, mainly because there is more product, not just film and television, but cable, streaming, and video games. Broughton said there is often not enough money to support so many composers because many budgets are so small. There are still big-budget films being made, he said, "but there are a lot of indie features getting by on a $36,000 budget and much, much less. By the time the picture is ready for music, the money for music has become pretty thin."[7]

As much as the technological production of music has changed and the demand for content has risen, the culture of these musicians has altered less. Reading sociologist Robert R. Faulkner's excellent studies of musicians in the Hollywood of earlier generations, *Hollywood Studio Musicians: Their Work and Careers in the Recording Industry* ([1971] 2013) and *Music on Demand: Composers and Careers in the Hollywood Film Industry* (1983), I am struck by two things: how much has changed and, also, how little. The culture of these businesses remains the same: it is heavily male dominated; personal relationships matter greatly in securing gigs and maintaining one's reputation; there is never enough time to get the work done (even less today than when Faulkner was writing); there are battles over creative autonomy; struggles with one's bosses (producers and directors); and more. *Working Musicians* offers more than an update, however, since it addresses themes and issues that weren't covered in Faulkner's books, particularly gender and diversity, and questions of money (the composers' union was in the process of disintegrating when Faulkner was writing, though he doesn't consider this). The theoretical frameworks I employ—from Marx, Bourdieu, Raymond Williams, and Tsing—are also completely different from Faulkner's, who, as a sociologist, was concerned with addressing questions of the sociology of work.

Working Musicians also differs from Faulkner's books in its focus on workaday composers and all those who labor with them: music editors, scoring mixers, recording engineers, performers, music copyists, composers' assistants. I am less focused on major composers, who labor in a comparatively rarefied world that is unlike the working environment of most musicians. A famous composer such as John Williams can enjoy all the studio recording time he wants, hire the best orchestrators and the best musicians, who will drop other gigs in order to record with him. Most of the composers I talked to are rarely able to hire any live musicians. Yet, as composer Christopher Wong told me, for every composer such as Williams making $1–2 million per film, there are "thousands of guys like me," working every day, making a living.[8] They are the subjects of this book (though I did speak with a few well-known composers—Bruce Broughton and Lalo Schifrin—to learn if their perspectives were much different), and some of the other music workers I interviewed are at the top of their fields, even if they are unknown to audiences.

Stephan Eicke's *The Struggle behind the Soundtrack* (2019), like Faulkner's books chronicling an earlier era, clearly demonstrate the differences between the big-budget composers he interviewed and the musicians considered in these pages. It is a different world in terms of the amount of money expended. Eicke mentions the film *King Kong* (2005), on which James Newton Howard employed eleven orchestrators; most of the musicians I interviewed can only dream of the opportunity of writing for an orchestra.[9] Still, even highly paid composers must do as they are told. Eicke also discusses the rise of a business devoted to acquiring the publishing rights of composers' films, which finance the recording of film scores in exchange for ownership of the master and publishing rights (41), but most of the composers I spoke to never brought this up, probably because soundtracks of their music are never released, or, if they are published, it's at the composer's expense.

Now let me offer a brief overview and critique of the creative or cultural businesses literature in order to situate *Working Musicians* in the existing literature. I am concerned in part with the conceptions of creative freedom in these writings, as there is probably nothing as desired, contested, and managed in the film, television, streaming, and video game businesses. While none of the workers I spoke to operates under the assumption that they possess total artistic autonomy, there are degrees of artistic freedom available to composers who are managed by their bosses—producers and directors. Composers, in turn, manage the creative freedom of all of those who work for them (the music editors, orchestrators, mixers, and more).

In recent decades, however, discourses of creativity have escaped the relatively enclosed realms of artistic production and the cultural businesses and have become commonplace in societies around the world; discourses of creativity are everywhere. In the 1990s, policymakers around the world began to realize that an important sector of their economies was derived from the creative or cultural sectors—among them, ABBA in Sweden, the Beatles and Shakespeare and Harry Potter (among other) "industries" in the UK—and governments began to pay more attention to this sector. In Europe, where universities must be more responsive to national governments than in the US, since education is funded by central governments, studies of the cultural businesses and their role in the economy have proliferated (see McRobbie 2016; Reckwitz 2017). Some years ago in Stockholm, I found myself in conversation with the former rector of the University of Stockholm, who, once he learned I was a music scholar, told me, with some bewilderment, that, post-ABBA, the Swedish economy made more money from exports of popular music than from exports of steel.

The growth of discourses about creativity has been diagnosed and analyzed in two main ways that are polar opposites: as a negative as well as an extremely positive symptom of neoliberal capitalism (the latter being what one might call creativity triumphalism). (There is also a more sober perspective somewhere in the middle represented by the authors listed above whose work I hope this book builds upon.) Let me tackle the two extreme perspectives, starting with the first.

Some argue that the influence of the state, specifically its validation of the creative economy, is a symptom of neoliberal capitalism, the proponents of which conceptualized people's skills and labor power as "human capital" (see Becker [1964] 1994 and Schultz 1959 and 1972), and, indeed, there are theorists who understand creativity mainly in this way—as a neoliberal ideology that encourages risk-taking while downplaying the potential for precarity (see Jones, Lorenzen, and Sapsed 2015; McRobbie 2016; Mould 2018; and Reckwitz 2017). Both Angela McRobbie and Andreas Reckwitz refer to creativity as a negative symptom of neoliberal capitalism, but to characterize it this way seems to me to go too far in emphasizing the "darkness" of creativity today (see Ortner 2016). McRobbie provides an example of a young woman who sacrificed a good deal to become a celebrity chef, which is meant to be a case of how neoliberalism encourages people to follow their dreams and risk precarity, but there's nothing particularly neoliberal about that; people have sacrificed in order to make careers in the arts (or risky fields, such as the restaurant business) for decades—centuries, even—most frequently facing precariousness, and many rural people, including in the Global North, also have faced precariousness for generations. Today's precarity—a term employed to label the growth of a "precariat" class group that lives without steady employment—is real but not simply because people have attempted to follow their dreams—rather, because the global economy is increasingly stacked against everyone but the already rich, so people whose occupations might have been safe now face the possibility that their secure jobs could disappear, that they could become part of a casualized labor force or workers in the gig economy.

There is also a strain of creativity triumphalism, a school of thought founded mainly by urban theorist Richard Florida, who champions creativity as the harbinger of a better future. In many ways, Florida's book *The Rise of the Creative Class* (2002) set the tone for the burgeoning cultural businesses literature in its unabashed and unquestioning embrace of whatever is thought to be "creative." He argues that the massive social changes in the few decades preceding his book are a result of "the rise of human creativity as the key factor in our economy and society. Both at work and in the spheres of our lives, we value creativity more highly than ever, and cultivate it more intensely" (4). I would say that this is less a "real" shift than a discursive one, however, and confined to higher class groups who enjoy the economic and cultural capital that permits them to think of themselves as creative.

Florida's ideas have found their way into more scholarly literature on the cultural businesses, which sometimes echoes his breathlessness about creativity uncritically. For example, the introduction to an edited volume entitled *Creative Industries* says, "The background to this book is the need to respond to the challenges posed in a world where creativity, innovation, and risk are general necessities for both economic and cultural enterprise, where knowledge and ideas drive both wealth creation and social modernization, and where globalization and new technologies are the stuff of everyday life and experience" (Hartley 2005, 1). There is much to unpack in an opening salvo such as this, perhaps especially the separation of "economic" and "cultural," the uncritical celebration of creativity and innovation, and the remarkable lack of historicity: as if capitalism hasn't always relied on people's creativity, innovation, and risk-taking; as if knowledge isn't always necessary; as if globalization and technologies are new and unprecedented. Volume editor john Hartley goes on to echo Florida's rapturous account of the "creative class," enshrining a quotation—"Creativity . . . is now the decisive source of advantage" (1, quoting Florida 2002, 5)—in a box and, later, considering the "new economy" that is based much more on the "creative industries" than in the past.

For Hartley and the other creativity triumphalists, everything is new or, rather, NEW. Another passage (this time the words are Hartley's) is placed in a box: "The idea of the CREATIVE INDUSTRIES seeks to describe the *conceptual and practical convergence* of the CREATIVE ARTS (individual talent) with Cultural Industries (mass scale), in the context of NEW MEDIA TECHNOLOGIES (ICTs) within a NEW KNOWLEDGE ECONOMY, for the use of newly INTERACTIVE CITIZEN-CONSUMERS" (5).

Such emphases on creativity in the scholarly literature represent, I think, an attempted corrective to the Horkheimer and Adorno position, that the production of "mass culture" was derivative and inherently uncreative. So, the Birmingham School's rejoinder to the Frankfurt School on cultural consumption has been mirrored in subsequent studies of the cultural businesses by simply swinging the pendulum back from an assumption that the cultural businesses and their products aren't creative to an assumption that they are (see also McRobbie 2016 for a lengthier treatment of this point).

One of the most frequent themes in the creative and cultural businesses literature concerns the question of creativity itself. Again and again, assumptions are made that workers in the cultural businesses perform creative work, whatever it is, and that what they do is qualitatively different from others who are not thought to be creative or who work outside the creative or cultural businesses. The cultural businesses are creative by definition, as opposed to businesses that manufacture more quotidian goods like automobiles or microwave ovens (see also Hesmondhalgh and Baker 2011).

Neoliberal capitalism has brought with it new usages and meanings of *creativity*. It has been a particularly spongy term since the nineteenth century but recently has become a potent component of discourses about the entrepreneurial self under neoliberal capitalism. Most of the people I spoke to didn't bring up the term since many don't often view their work as creative. Nonetheless, the discourses currently in circulation about creativity and the cultural businesses—discourses that circulate both in and out of these businesses—are symptomatic of a neoliberal emphasis on the concept.

One of the goals of this book is to problematize the Romantic conception of creativity in the existing literature, which often posits the sort of labor that cultural businesses workers are engaged in as "creative" (or "immaterial"; e.g., Hardt and Negri 2000 and 2004). Other authors offer characterizations and classifications of the products of the cultural businesses, arguing that they are special sorts of commodities, different from everyday commodities (e.g., Miège 1989). But it seems to me that creating taxonomies of businesses or labor or its products goes down the wrong path (see also Graeber 2006), provoking endless and fruitless debates about where something goes in a particular taxonomy or if it belongs there at all. The cultural businesses are in the business of producing commodities, and the workers' labor is productive in Marx's sense—they create surplus value for capitalists. The task should not be to taxonomize businesses, labor, or commodities—which only produces more and more complex taxonomies and endless quibbles over them—but to think more ethnographically about how workers and bosses themselves conceptualize capitalist businesses, why workers devise the sorts of classifications of labor that they do, why some of those forms of labor are valued over others, and how consumers value such commodities in the ways they do.

I address these and other issues in *Working Musicians*, for which the following is a brief overview. I view the cultural businesses as patriarchal and capitalist businesses and those that labor in them, workers. Composers are seen as laborers whose creativity is culturally coded as feminine and whose products are seen as a natural resource, acquired through accumulation by dispossession and managed by their bosses—directors and producers. The product of composers' work undergoes various labor processes and moves through the music supply chain—itself embedded in a complex of supply chains—refining it and defeminizing it for its ultimate use-value of supporting what is on screen. Music doesn't move in a supply chain from one disconnected group to the next, but within an interconnected group whose members view social and symbolic capital as paramount: who you know, with whom you have worked, and your credits are the only forms of capital that matter. Directors and producers hope that the use-values generated by music workers will be those desired by consumers of their commodities, producing exchange-value and ultimately surplus-value for the studio. Group production predates neoliberal capitalism, but this form of capitalism has shaped this mode of production in the past few decades in three important ways: it has introduced digital technologies—culturally associated with men—which have effectively increased the speed of production, put many live musicians out of work, and made possible the outsourcing of recording to cheaper locales, especially in Eastern Europe; ushered in new pay structures in the form of the package deal, which brought the rise of the composer-as-entrepreneur-manager; and busted the composers' union in the early 1980s. Finally, since creativity is thought to be a masculine quality and most of these music workers are men, there is a discussion of gender in these patriarchal businesses.

After this introduction, the next chapter begins to theorize how to understand cultural production not by individuals, but by groups, employing approaches from Raymond Williams on group production, Pierre Bourdieu on fields of cultural production, Marx on use-value and the collective laborer, and Anna Tsing on supply chains. The raw material of the composer is refined by orchestrators, music editors, and others as the composer's work slowly wends its way into the final version of the film, episode, or game. This chapter also discusses the forms of capital that circulate among workers in these fields; social and symbolic capital are paramount: no one cares about musicians' economic capital or cultural capital (including if, or where, they went to college). One's past performance and who one knows are all that matter.

Chapter 2 historicizes and problematizes the Romantic conception of creativity that exists in these fields and, in some studies of them, that is employed both to honor and justify the management of those who are thought to be creative, endowed with what I call, drawing on Foucault, the creative function. The creative work of composers is treated as both a natural resource—a raw material in need of refinement that is acquired through accumulation by dispossession—and a critical component of a complex cultural product that is made to order. This chapter also examines the Western construction of creativity as an exclusively male faculty, an idea promulgated since the nineteenth century that continues into the present even though creativity is a human faculty. We also hear from my interlocutors in this about how they view their own creative freedom and agency.

The next two chapters lay out just what it is these workers do, since very little is known outside of this world about these workers' labor (save for the very few composers who have gained enough fame to be interviewed in the mainstream media). Composers write the music requested of them by their bosses, raw material that, if it is notated music, then enters an analog supply chain, first going to an orchestrator and then to a music contractor who hires the requisite number of musicians for a recording session. The digital files generated by the composer (if no live musicians are involved) or recording engineer (if there is one) must also be refined, entering the digital portion of the music supply chain that includes mixers and music editors. Chapter 4, which considers workers below composers in the supply chain hierarchy, also addresses issues of the transformation of work as these businesses neoliberalize.

Chapter 5 addresses the challenges faced by workers in these fields, challenges generated by the diffuse nature of group production. This sort of production often results in confusion about who is in charge; despite long-established hierarchies and chains of authority, music workers frequently say it isn't always clear to whom they answer, and they are often given multiple sets of sometimes contradictory instructions. These workers must learn to cultivate a kind of ethnographic sensibility in order to discern whose directives to follow. For them, the questions are about who is in charge, which order to execute, and how, if at all, they will be allowed some creative autonomy. Another frequent complaint, and challenge, concerns communication with nonmusical bosses about music.

The next chapter focuses on the gendered nature of cultural production in these fields. Workers (mostly male) toil in an adrenalized culture in which everyone works too fast and too hard, frequently relying on wives and girlfriends to take care of quotidian matters. Most male composers work in what are essentially man caves, elaborate home studios full of computers and other electronic gear, though one person told me that having children necessitates moving the studio out of the home in order to be able to work without being disturbed.[10] I also interviewed a number of women musicians to learn about their experiences and found something of a generational divide between older women who maintained that they forged ahead and persevered and a younger generation whose attitudes were more militant in the era of #MeToo.

While, as I said earlier, there are many ways in which music production remains unchanged over the decades, the advent of neoliberal capitalism hasn't just shaped cultural production by joining with other forms of the production of value; in some ways, it has utterly changed how music is produced, and how musicians are paid, developments considered in chapter 7. One of the most significant shifts, commented on by everyone I spoke to, has been the rise of digital technologies. Many of my interlocutors articulated great ambivalence about these technologies for having obviated some mundane tasks performed by humans, offering workers new ways to exercise creative freedom. But virtually everyone commented that digital technologies have also resulted in people working longer and harder, as, unlike in the past, their bosses know that changes can now be demanded and effected at the last minute. These technologies can also be strategically employed to limit others' creative options downstream in the supply chain. This chapter also examines how musicians are paid, which was the most frequently recurring concern of everyone I spoke to. Composers are paid by the studio, but in recent decades they have frequently been given a kind of block grant, usually referred to as a "package deal," out of which they must pay not only themselves, but their music editors, any performing musicians, and others involved in the production of their music, a payment scheme that has essentially turned composers into managers. This has resulted in composers making less money, so some have also begun to take on many more jobs than they can possibly handle themselves, hiring teams of composers, thus introducing a sort of entrepreneurial-capitalist mode of musical production by groups.

The concluding chapter steps back to reflect on the usefulness of the eclectic theoretical approaches this book has taken, its combination of classic Marxian perspectives with more recent arguments about how value is created or refined through supply chains, as well as thematizing issues of patriarchy and gender. The use of these approaches shows how neoliberal capitalism can infiltrate, work alongside, and cooperate with other forms of the production of value, not necessarily subverting or overwhelming them, even as it becomes increasingly hegemonic. And there has been another, familiar, shift with the arrival of neoliberal capitalism: those at the very top earn more; everyone else, less.

Finally, a note on methodology. This study is based in Los Angeles and is not comparative, however tempting (though impracticable) such a study might be.[11] I am not only US-based, but Los Angeles-based, and this study concentrates on these cultural businesses as they exist here. I began interviewing in 2012, then needed to attend to other obligations before resuming interviews in various periods between 2017 and 2020. The gap in time from the first interviews to the second helped me gain a somewhat more diachronic perspective, as much had changed in the interim, in particular, the meteoric rise of streaming services and changes in attitudes toward gender and diversity, all of which I discuss in the following chapters. Since I allowed all my interviewees to review their quotes, it also proved to be interesting that several asked me to change masculine pronouns to inclusive pronouns; two men asked their wives to edit their quotes; one person asked his publicist to read over his.

It's also necessary to say what I mean by *ethnography*, for a study such as this faces constraints that obviate the possibility of a more *classical* sort of ethnography in which one lives with one's interlocutors and enjoys virtually unfettered access. But restricted access doesn't foreclose the possibility of an ethnographic study. Even though the pace of change of theoretical frameworks and orientations seems to be faster than ever, I still see no reason to abandon Clifford Geertz's insistence that ethnography should be about what is meaningful to the people we study, that meanings are shared by members of the same culture and are organized, to varying degrees, in systems (1973). There are those, of course, who might object to Geertz's understanding of the systematicity of culture, and it is certainly more difficult to discern as cultural forms traverse the globe ever more quickly. But people, even if remote from one another, still make meanings, and meanings are organized in various ways, shared, and contested. The main point is to attempt to discover what is meaningful to the people we study, not induce them to tell us what is meaningful to us or impose our synthetic frameworks on them.

I am thus thinking of the production of film and television broadly, as a kind of cultural system, and the production of music as part of this broader system. What interests me is what my interlocutors find to be meaningful in what they do. Learning that doesn't require the sort of access that ethnographers were once (more) freely given.

It is also important to emphasize that ethnography in the Geertzian sense is a perspective as much as it is a method; conducting fieldwork isn't necessarily conducting an ethnography. One can be an ethnographer while working in an archive. And one can be an ethnographer as a reader; the trade press, which I perused extensively, was useful both for information and for the insights it provided into the cultural system of film and television music workers.

I found my first interlocutors through personal connections: family, neighbors, friends, spouses of friends, all of whom were happy to make recommendations of additional people to talk to. I told my interviewees I could meet them whenever and wherever they liked, which often resulted in offering up some ethnographic data. I met some in their home studios, which gave me a glimpse of how they lived (though studios in Los Angeles often occupy former garages, so I didn't always get a look inside the house). I met some in cafés, from Starbucks to hipster establishments. I socialized with a couple of my subjects, mainly because they were neighbors. What I didn't do is accompany people in their work, since most of them labor alone most of the time. There are only a few instances when these workers might not be left alone: spotting sessions (when they meet with those in charge to hear what sort of music and where it should be placed, though these sessions had become as rare as face-to-face meetings even before the COVID-19 pandemic) and recording sessions, which aren't that common among the musicians studied here because most of them work with limited budgets that preclude the use of live musicians. Most of my meetings with these musicians were in person (until the pandemic). I followed up with some via email or telephone.

Some of my interlocutors said things that they later thought were too sensitive and didn't want attributed to them; one person didn't want their name used at all; and another never got back to me after several attempts to get them to edit or delete their quotes. So I have devised a way of referring to all of these individuals in an effort to respect their wishes. The person who didn't want their name used is given a pseudonym, and the date and place of our interview is in the notes; the same for the person I never heard back from. The remainder are referred to by their real names (with the place and date of the interview in the citation); for their sensitive quotes, they have their own pseudonyms, and the citations list only the year, not the precise date or place of the interview.

Most people I contacted were happy to meet with me, since this study is not about famous musicians whose time and access are extremely limited. This is not a study of film and television (and video game and streaming) composers, but a study of those who work on music. Its value is both empirical, shedding light on what little-known musicians do, and analytical, using ethnography to make an argument about how value through various musicians' creative and technical labor is created through a music supply chain.

But the main point in this discussion of ethnography is that ethnography and, indeed, the sort of work I try to do no matter the methodology centers on what is meaningful to my subjects. Geertz (1973, 15) wrote, "Nothing is more necessary to comprehending what anthropological interpretation is, and the degree to which it *is* interpretation, than an exact understanding of what it means—and what it does not mean—to say that our formulations of other peoples' symbol systems must be actor-oriented." *Working Musicians* begins and ends with this premise.

The result, I hope, is a study that usefully pulls together insights about supply chains and the creation or refinement of the value of cultural goods, which begin as the "natural" products of composers' creativity, which is culturally understood as male but with such culturally attributed "feminine" qualities as unpredictability and moodiness. Composers' work is refined and rationalized through the music supply chain at the same time it is defeminized in this deeply patriarchal system.

GROUP PRODUCTION, THE COLLECTIVE LABORER, SUPPLY CHAINS, AND FIELDS

A major Hollywood film can employ over three thousand people. Indie films hire far fewer workers, but nonetheless, in recent years, the average film employs nearly three hundred people per production (see Follows 2020). Network and streaming series' employee numbers vary widely, in the hundreds and up. The point, however, isn't numbers, but that these media require many—sometimes, very many—people working together. How?

There are various ways of attempting to understand how people working together can produce an artwork or commodity. A good deal has been written about the forms of organization in film and other cultural production (for a useful overview, see Dwyer 2015). Much of the scholarship rests on characterizations of the cultural businesses as industries. The use of the term by workers in these businesses to describe themselves has been widely accepted by scholars (including, foundationally, Max Horkheimer and Theodor Adorno), without always interrogating what using the term actually means, what it implies. Marx theorized the capitalism of his day— industrial capitalism; Horkheimer and Adorno believed their capitalism to be different, terming it "late capitalism," but they nonetheless assumed that the culture industry was an industry that mass-produced identical commodities. But just because the industries call themselves industries doesn't mean they're industries, and just because people work together doesn't mean that they constitute an industry. And, yes, these cultural businesses produce commodities (though it's complicated with respect to broadcast television, as we know from Dallas Smythe [1977] and later authors), but just because the cultural businesses produce commodities doesn't mean they're industries like the automobile or computer industries.

Considerations of the cultural businesses as industries range from those who view it as a kind of Fordist assembly line (most famously, Janet Staiger in Bordwell, Staiger, and Thompson 1985; see also Prasad 1998) to coordination and management of artisans or craftspeople (Banks 2010; Garnham 1979; Ryan 1992) to a flexible sort of creative production (Caldwell 2008).[1] Whatever their perspective, these arguments rely on assumptions or assertions of what constitutes standardization and where it lies—in labor processes and/or in the final product. Horkheimer and Adorno's argument is that the culture industry produces standardized products, but they fold two supposed standardizations into their indictment—the standardization resulting from mass reproduction and what they claim is the sameness of all the products of the culture industry ("its element is repetition," they write [2002, 108]).[2] Horkheimer and Adorno and some others thus conflate mass production with mass reproduction.

Every good produced by the cultural businesses is unique; no matter how derivative a film can strike us, no matter how much an episode seems to be like any other, it is nonetheless the product of vast amounts of concrete labor: a writer authoring a particular screenplay, a set designer devising a particular set, a composer writing a particular score, and on and on. Even the most derivative films or episodes will have different sets of workers who are subject to different amounts of supervision by managers whose behaviors will vary. That the result of all this labor is mass-reproduced should not obscure the fact that all this labor is unique, made for a single cultural good. The distinction to be made is that, in my view, the preponderance of concrete labor is what makes this form of production more artisanal than industrial. Factories attempt to render labor as abstract as possible, something that can be performed by anyone with the same result. The film and television businesses strive to transform their workers into providers of abstract labor as much as possible, but since every product is different, this is ultimately impossible.

Joseph Lampel and Jamal Shamsie (2003), along with Nathan Rosenberg (1963), argue that that filmmaking involves a specialization around "a homogenous collection of resources" (Rosenberg 1963, 220). Lampel and Shamsie view filmmaking not as a technical or creative endeavor, but as the coordination of an assorted group of resources into a finished product. Paul Dwyer (2015, 99) emphasizes that in terms of project production, the production of media challenges Taylorism because there are two competing sources of authority, those who manage the uncertainty of the market and those who possess creative autonomy to make something that is intended to attract mass audiences. This seems to be to be another way of characterizing the business and creative sides of these businesses.

The Lampel and Shamsie approach is promising because it is not a one-size-fits-all theory, and I also agree with Dwyer about the necessity for specificity, for looking at particular media and how they are produced. That is as far as I think we can come to a model, of which I am leery. What must be emphasized is the variability of production, even if the end result seems to be yet another derivative blockbuster. Media production affords many individuals—not just directors and producers—creative opportunities, or at least, choices, which are often made with the knowledge of who is in the supply chain; a director or producer can hire a composer with whom they have a particular relationship; a composer can write something for a particular musician; recording engineers and music editors can create stems (bundles of recorded tracks) in a certain way, and on and on. Nothing will necessarily be done the same way twice.

This preference for a more capacious view of media production comports with my use of the term *business* instead of *industry*; *business* is common enough in every usage but doesn't carry the baggage of *industry*. Businesses can be organized in a variety of ways and do not connote the assembly-line, standardized production of *industry*.

To understand these businesses from the perspectives of their laborers, I take a somewhat eclectic approach, bringing together Pierre Bourdieu on fields and Marx on the collective laborer with Raymond Williams on group production and Anna Tsing on supply chains and value. The aim is to show how people work together through the music supply chain to produce a use-value of an intellectual property commodity but do so in fairly constrained fields in which specific forms of capital circulate.

In a good deal of other work, I have employed Bourdieu's various writings on fields of cultural production, a set of approaches and perspectives that I have found to be exceptionally useful, enabling insights into the dynamics of such fields, identifying the forms of capital, and positions and position-takings that circulate in particular fields, the habitus of the participants and how it shapes their maneuvers in the fields in which they find themselves. But this project is different. However useful Bourdieu's work on fields of cultural production is, it nonetheless must be said that it is of little help in understanding what Raymond Williams (1981) called group production. Bourdieu's concept of the field is predicated on the idea that fields are composed of individuals—writers, painters, composers—who compete or form alliances as individuals; fields are battlefields in which people struggle against each other to decide what counts as capital in particular fields; they play against one another to define which positions (and position-takings) are legitimate and worthy and which aren't.[3]

In fields of group production, there is still competition, but it takes place among people who have the socially determined right to wield authority in a hierarchically organized business, to be the exclusive creative agents in these fields; everyone else is a worker doing what they are told. These workers are freelancers, they work for hire, and they all have bosses, including the composers, who make music to order. Composers aren't battling over aesthetic ideals, positions, as in a Bourdieusian field. They aren't writing or recording music they hope someone at a record label will like enough to offer them a contract. There may be competition, so in that sense this is a battlefield, but it's not direct. Composers and others don't necessarily know the people they are competing against when being considered for a job. And once they win it, they must do what they are told. If they want to try out a particular style in accord with, or to oppose, something they have heard in another film or program, they may only do so if they can convince their bosses that this approach serves their interests.

Creative authority lies with those workers considered to be "above the line": screenwriters, producers, directors, lead actors. They—especially directors in film and showrunners (executive producers) in television— parcel it out in various measure to below-the-line workers, a category that includes composers and all other music workers. But the latitude given can vary tremendously based on a particular director's or showrunner's management style and their relationship to the composer. The fame of the composer doesn't matter; unknown and well-known composers can be micromanaged or left alone. As famed composer Henry Mancini told *Variety* in 1989, "I've worked with some directors who couldn't care less, strange as that may seem. With others, they almost go with you to the laundromat" (Zimmerman 1989).

Much has been written about the art versus commerce dichotomy that faces workers in the cultural businesses, but this debate is often discussed in terms that are too broad; none of the workers I spoke to ever mentioned it. What matters most are the internal dynamics of the field of cultural production, which for them means simply trying to do a good job, getting along with others, in the hopes that good work and good behavior will lead to more, and perhaps better, jobs and thus higher and higher amounts of social, symbolic, and economic capital. And some of these workers—the composers at least—want to be able to exercise some degree of creative freedom as they conceptualize it. Their desires for this aren't waged against the money people in an art-versus-commerce battle, but against their bosses, directors, and producers who want to retain what they consider to be creative freedom for themselves as much as possible. It is they who are structurally permitted to engage in art-versus-commerce clashes.

Group Production and the Collective Laborer

Since films, episodes, and video games are not produced by a single individual, I need to spend some time examining what Raymond Williams called group production as well as Marx on the collective laborer. I also am concerned in this section with the movement of music through a supply chain composed of many workers.

For this system of supply chains to work, everyone involved must understand that there is a hierarchical arrangement of power. Everyone below the top level of producers and directors understands that they are subordinate to their authority. One of the most striking discourses I encountered in many interviews was the way musicians talked about how they surrendered themselves to the collective process. Even middle-class, educated (and white and male) musicians were willing to set aside their own creative impulses and desires to satisfy those above them. Musicians justified this in various ways. One was simply that they knew that's how the business works, that producers and directors are in charge, and that the price of admission to working in this field is the subordination of one's own artistic desires to those of bosses. Others described how they were motivated to be involved in the storytelling process. Still others spoke of the satisfaction they derived from collaborating with other people. And some musicians find the world of composing for film and television less demanding than the life of the performing and touring musician and are willing to accept some diminution of their creative freedom.

Raymond Williams on Group Production

In *Marxism and Literature* (1977), Raymond Williams—whose work is still essential in my view—critiqued Marx for his characterization of cultural producers vis-à-vis workers, in which Marx writes that the manufacturer of the piano is engaged in productive labor while the player of the piano is not. "The extraordinary inadequacy of this distinction to advanced capitalism," Williams writes, "in which the production of music (and not just its instruments) is an important branch of capitalist production, may be only an occasion for updating" (93).

Williams provided more than an update in his next monograph, simply called *Culture* (1981), which considers cultural production. Among other things, Williams theorizes group production, a mode of cultural production that has a long history (113–14) and is useful for my purposes. Williams says it became more complex under capitalism, which introduced a class system and then the division of labor; different fields of cultural production took on divisions of labor that can be markedly different from one another, even when the fields might appear to be similar. It is clear in this and many studies, for example, that film is a director's medium, while television is a producer's medium (the television showrunner is usually credited as an executive producer), though this situation hasn't always been the case for both media.[4]

Williams notes that there were processes of specialization and the division of labor in group production before the rise of capitalism; division of labor in cultural production such as classical Greek drama was generally organized around professional duties: participants were actors, musicians, dancers, writers, though we don't know much about the internal coordination of these people; no abstract or general authority or hierarchy was established. Even in Elizabethan theater, he says, it's not clear how internal dynamics of authority worked. No figure such as the modern producer or director existed until the late nineteenth century, though this figure was preceded by the actor-manager.

A stable and regular division of labor that was based not just on professional duties, but on the emergence of what Williams (1981, 114) calls "conscious management" marked a new phase in cultural production. For Williams, this trend is clearest in the theater, where the producer, director, or manager appeared when production was totally coordinated, encompassing not just acting, but new staging techniques, including new approaches to design and lighting. Williams says that earlier such figures were still actors or writers, but by the mid-twentieth century, the director emerged as the primary force in cultural production (114).

New technologies of reproduction, especially in film and television, continued to shape the roles and hierarchies of authority. More regular and formal divisions of labor, based in part on greater professionalism, were also accompanied by what Williams calls more "conscious management." New laborers joined the productive forces—sound engineers, camera operators, and more. And people who built, maintained, and repaired equipment, sets, and others became necessary. Here, Williams (1981, 114) says, class lines were drawn in these fields of production. I think Williams is quite right about the class divisions, but at the same time, his argument strikes me as technologically deterministic in part. The growth of bureaucracies and the rise of the "organization man" after World War II serve as cultural context, as the cultural businesses became more bureaucratized. And the rise of auteur theory in film, which had a result of vesting creative authority definitively in the hands of the director, surely had organizational and hierarchical effects.

The Collective Laborer and Supply Chains

Marx's writings on the collective laborer and Anna Tsing's on supply chains provide the next parts of the theoretical apparatus of this chapter. Marx is useful here because he offers a way to understand production by groups in which some people are more closely involved with the production of a commodity while others play more remote roles but nonetheless contribute to the value of the commodity. Production can occur through supply chains, through which, as we know from Tsing, value is created or enhanced.

With the rise of industrial production and the increasing division of labor, Marx theorized in *Capital* the advent of the collective worker or collective laborer. Before capitalism, labor processes that required multiple tasks were carried out by people known to each other, but under capitalism's greater division of labor, tasks are separated out and assigned to different people; mental and physical labor become separate and hostile to one another. The direct product of an individual's labor becomes a social product, "the joint product of a collective laborer, i.e., a combination of workers, each of whom stands at a different distance from the actual manipulation of the object of labour" (Marx 1990, 643). The concept of the collective laborer necessitated broadening Marx's theorization of productive labor and his ideas about the "bearer" of that labor, since not every worker contributes to surplus value as clearly as others: "In order to work productively, it is no longer necessary for the individual himself to put his head to the object; it is sufficient for him to be an organ of the collective laborer, and to perform any one of its subordinate functions" (643–44). Marx is saying here that the production of surplus-value—the fruits of the productive labor of workers owned by capitalists—is produced collectively, not by an individual worker. Individual workers produce use-values by themselves only rarely with the spread of the division of labor, but the collective of workers does produce a use-value and therefore is engaged in productive labor.

In *Theories of Surplus Value* (n.d.), Marx wrote that in the capitalist mode of production, where many laborers work together to produce the same commodity, "the direct relation which their labour bears to the object produced naturally varies greatly" (398). Unskilled workers perform substantially different tasks from those of skilled workers, and, of course, there are overseers as well, one step away from those who work with raw material; and some workers, such as engineers, work mainly with their brains. But, Marx says, all these laborers work together to produce the result, a commodity, having exchanged their labor for capital and reproducing the capitalists' money as capital, as "value-producing surplus-value" (398–99).

Marx writes that it is characteristic of the capitalist mode of production to separate different kinds of labor from each other, including mental and manual labor. "This however," he writes,

> does not prevent the material product from being the *common product of* these persons, or their common product embodied in material wealth; any more than on the other hand it prevents or in any way alters the relation of each one of these persons to capital being that of wage-labourer and in this pre-eminent sense being that of a *productive labourer*. All these persons are not only *directly* engaged in the production of material wealth, but they exchange their labour *directly* for money as capital, and consequently directly reproduce, in addition to their wages, a surplus-value for the capitalist. Their labour consists of paid labour plus unpaid surplus-labour. (399)

Much has been written about these overseers and managers, and I don't need to rehearse those discussions here.[5] The main point is that there are workers who perform the labor that actually produces the commodity, but there are plenty of workers whose efforts do not directly lead to the production of that commodity and who are nonetheless necessary.

Such divisions of labor lead to social divisions in workplaces, which, in the cultural businesses, concern who is allowed to be creative and who is managerial, but sometimes these distinctions can become blurred because they are roughly coequal: A studio executive or producer can tell a director what to do, can wield financial power over their project, but a producer or director can sometimes resist and prevail in such battles.

The products of today's cultural businesses—perhaps, especially, scores for film, television, and games—are no less commodities than industrial commodities theorized by Marx, the only difference being that the raw materials that commence the production process are found not in nature, but in people's imaginations. But once artistic works became produced as commodities by groups, much of what Marx theorized—about the division of labor, forms of value, and more—becomes analytically pertinent.

Labor processes consist of people who contribute directly to the creation of value and those who don't. Supply chains employ both sorts of laborers. Here, I consider supply chains as theorized by Anna Tsing (2009, 2013, 2015), ways that leading firms create capitalist value. In contrast to Tsing's case—matsutake mushrooms gathered in Oregon that end up as expensive gifts in Japan after multiple processes of sorting, which, as she puts it, takes the gift out of these goods and "translates" them into commodities—I am considering a case of cultural production. Composers create a kind of raw material (either a written score or set of audio files) under the supervision of directors or producers that must be refined as it traverses the supply chain: if notated, the composer's score must be orchestrated, proofread, then recorded, and audio files must themselves be refined—mixed both to improve the sound and to balance everything and finally edited to fit to the picture and mixed with the other audio of the film. In practice there are two different supply chains, though they later converge: One supply chain I am calling analog, and it begins with a composer's written score, which is then orchestrated, performed, and recorded; the other I am calling digital, and it begins with an audio recording. The supply chains converge once there is an audio recording, which is then mixed, edited, and incorporated into the film, episode, or game.

What interests me here (as elsewhere; e.g., Taylor n.d.a) concerns the many ways that supply chains are used to create value. In the case of scores for films, episodes, and games, I would not say that capitalist value is being created as the composer's work moves through these supply chains. Rather, through labor processes of refinement, value is translated from an artisanal product into a component of a product ready to be a mass-reproduced commodity. The value that is created is use-value—music that, in the view of the producer and director bosses, supports and sometimes adds to what is on the screen. I am subscribing to the idea that cultural goods are (or were) produced not in a sort of assembly line, but in the sort of supply chain theorized by Tsing.

Musical scores or digital files moving through a supply chain that includes productive workers and managers do not terminate in a commodity with an exchange-value (a commercial soundtrack is never a guarantee). Music scores are made and refined through a supply chain for their use-values. Concrete labor is expended to produce use-values, but this concrete labor is part of the collective labor of all workers involved. The extreme focus on the use-value of film and television scores precipitated a strike by the Composers and Lyricists Guild in the early 1970s (for a capsule history, see Burlingame 2010; for longer histories, see Eicke 2019 and Taylor n.d.b).[6] It was the desire of composers to realize exchange-value from their work that led to a strike against producers in the 1970s—composers wanted to own the publishing rights to the music they had written so that they could benefit from making recordings of their music and exploiting it in other ways. But they lost; their union was busted in 1982, and the use-values of music envisaged by composers' bosses prevailed.

Creating value through supply chains is a group effort. A composer who is home alone writing symphonies doesn't enter their music into a supply chain; their work is complete when they believe it to be (though, of course, it is sometimes performed and recorded). Even in the realm of popular music, which involves more workers, the supply chain is smaller (and creative authority can be shared between musicians and producers). Scoring mixer Oren Hadar made an interesting comparison of music for television and music in a recording. Composers make a rudimentary mix for whoever has to approve the "cue," what an individual chunk of music is called. Hadar said that when he receives a cue for a television program or film, it has already been approved by the producer and director, who have been listening to a mix the composer has given them; this music has already gone through much of the supply chain, its use-value partly refined. So, when Hadar receives a cue, it has already been subjected to a good deal of back-and-forth, already listened to by many people. Hadar therefore cannot deviate very much from that mix. If he does, when everyone congregates on the dub stage (where the final mix of all audio is made), a producer could object, saying they hear something they haven't heard before. But with records, Hadar said, there is a much shorter supply chain, fewer people involved. A record is less in need of refining, and Hadar said that with records he has much more latitude to make aesthetic decisions. He told me, "The mix engineer really has a lot of freedom to reimagine and can just take out things—'this is extraneous; we don't need this guitar part.'" Hadar told me what he said is a famous story (among mixers, at least) of a song by the band INXS: "Originally it was this huge production with all these different elements, and the mix engineer just went mute, mute, mute, mute— 'Here's your song.'" This isn't the sort of intervention a mixer can make in a film or television score.[7]

Theorizing Group Production/Collective Laborers in Fields of Cultural Production

Even though I am concerned with group production, groups are made of individuals who possess different volumes and sorts of capital. That is, members of groups exist in fields as theorized by Bourdieu. In this section, I examine film, episode, and video game music as fields of cultural production. In bringing together Raymond Williams on group production and Marx on the collective laborer, I am not proposing a different sort of field of cultural production but endeavoring to show how field theory can be used to understand group production, at least in the cases here. My first point is that Bourdieu considered fields in terms of those who occupied the apices, individual creators such as a poet in a restricted field (he never really considered large-scale fields; see Hesmondhalgh 2006; Taylor 2017). In both types of fields, there are plenty of workers below those at the pinnacle. All but the most hermetically isolated artists in restricted fields of cultural production (Bourdieu's term that contrasts large-scale fields) require others to produce, reproduce, distribute, advertise their work, and still more, as Howard Becker (1982) famously argued.

First, let me quickly revisit some of Bourdieu's main points in his field theory before proceeding, so I can begin to argue for what I think is still necessary in understanding group production, what isn't, and what needs to be altered. What is commonly misunderstood, or not fully understood, in many of the writings I have seen that employ Bourdieu is that his thinking lays out a comprehensive and systematic conception of how the social world is constituted and continually reconstituted. It's not possible to discuss one aspect of it without considering the others. Individuals possess a "disposition," a habitus, defined by the volumes of various forms of capital they possess: cultural, social, and symbolic, in a particular social space or field, which is reliably reproduced though the symbolic power of dominant groups. In the social space of French society considered in *Distinction* (1984), these forms capital are of the broadest sort, present (or absent) across the entire social space. Bourdieu came to view fields as fairly rare, so his idea of social space eventually superseded it in large part. Loïc Wacquant argues that, for Bourdieu, social spaces are "multidimensional distributions of socially efficient properties (capitals) stipulating a set of patterned positions from which one can intelligibly predict strategies" (Wacquant and Akçaoğlu 2017, 62; see also Wacquant 2013). Fields are less common, are predicated on a fairly high degree of social differentiation, and possess "institutionalized boundaries," "barriers to entry," and require "specialists in the elaboration of a distinctive source of authority and sociodicy" (Wacquant and Akçaoğlu 2017, 63; see also Bourdieu 1989)—all of which we have in the fields to be considered here.

Bourdieu's concept of field thus remains helpful in understanding particular social formations, such as a field of cultural production of literature in nineteenth-century France. These fields interface with the broadest social space, but at the same time, they host their own forms of capital that are defended and contested by members of those fields. An example familiar to musicians would be of the contemporary composer who must decide whether or not to write tonal music and who mobilizes forms of capital in this field—such as placing oneself in a lineage of famous tonal composers—to defend this position-taking, which itself is defended against those who write atonal music. They, in turn, attack their antagonists. Any consideration of a field of cultural production (or other field or social space) must sort out the forms of capital, the positions and position-takings, that are in that field as well as the habitus of the participants. Bourdieu's writings on fields of cultural production remain valuable in focusing analysis on the forms of capital that circulate in the fields of cultural production examined here, which I will take up in the next section.

Forms of Capital

Some forms of capital in the fields considered here take on outsize importance in fields of group production, and some matter less than in other fields of cultural production. Cultural capital doesn't count for much. The point isn't just that some forms of capital take on greater importance, but that others are suppressed from above through the constraints on the field. In group production, forms of capital don't flow freely but are constricted by those at the top of the supply chain hierarchy. The symbolic capital derived from having attended a particular educational institution matters less, if at all—noone cares if a composer or music editor or other music worker attended the Yale School of Music or never finished high school. Attendance at a prestigious school only matters to the extent that it introduces people to others with high amounts of social capital.[8] As everyone told me, succeeding in this business is about knowing people and knowing how to get along with people.

In these fields, economic capital is generated by social and symbolic capital. People are willing to work for nothing or for very little—sometimes losing money—in order to accrue the symbolic capital of credits, slowly attempting to gain not just more credits, but employment on higher and higher quality work that pays better and garners more attention, critical and popular (see Faulkner 1983)—more and more symbolic capital.

SOCIAL CAPITAL

Let me dig into Bourdieu on social capital, since it is a concept that is employed less often than cultural or economic capital, at least in my corner of the softer social sciences.[9] Bourdieu (1986, 51) defines social capital as "the aggregate of the actual or potential resources which are linked to possession of a durable network of more or less institutionalized relationships of mutual acquaintance and recognition—or in other words, to membership in a group—which provides each of its members with the backing of the collectivity-owned capital, a 'credential' which entitles them to credit, in the various senses of the word." These relationships, Bourdieu says, can materialize simply through practical exchanges but can also be socially instituted through the use of a family name, class, tribe, school, political party, and more. Such relationships are enacted, maintained, and reinforced through exchanges both material and symbolic (51).

Networks of relationships, according to Bourdieu, are the products of "investment strategies, individual or collective, conscious or unconsciously aimed at establishing or reproducing social relationships that are directly usable in the short or long term, i.e., at transforming contingent relations, such as those of neighborhood, the workplace, or even kinship, into relationships that are at once necessary and elective, implying durable obligations subjectively felt (feelings of gratitude, respect, friendship, etc.) or institutionally guaranteed (rights)" (1986, 52). These strategies are accomplished through "the alchemy of *consecration*," constant acts of exchange that transform "the things exchanged into signs of recognition," which also have the effect of reaffirming the limits of the group (52).

Bourdieu writes of social capital in terms of volume as he does with other forms of capital. The amount of social capital an individual possesses is determined by the size of their network but also by the volume of the other forms of capital possessed by the members of the network. People tend to exchange with others in their network based on similar amounts of the forms of capital they possess as individuals, and this can have what Bourdieu calls a "multiplier effect" on the volume of social capital possessed by an individual. Social capital in the fields of production of film, television, and games leads to everything else: You get gigs based on who you know. You get more gigs based on what you have done in the past, which is based on who you know. There is a meritocracy in operation, but you have to pay your dues and build and exploit your social capital in order to get in the game.

Bourdieu also mentions people who have inherited a "great name" from which they derive a high amount of social capital (and therefore also possess high cultural and economic capital) and who, he says, "are able to transform all circumstantial relationships into lasting connections. They are sought after for their social capital and, because they are well known, are worthy of being known ('I know him well'); they do not need to 'make the acquaintance' of all their 'acquaintances'; they are known to more people than they know, and their work of sociability, when it is exerted, is highly productive" (1986, 52–53). Bourdieu's discussion of social capital mentions family names, and employing them has been useful for a number of people I interviewed. Probably the most notable is a composer who changed his surname from his father's to his mother's because she was a member of a well-known family of film music composers.

Everyone I have spoken to—including those with "great names"—say that getting hired depends on who you know as well as some luck and a good deal of perseverance. Who you know could be relatives or friends in the business, but networking with people you don't know is also crucial.

Composer Ben Decter, who studied history, not music, as an undergraduate at Harvard, said that, even after a couple of decades in the business, most of the jobs he gets come from college classmates, including the program for which he won an Emmy Award, "Operation Homecoming:

Writing the Wartime Experience" (2007). This was a documentary for the PBS series *America at a Crossroads*, which was produced by a college classmate about fifteen years after graduation.[10] Composer Zach Robinson told me that when he was finishing his undergraduate studies at Northwestern, he realized that people in his cohort would be developing their own programs and movies, people who had asked him to write music for their short film. "I have more and more people coming to me saying, 'Hey we have this animated show for you,' or, 'we have this show for you.'"[11]

Whether one's network is based on college connections or something else, having connections is all that matters. Composer Joey Newman told me that the business is all about finding personal connections, that getting gigs is founded on relationships, not agents or anything else. "It's all based," he said, "on the cycle of how a composer meets producers/directors somewhere and they vibed. Or, maybe, they heard the composer's music somewhere else from an editor's temp score [preexisting placeholder music], live show—especially if they're a performing artist—or music supervisor and they like how the composer's music is working in their film. The one reason why we work or not is that somebody out there champions us, likes our personality, and wants to work with us over somebody else for a long time."[12]

No matter what one's location in a field, whether a composer (the beginning of the music supply chain) or the lowliest, entry-level composer's assistant (a position through which many composers get into the field), one's network and connections are virtually all that matter. Recording engineer Alan Meyerson said that getting jobs is through "word of mouth; it's your reputation; it's the quality of your work, and then people like the experience of working with you."[13] And recording engineer and scoring mixer Michael Stern told me that getting a job is based on relationships. He said there are networking events in his field where he can meet young, up-and-coming composers and get jobs that way, but most of the jobs he gets are through word of mouth. "As big a town as Los Angeles is, you can say that in the industry it's a small town because everybody starts to get a sense of who is doing what."[14]

Sometimes, a musician can make a connection through happenstance. A young composer's assistant (who didn't want to be named; I'll just call her Flora) also spoke of the smallness of Los Angeles, how it is possible to meet people socially or by chance and find work that way. Sometimes, it can be quite accidental. Flora told me, "I was in a movie theater two weeks ago and stuck around to watch the credits, and this guy just turned around and started talking to me about the film, and then I found out he was a filmmaker, so we're going to start potentially working on a documentary that he's got coming up."[15] Flora also told me that, in Los Angeles, it's not that difficult to run into people, especially people in the same age group.

Some people have found work through ethnic networks. Music editor Andrés Locsey told me that he met Mark Robertson, an LA-based orchestra contractor (the person who hires musicians for recording sessions), and approached him to ask advice about getting work and was told he should speak to Gustavo Borner, an Argentinian studio owner. Locsey thinks Robertson had heard his accent and asked if he was from Latin America, which Locsey, who is Mexican, confirmed. When Locsey graduated from the Berklee College of Music, he moved to Los Angeles and sent many emails to potential employers, but none answered. Then he remembered Robertson's recommendation. "I emailed Gustavo in Spanish, and within five minutes he answered. Right away from the start, I noticed how important it was to know someone or have a referral. So, I started interning at Igloo [Music], his studio."[16]

Orchestrator Tom Calderaro noted the extent to which people who make recommendations need to safeguard their credibility. Getting jobs depends not just on who you know, but who knows you, who is willing to recommend you. "You have to have people want to recommend you," he told me. "You have to have them feel that not only do they think that your work is at that level, but that it's good for them to provide somebody with a good recommendation. You have to have an advocate out there, somebody who just can't wait to say your name." Calderaro said that because everything is done so quickly, there's not a lot of time to search for workers, so those who are known to be good and reliable will be called.[17]

In southern California there are countless networks, overlapping, expanding, contracting. People with little or no cultural capital beyond a high school education nonetheless have networks. One could begin their career with access to a network that might not include many members with large amounts of social and symbolic capital, but since social capital can be accumulated, they can try to work their way up. A foot in the door is all one needs to start building the network, acquiring social and symbolic capital. People in these fields are constantly attempting to improve their networks, make acquaintances, and get hired by more and more famous people. If a musician starts in a modest network, they attempt, and hope, to parlay that into more famous contacts and more prestigious gigs.

Miriam Mayer, who grew up in Los Angeles, told me of her high school music teacher, who also worked as a freelance studio musician and composer and who encouraged her to develop her skills as a performer and composer. That was her opening.[18] Orchestrator Tom Calderaro got his start in community colleges in Orange County, California, close enough to Los Angeles that there were many major musicians who taught or passed through, musicians with networks that young and aspiring musicians could attempt to benefit from. Through this network, Calderaro met Alf Clausen, most famous as the longtime composer for *The Simpsons*, who gave him private lessons and who helped him get his first job, which launched his career. "That was pretty much it," he told me. "A typical story of boot-strapping up a career: You meet people, you take jobs, you work everywhere you can with everyone you can, trying to develop relationships and contacts and get better at what you do."[19]

Making connections and entering into a network through one's teachers in southern California is one strategy, but not all composers and other musicians hail from southern California. Unless one has a connection, the only way to generate social capital when one enters the field from outside is through brute-force perseverance. Composer Jan Stevens, best known for writing the music for the network comedy *Scrubs* (NBC and ABC, 2001–10, 187 episodes), told me that in order to make a living, he had to be incredibly persistent. Like all composers, he built up more credits and more pieces for his reel (a collection of samples of one's work). He developed a system: Every time he went to a party or event where he might meet someone involved in film and television, he'd get their name and number. "I compiled many numbers," he told me. He also "kept a call sheet, contacting everyone on the list every three months" and keeping a record of what they had discussed. And still, he persisted. "The guy who gave me my break in television called me 'the icon of perseverance.'"[20]

Not only is a network necessary to find work, but it is also necessary to get work done. Composers rely on other workers in order to do their jobs (as I will detail in chapter 3): music editors, scoring mixers, and, sometimes, orchestrators and composers to write additional music. Composer Zach Robinson, who worked with leading film composer Christophe Beck, learned more than just technical aspects of the composer's job from Beck. He said that since composers work with everyone involved in music production, they have to develop relationships with music contractors, musicians, engineers, mixers, and more.[21]

People are not only constantly attempting to improve and expand their networks; they are also busy maintaining the networks they have. In his consideration of social capital, Bourdieu (1986) also argues that the "unceasing reproduction of social capital depends on an unceasing effort of sociability, a continuous series of exchanges in which recognition is endlessly affirmed and reaffirmed." This work requires time and effort, which, Bourdieu says, means that it draws, directly or indirectly, on economic capital. It's necessary to obtain and maintain knowledge of genealogies and other connections and employ them with skill. One must not only acquire this competence, but learn a disposition to acquire and maintain it, both integral parts of this form of capital (52).

As a quick and preliminary example of this point, I have an acquaintance with whom I occasionally socialize who is highly placed in the entertainment business, and it has been striking over the years to see him in action in social situations. If someone famous in his field makes an appearance (fairly common with this friend), he thinks of someone famous whom he knows and whom he is sure the present famous person knows and approaches that person by name-dropping their mutual connection. Before introducing me to a friend, he often provides a genealogy by naming famous relatives of the person, or how that person improved their social capital. He once spoke admiringly of someone in his field who, as a teenager, had moved of his own volition to a wealthy Los Angeles neighborhood and lived in a friend's basement, all so he could build a network of the children of famous people at the local high school. Before he was forty, he was a major executive in his entertainment field.

The sociability that is a part of Bourdieu's conception of social capital also takes the form of knowing how to get along, about disciplining one's conduct. Many people told me that playing well with others is an important skill to possess in this business. While most of these workers do what they do alone, there are moments when groups of them come together, such as spotting sessions, recording sessions, and other such situations, when knowing how to get along matters greatly. Composers seem to be able to get away with more mercurial behavior—at least to those below them in the supply chain and depending on their level of fame—in large part because they are at the origin of the music supply chain. But everyone else learns how to comport themselves, including composers when they are dealing with their superiors.

In understanding how the exercise of power works in these fields, Foucault's writings illuminate. Foucault (1982, 208) says his work is about how people are turned into subjects—through the disciplines that call themselves sciences, through what he called "dividing practices" (labeling the sane and the mad, for example)—and how people turn themselves into subjects through, for example, the "domain of sexuality," that is, "how men have learned to recognize themselves as subjects of 'sexuality.'" "Creativity" is another such endeavor, except that these musicians' freedom to act on their own creative desires is highly managed and sometimes denied altogether. I will discuss this at greater length in the next chapter.

Foucault's conception of power is what one could call cultural; it is not direct confrontation, operating through cultural and social channels and understandings: "What defines a relationship of power is that it is a mode of action which does not act directly and immediately on others. Instead, it acts upon their actions: an action upon an action, on existing actions or on those which may arise in the present or the future" (1982, 220). The exercise of power, Foucault writes, "is a total structure of actions brought to bear upon possible actions; it incites, it induces, it seduces, it makes easier or more difficult; in the extreme it constrains or forbids absolutely; it is nevertheless always a way of acting upon an acting subject or acting subjects by virtue of their acting or being capable of action. A set of actions upon other actions" (220).

Foucault employs the term *conduct*, for that word "is at the same time to 'lead' others (according to mechanisms of coercion which are, to varying degrees, strict) and a way of behaving within a more or less open field of possibilities. The exercise of power consists in guiding the possibility of conduct and putting in order the possible outcome. Basically power is less a confrontation between two adversaries or the linking of one to the other than a question of government" (1982, 220–21). Foucault employs the term *government* in the broadest sense, not just for political entities but also to designate "the way in which the conduct of individuals or of groups might be directed," as the term was used in the past (221). "To govern, in this sense, is to structure the possible field of action of others" (221). Wendy Brown's exegesis and extension of Foucault's concept of political rationality shows how today's neoliberal capitalism works: "A political rationality, such as neoliberalism, is that by which we are ubiquitously governed even as there will also be discourses crosscutting and incompletely contoured or controlled by such a rationality" (2015, 117). I'll discuss later in this chapter the sorts of conduct adopted by musicians at all levels because of this political rationality.

Foucault's thinking here is not far from Bourdieu's on the habitus. Bourdieu (1990, 55) argued that people with a particular habitus are faced with a certain array of "thoughts, perceptions and actions" but only these. Foucault's emphasis is not on the classic practice theory problem of structure and agency (however circumscribed the latter concept may be in Bourdieu's thinking); Foucault is famously less interested in individual agency and more concerned with the disciplining effects of societies and cultures on conceptions of selfhood.

Foucault's notion of power is based on the idea that social actors are free subjects: "Power is exercised only over free subjects, and only insofar as they are free. By this we mean individual or collective subjects who are faced with a field of possibilities in which several ways of behaving, several reactions and diverse comportments may be realized" (1982, 221). In these pages, *freedom* refers to musicians' abilities to exercise their own creative freedom.

Foucault develops his conception of the exercise of power to make it more explicitly cultural, writing that the exercise of power should be seen as "a way in which certain actions may structure the field of other possible actions. What therefore would be proper to a relationship of power is that it be a mode of action upon actions. That is to say, power relations are rooted deep in the social nexus, not reconstituted 'above' society as a supplementary structure whose radical effacement one could perhaps dream of. In any case, to live in society is to live in such a way that action upon other actions is possible—and in fact ongoing" (1982, 222)

Foucault's analysis of power relations is based on several areas of analysis: the "system of differentiations" that permits one to act on the actions of others, which could be legal, traditional, economic, or something else; the types of objectives pursued by those who act on others' actions, such as privileges; the means of bringing power relations into being, such as armed threats or surveillance; forms of institutionalization, such as hierarchical structures; and the degrees of rationalization (1982, 223). This last locus of analysis is the most relevant here, of course; the film and television businesses are hierarchically organized, though, as I will discuss, there are many ways in which hierarchies can be disrupted.

Successful composers learn that they need to know how to conduct themselves in order to make themselves the sorts of people others want to work with; this is perhaps an effect of the overcrowded field of film and television music production (Coleman 1993). As one film and television music agency owner said in the 1990s, personality was at least as important as talent for composers, a situation that hasn't changed (Coleman 1993). Producer J. J. Abrams, when asked why he chose Michael Giacchino to score his hit series *Alias* on ABC (2001–6), put the issue of personality at the forefront: "Part of it was I wanted to find someone who felt like one of us, who would have the same instincts and sense of humor I have; Michael and I have that in common" (Krogh 2002b). Edward Trybek, who works mainly as an orchestrator, told me of being asked to orchestrate some cues as a kind of audition and, having passed, was then asked to be interviewed by a composer with whom he now regularly works. He told me, "I think that interview was to make sure you're not a psychopath."[22] How-to books by business insiders discuss personality; Richard Bellis's *The Emerging Film Composer: An Introduction to the People, Problems and Psychology of the Film Music Business* (2006) places "psychology" in the subtitle of the book and urges readers to acquire a "team personality" (8). It also includes a tip on how to dress: "If I note that the director always dresses kind of sharp, I try to wear similar attire. If he or she is always in jeans and a T-shirt, so am I. It's a way of easing concerns about whether we think alike—whether I'll *get* what they have to say or not" (9).

Many people told me of the strategies of how they learned to modulate their behavior; an easygoing personality and agreeability are traits composers and others learn to cultivate. While this seems to be a necessity for everyone, there was perhaps even greater pressure on women and BIPOC workers to get along. "If you cannot be entertaining, then nobody is going to be interested in working with you," said the pioneering woman composer Shirley Walker. Continuing: "I am totally shy, but I have had to become a performer because it's a necessity for my career. You have to have tremendous confidence in yourself and your talent, and you have to be able to verbalize that" (Coleman 1993). When composer Kurt Farquhar, one of the few people of color I was able to interview, elected to concentrate on television rather than some other corner of the music business, he decided how act in order to succeed. He told me he was going to take charge of everything under his control: He would be on time or early for everything and be the most prepared person anyone had ever seen. And, he said, "I was going to be a person who's agreeable, who you could spend time working with because that matters. I'm in a dark, windowless room for sixteen hours a day. You get concerned about who you want to be with, and so I thought, 'I'm going to be a decent person to be around.'" Farquhar cultivated an agreeable attitude and has tried hard to be "the guy who, when they're nervous about telling their staff, 'Oh my God, we're going to have to work until two in the morning; everybody buckle up,' I'm not the person that they have to get nervous about saying that to. My attitude is, 'Cool; when do we start?'"[23] Orchestrator Edward Trybek said he's gregarious, but nonetheless, he has learned how to be adaptable to whatever work environment he finds himself in or personality he finds himself next to. Trybek said he doesn't actually try to change his personality, "but the way you might approach a topic or the way you might speak might shift a little bit. I talk fast; I'm very caffeinated, and I go, go, go, go! And I have to keep telling myself, 'Slow down and chill out.'" But then other people might want him to work fast, so he needs to ask himself, "Do I need to be high energy, or do I need to slow down?"[24] Social capital is thus not just the cultivation and improvement of networks; it also requires maintenance through constant acts of renewal and sociality.

Composers in particular need to exert a calming and reassuring sense of authority, since they enter the film, television, and game production process so late. Agent Richard Kraft said that when a screenwriter starts a job, it's all about their hopes for what the film can be. But then, in the production process, the stars fight, someone leaves the set, the love scene doesn't work, and on and on, so the composer has to be able to appear and say, "'I'm going to put my magic salve on everything, and it's all going to be OK.'" Kraft says that some people can inspire that confidence, and others can't (Coleman 1993).

Not having an easygoing personality is a detriment. Music editor Craig Pettigrew told me that while a lot of people can technically do the job, "There are a lot of people who producers just don't want to work with. They walk into the room, and they bring the room down because their attitude is blah. You spend a lot of time in a dark room with somebody, you want them to be fun to work with." Being easy to get along with extends outside of the studio, Pettigrew said. Workers don't only need to know their business, they must possess, or cultivate, a personality that makes them interesting to be with because, Pettigrew said, "you don't talk about the job when you go to lunch; you get to know somebody on a project, and it's nice to have somebody on the stage you want to get to know a little better, so despite all the technical stuff that goes on, being an interesting human being is a huge part of the job." Pettigrew mentioned a person who is talented and smart but never stops talking and, because of that, rubs people the wrong way.[25] It is probably also relevant that this person is a woman in a man's world.

Bourdieu (1989, 17) writes that symbolic capital is "the form that the various species of capital assume when they are perceived and recognized as legitimate," elaborating that "symbolic capital is nothing other than economic or cultural capital when it is known and recognized, when it is known through the categories of perception that it imposes" (21). All other forms of capital can be read by social actors as symbolic capital—honor, prestige—which means that symbolic capital can be considered to be a kind of overarching form of capital. And symbolic capital can accumulate to give symbolic power to its holders. Symbolic power, according to Wacquant, is, with the idea of social space, the other foundational concept in Bourdieu's theoretical universe, and he defines it as "the capacity for consequential categorization, the ability to make the world, to preserve or change it, by fashioning and diffusing symbolic frames, collective instruments of cognitive construction of reality" (Wacquant and Akçaoğlu 2017, 57; see also Wacquant 2013).

Bourdieu's own words on symbolic power make it clear that he is essentially following the Marxian conception of the ownership of the means of intellectual production as Marx and Engels famously theorized in *The German Ideology* (1970). Bourdieu (1989, 23) writes that "to change the world, one has to change the ways of world-making, that is, the vision of the world and the practical operations by which groups are produced and reproduced." The form par excellence of symbolic power "is the power to make groups," which rests, he says, on two conditions, the first of which is the most relevant here: Symbolic power needs to be based on the possession of symbolic capital. Bourdieu writes that "the power to impose upon other minds a vision, old or new, of social divisions depends on the social authority acquired in previous struggles. Symbolic capital is a credit; it is the power granted to those who have obtained sufficient recognition to be in a position to impose recognition" (23). This is how the status quo in these and other fields of cultural production is maintained: Symbolic power is wielded by those above the line to define the field as they do, though this is a constant battle.

Symbolic capital, like social capital, also assumes greater importance in the fields studied here than in Bourdieu's thinking, since the other forms of capital theorized by Bourdieu matter less in terms of people's positioning in this field. Symbolic capital manifests in two registers. The first is a simple numerical calculation of credits: how many credits (film, television, other media) a particular composer has amassed (see also Faulkner 1983). It is "volume" that is relevant here. But at a certain point, it's less about numbers, and other metrics kick in, such as awards and the prestige derived from working with famous directors and producers.

Symbolic capital can also be lost or subtracted. Stephan Eicke (2019) and Robert Faulkner (1983) write about how being associated with a flop causes harm to one's reputation, but no one I talked to discussed this. It may be that these fields have become so volatile, with television series running perhaps only thirteen episodes before they're canceled, films declared to be unsuccessful after the opening weekend unless they make tens of millions of dollars, that everything moves too fast for a flop to be registered or for its taint to stick. Also, however, since most of the musicians represented in these pages aren't famous, they aren't working on films with large budgets that can be huge flops financially.

Amassing symbolic capital through the acquisition of credits means that most composers, at least early in their careers, work gratis or for very little remuneration on student films and very low-budget independent films in order to build up their list. Composer Ryan Shore, for example, got his professional start working for his uncle, the well-known film music composer Howard Shore. Ryan first scored about a dozen short films at New York University. Any funds that were available he put directly into the actual recording of the score, and he didn't take anything for himself. He also composed music for the theater, conducted, orchestrated, arranged, copied music, managed people's electronic gear, and more. From these experiences, he landed his first feature film job. "And then, one feature film would lead to another, and that began the feature writing. Building your career can be a very progressive endeavor."[26] Family, friends, networking, perseverance, luck, and more are the keys to success, but they don't guarantee it. Finding success has become more difficult, even in this era when more and more content is being produced.

One of the obstacles to acquiring symbolic capital is that one needs it in order to accrue more. Jan Stevens and other composers expressed frustration that it was impossible to land a network series unless you had worked on one before. "It's a catch-22," he said. "You cannot get a job doing network television unless, somehow, you've done network television. Well, how do you do get to do network television unless someone's going to let you?" Stevens said that this is a trust issue for producers and networks. "Producers are not going to give you a chance to compose for a series unless you are a proven commodity. It doesn't even come down to how good your music is.

The producer will ask, 'Has this person done anything? Can I trust them to deliver the music on time?'"[27] Composer Matt Hutchinson said much the same thing. Producers can see that a composer has credits for having written or cowritten additional music, but, he said, they're thinking, "You don't have your own show yet, so we can't really hire you. We need you to show us that before we'd be confident in hiring you."[28]

For music workers other than composers, symbolic capital also matters; it can accrue to musicians who work with famous directors and producers. Miriam Mayer told me that if a contractor calls a musician to play on a John Williams score or a score by another famous composer, they'll ditch whatever gig they may have already booked in order to play on the more prestigious one (though perhaps not, she said, if you get to be the principal in your section, which confers a different sort of symbolic capital).[29] Recording engineer and scoring mixer Phil McGowan also said it's important to try to get a few big-name clients. Workers such as himself who are largely unknown make their reputations by working for famous people. He told me, "I've always felt that mixers and orchestrators, people like myself, we honestly do ride on the coattails of our clients," and he gave a couple of examples of recording engineers who are famous because they work for well-known composers. Famous clients "get you to where you are," he said, but acknowledged that you have to do a good job. McGowan noted that in interviews, engineers always list their clients. McGowan said he has learned over the years that "it really is important to establish one or two really big, huge clients to move into the upper echelon of whatever you do. A lot of people will hire engineers and orchestrators—people like that— just because of who they worked with." McGowan said that the people who hire recording engineers or mixers don't necessarily hear what makes them distinctive; it's people's reputations that matter. Sometimes, he said, composers can hear what an engineer or mixer has done, but many times, composers "hire people because they're thinking, 'Oh, well, you've mixed all of the scores for XYZ huge composers. You must know what you're doing.' That's really where a reputation comes from, our clients' work and what we've done with our clients."[30] Symbolic capital is everything.

Most of the time. Occasionally, success can work against you, at least for composers. Composer Matt Hutchinson told me that either a composer can't get a big job because they haven't worked on one before, or, the fact that they're successful marks them as someone established, not cutting-edge or up-and-coming.[31] Some composers are also concerned that their success in a particular television genre can lead to being typecast as someone who can only do what they have been doing. Joey Newman spoke of this with some frustration; he was the composer for the single-camera comedy *The Middle* on ABC for its entire run (2009–18). Even though Newman started his career scoring hour-long dramas, he said some people now view him as a "network guy" or "network comedy guy" or "sitcom guy," but he is capable of writing for a variety of programs in many musical genres. Newman said that, as much as he enjoys writing for half-hour shows, he began to realize that he needed to try to work on different types of projects, to push himself in order not to be pigeonholed. "I want to continue to progress," he said, and if he doesn't, "I will become that stereotype." This was the biggest challenge he faced at the time of our first interview; even though he's not that old (in his early forties at the time of that interview), he said that "younger filmmakers are coming up in the industry, and their relationship to picture and music can differ widely from my other clients who are my age or older."[32]

Matt Hutchinson also discussed that attitude, where a composer's very success might mark them as established and not cutting-edge, fearing that producers and directors might think "'he's really great, but he's an Emmy award–winning composer. Don't you think we want some fresh blood on this?'" Hutchinson said, with some surprise, "They lose the gig because they're an award-winning established composer, and they want somebody who's new." This situation is something of a double bind for composers, who need to demonstrate success before being afforded more prestigious opportunities, but winning those may work against them. Hutchinson said this happens frequently in the world of streaming, where people who may have never scored a show before—recording artists, bands— are being hired.[33]

Such concerns demonstrate that symbolic capital in these fields has been destabilized in recent years. When I was researching my book about the history of music in advertising (Taylor 2012), it was clear that there was a definite hierarchy of prestige, with film at the top, television in the middle, and commercials at the bottom (Faulkner [1983] found the same thing in an earlier era). Composers in the middle or bottom tiers were constantly hoping for a better gig, to move from commercials to a television series or from television to film. But the rise of streaming has upset the rigidity of this hierarchy. Streaming programs are seen by many as edgier (by which is meant more anti-mainstream, anti-network; see Ortner 2013), cooler, and some composers worry that their symbolic capital that used to count for something—writing music for a network show—now counts less than writing music for a streaming series.

Part of this concerns what is considered to be symbolic capital. While it once was a matter of a hierarchy of prestige with film at the top, now it is more likely to be about what is thought to be hipper, cooler, edgier. Because streaming programs are thought to be edgier than network television programs, more symbolic capital is to be found there in today's cultural businesses (see Taylor 2016). Composer Deborah Lurie told me that in her twenty years in the business, one of the most dramatic changes has been the re-ordering of prestigious gigs; film was once almost exclusively at the top, but now there are high-quality shows that are streaming or being aired on certain cable television networks, so it's hard to know where the best content might come from. "In general," she said, "it's not just Fox and Sony and whatever now; it's also Amazon and Hulu and Apple. The bosses are different, the game is different, the budget concepts are different."[34]

Few people I consulted brought up the question of age, though ageism is clearly a factor that shapes people's conceptions of these workers' symbolic capital. Virtually everyone I met who was born in the 1950s or earlier culti-vated a youthful look, dressed in hip and cool clothes, and tried to maintain a youthful-looking body. Writer/producer Kamran Pasha told me that in his world, one ages out at around forty-five. He said that young people who are very good, but inexperienced, are nonetheless winning jobs as showrun-ners, and he told me about working on a show with a twenty-nine-year-old showrunner who was uncomfortable operating with anyone older and, so, made sure to be surrounded by inexperienced people in their twenties. Pasha said that studios are pandering to young people, thinking that young workers will be able to speak to their generation and therefore attract such viewers, but Pasha thinks their lack of experience can result in films or pro-grams that aren't very well done.[35]

Young people are thought to be more organically hip and cooler than older people, and hip and cool people are thought to be more likely to produce edgy work that goes against mainstream norms in film and television production. Conceptions of hipness and coolness suffuse these fields, which are well known to be ageist and not just with respect to those appearing on cam-era. Cultural businesses workers wear their symbolic capital as cultural businesses workers. The "creative" lifestyle has a long history, going back to the bohemians and flâneurs of the nineteenth century, the Beats of the twentieth (see Taylor n.d.a). Living in Los Angeles, it is relatively easy to spot workers who present as workers in a creative business. They try to look youthful, act hip and cool, and are early adopters of the coolest technologies, whether the latest iPhones or Teslas. I was struck, some years ago, by meeting a pair of directors after the release of their first feature film, which had become rather hot; previously, they had directed advertisements and music videos. But their hexis, dress, and overall presentational style were of hip, young, "creative" people. They were creative people, no matter their work, possessors—and displayers—of what Bourdieu (1995, 111) called the "new social personality" of the artist updated for today's hip and cool cultural producers (see Taylor n.d.a).

Studio pianist Bob Alberti, who worked on many television programs in the 1960s and 1970s, writes in his autobiography that all Hollywood studio musicians—including, I would say, composers, except for a very few—suffer the same five-stage career trajectory:

1 "Who's Bob Alberti"?
2 "Get me Bob Alberti!"
3 "Get me someone who sounds like Bob Alberti!"
4 "Get me a young Bob Alberti!"
5 "Who's Bob Alberti?" (Alberti 2003, 116)

The business is youth-centric and ageist from top to bottom, not just in the realm of composers (or actors). All workers, except for a very few at the absolute top of the hierarchy, must appear to be young and cool and hip, capable of producing edgy work.

Conclusions

In the following chapters I will continue to flesh out what group production in these particular fields of cultural production looks like, what workers in these fields do, and how they manage their positions in these fields with this constricted set of capital at play. For now I will simply say that, while the necessity for high volumes of social and symbolic capital hasn't changed in these fields, today's musicians find themselves in a period of considerable flux due to the landscape of production shifting under their feet, with an increasing number of content providers entering the scene and with more on the horizon; the uncertainty surrounding the future of cable television as well as struggles to define what sort of platform (streaming, cable, network) is hipper and cooler than another and, thus, which provides more symbolic capital; and changes in payments and royalties (to be discussed at length in chapter 7). Some would argue that the future of high-quality television is at stake given the current struggles in the Writer's Guild of America, which could result in television becoming a director's medium rather than the writer's medium it currently is.[36] The point for now is that such struggles—over what counts as symbolic capital as well as attempts to improve and widen one's social capital through their network—never stop.

CREATIVITY

While all the people discussed in these pages would probably describe themselves as creative workers, or people who are employed in a creative industry, the freedom to be creative is denied to most; this is the province of the above-the-line workers. Composers are the only workers in these pages who have a hope of realizing some of their own creative decisions, but that depends greatly on for whom they are working. Some producers and directors like to afford their composers a good deal of leeway; others do not. The protection of the power of creativity is such that all the other below-the-line workers sometimes think of their work as creative, sometimes not, but they have mostly bought into the conception of creativity that circulates discursively in these fields, which is evident from how they dealt with my questions about the creative nature of their work. They don't view themselves as uncreative, just not the sort of worker who is permitted to exercise all of their creative choices. But if the Romantic discourse of creativity, which still dominates in these fields, involves at least in part the freedom to make choices and decisions based on one's judgment—derived from education, experience, and taste—then the below-the-line workers are creative as well, if not authorized as creative.

What we now call *creativity* was constructed out of various discourses, as Christine Battersby (1989), Camilla Nelson (2010), and Keith Negus and Michael Pickering (2004), show, but today it exists in a distilled form that permits those who are thought to possess it authority in these fields. In other words, I view creativity as a discourse in the Foucauldian sense, and those associated with it are the only workers in these fields who can act as authors or, to continue my debt to Foucault (1984), exercise an author function. So, let's use the term *creative function* (with *creative* as a noun, as the term is used in the cultural businesses; some workers are creatives, others not). Foucault's argument is well known and doesn't need much rehearsal, but I will emphasize a few points. Foucault notes that not all discourses contain author functions and characterizes those that do as "objects of appropriation," which he describes in binary terms—sacred and profane, licit and illicit, and more. This appropriation becomes caught up in systems of ownership of texts (109–10). Foucault also points out that the author function doesn't simply apply to an individual, but "is, rather, the result of a complex operation which constructs a certain rational being that we call 'author'" (110). Even if an individual is anointed with the term *author*, Foucault says that "these aspects of an individual which we designate as making him an author are only a projection, in more or less psychologizing terms, of the operations that we force texts to undergo, the connections that we make, the traits that we establish as pertinent, the continuities that we recognize, or the exclusions that we practice" (110).

In the fields of cultural production considered here, there have been myriad operations constructing people with certain roles as authors while marginalizing everyone else. A film has become something that can be authored by virtue of the creativity thought to be possessed by people working in these roles. Think of the language film and television workers use to describe what they do. A director, producer, or an actor can say they "made" a film, though no one else can (not even the writer).

My argument in this chapter is to finish laying out the theoretical orientations of this book by showing that the creative function is accessible to a select few in film and television production, which gives them power that is expressed through discourses of creativity, while most others are denied access to the creative function.[1] It's not a simple matter of above-the-line workers concerning themselves with the creative vision of the enterprise and below-the-line workers tending to minor or technical details; above-the-line workers, especially producers and directors, are empowered to opine on anything, from the script to the minutest musical detail. There is no clear line between what people think is a creative decision and what isn't, something more technical, less consequential: It is the prerogative of who can deploy the creative function to weigh in on whatever they want, honoring their intuition. Being a worker who has the structural authority because of their status as a creative person shows that the entire system is really about power. Creative authority is simply authority. This is perhaps the main reason that discourses of creativity are historically rooted in the patriarchy and why they are still so protected.

Creativity is as much discursively produced within these fields of cultural production as without. Workers might refer to themselves as laboring in the creative industries or being creative workers, but in practice, it is a matter of these workers possessing various degrees of agency—depending on how much they are afforded by bosses and by their position in the supply chain—to do what they want in their work, whether it is writing music or mixing a recording. As music moves through the supply chain, the work performed tends to become increasingly technical, more difficult to characterize as creative, yet there are nonetheless options to be considered, decisions and choices to be made, and these are informed by the training and judgment of particular workers.

This chapter begins by examining the historical constructions of creativity as a natural male faculty, except that the markers of creativity are culturally coded as feminine. Creativity as a natural resource is available to be captured and molded by directors and producers through accumulation by dispossession. In group production, creativity becomes linked to, or even a form of, agency; that is, if one is faced with structural constraints, then the freedom to act on one's creative impulses or desires becomes a question of agency. This chapter also considers how film and television workers conceptualize their labor. What emerges is not a simple story (or series of them) of people going to work and being creative all day. Rather, these are mostly stories of how people struggle to find ways to exercise agency in what they do. Still others, particularly composers of film music, view their real creative freedom as lying mainly outside of what they do in the cultural businesses, instead concentrating on what they call "concert music," music written not for the screen, but the concert hall.

Creativities

Here, let me pick up from the discussion of creativity in the introduction. Having spent a good deal of time in my youth performing various sorts of agricultural labor, the idea that somehow this sort of labor and other forms of manual labor are uncreative compared to the labor of people who work in the cultural businesses doesn't make much sense. People are creative: To be human is to possess creative capacities, and those capacities are exercised all the time and in myriad ways, in the kitchen, in the field, in the studio. So why is it that certain kinds of labor are thought of as creative and others not?

With a term as complex and culturally loaded as *creativity*, any attempt to answer this question will necessarily by complex and multifaceted. The word, as we know from Raymond Williams, is one of the most fetishized and romanticized in the English language as well as a highly gendered concept. Williams's history of the word in English is fascinating. The term originally was used in the sense of "make" or "produce" and was mainly employed in connection with God's creation of the world and its creatures, a term that shares the same root. According to Williams, in the era when *create* was used this way, creatures were seen as creations unable to create themselves. This meaning was in use until at least the sixteenth century. What changed was the advent of the Renaissance, a period when men believed themselves to be able to create. Williams (1983, 82) quotes Torquato Tasso: "There are two creators . . . God and the poet." The shift to this meaning, writes Williams, is the specific source of the modern usage of the term, even though there was some ambivalence about it as the earlier meaning was retained by some. But by the seventeenth century, *create* and *creation* in the current meanings were in widespread use, and by the eighteenth century, the term became associated with art. *Creative* as a term was coined in that century. Writes Williams, "The decisive development was the conscious and then conventional association of *creative* with *art* and thought" (83). By the early nineteenth century, he writes, the term was "conscious and powerful"; by the middle of the century, conventional (83). *Creativity* as a term describing a faculty, which emerged in the eighteenth century, became a general word for that faculty in the twentieth century. Williams writes that the term's "emphasis on human capacity . . . has become steadily more important" (83). Williams discusses what he characterizes as the difficulty of the term, which, he says, emphasizes originality and innovation, which then requires making distinctions between innovation and novelty. But *creative* has become so commonplace that the term can be used to describe almost anything, such as the production of advertising, as I have discussed at length elsewhere (Taylor 2012; see also Nelson 2010).

My goal here is different, to assert that analysis should consider how workers themselves view their own labor and how particular cultures of production have awarded access to the creative function to some workers but not others. I want to think historically and ethnographically about how and why certain sorts of labor are classified the way they are and why some sorts are valued more than others (see also Mayer 2011; Hesmondhalgh and Baker 2011). Specifically for this study, I am concerned with how people conceptualize their own labor and creativity, how workers are managed by those above them in the power structure of their business or field of cultural production, how they push back against that management when they do, how they manage those below them, and more.

Naturalization of Creativity

My concern here is with creativity not just as a discourse, but as a discourse that has deep roots in Western history, the product of multiple histories. Beyond what I have already discussed, I am particularly interested in a couple of aspects of the Western discourses of creativity, those that naturalize it, and, later, those that naturalize it as an exclusively male faculty. This is in service of an argument that businesses treat creativity as a natural resource that can be accumulated by dispossession.

I am guided on this issue, as I have been for some years, by Christine Battersby, whose classic *Gender and Genius* (1989) remains essential (see also Negus and Pickering 2004). Battersby writes of the shift to the concept of genius, which, by the end of the eighteenth century, became closely related to the idea of creativity. "It was creativity," she writes, "not reason or talent, that made man resemble a god . . . made him more than an animal and made some men superhuman and superior to others" (2, ellipsis in original). The idea of artistic creativity in Romantic aesthetics was founded, she writes, on Kantian epistemology, which holds that, since we can never know the world in itself, we must construct a stable self, living our lives in a fiction we have made ourselves; Kant placed humans at the center of the knowable universe. Everyone's "I am" creates the world they live in. Kant imagined a human being who could, Battersby writes, "literally think himself into existence, unlike a human being who can only think into existence the self he appears to himself to have" (44).

Battersby also writes of the naturalization of the creative product by the Romantics in the nineteenth century. Creative individuals were expected to work hard, to suffer, but, she says, "the outcome was not a soulless 'mechanical' product." Rather, she says, "it was 'natural' and 'organic,' and was likened to the (previously despised) processes of being impregnated and giving birth" (1989, 73). Battersby writes that terms taken from nature were frequently employed to characterize the sort of labor that was valued in creative work: "The early Romantics appealed to spiders spinning webs, bees building hives, seeds sprouting, and plants burgeoning and blossoming" (73). According to Battersby, such organic labor was, at first, only occasionally described with animal metaphors, but the language of male motherhood, and male midwifery, became increasingly common in the nineteenth century. "The artist conceived, was pregnant, labored (in sweat and pain), was delivered, and (in an uncontrolled ecstasy of agonised—male—control) brought forth" (73). I will leave a consideration of this shift in the discourse for a little later. For the Romantics, the genius was the ruler in the art world, "a kind of junior God-the-Father who shapes matter into form according to rules." The Romantic genius (male, of course) exists in an artistic reality that is "as highly structured as the cobweb spun out of the bowels of the spider, or the child that emerges from the womb" (76).

Musicologists will recognize such discourses about the organic because the conception of composition of music with what was known as *organic unity* was common in the nineteenth century. Ruth Solie's classic article on the subject builds a strong argument for the importance of unity in Western European music. Solie (1980) also notes the importance of organic unity in the literary arts, an idea promulgated by Samuel Taylor Coleridge and others. And she quotes the influential music theorist Heinrich Schenker saying that he has found the secret to the works of the "great masters," which is "the concept of organic coherence" (151). Organically produced genius begets organically produced work.

The assumption of creativity as a naturally occurring faculty is perhaps clearest today in discourses around world music. I've written elsewhere (Taylor 1997, 2016) of the Western popular musicians' treatment of non-Western musics, frequently constructing them as raw material in need of refinement. The difference here is that non-Western musicians aren't assumed to labor, sweat, struggle, practice; their so-called natural creativity results in rough products that are left to Westerners, as either collaborators or intermediaries, to refine for Western audiences. Western creators produce creations; people classified as Others can't, by definition, be creators. They emit raw materials like women give birth, but what they produce needs to be refined. Nowhere was this clearer than in the controversy surrounding Paul Simon's *Graceland* album. After the album's release in 1986, Simon appeared at Howard University and took questions. A student accused Simon of stealing African qualities for his music, which, he said, people have done for a long time. Simon protested, pointing out that he was invited by South African musicians to be there—because they wanted money, interrupts the student—but Simon said that's a valid reason. Then he said, "You try and make a hit out of that!"[2] The West constructs non-Western musics as natural so it can exploit them as it exploits natural resources (see Taylor 1997).

This discussion is relevant because I am interested in the ways that creativity and its products are conceptualized as raw materials that are needed to complete the finished product, whether film, episode, or game. Film and television composers are viewed through both discourses: They are (or can be) respected as creators in the Romantic sense, whose creativity is a natural gift, but at the same time, what they create isn't viewed as a finished product; it must go through processes of refinement. A film or television composer's product is potential use-value that needs to be managed by directors and producers in its initial production, then refined as it passes through a supply chain, and finally fitted into its ultimate destination to perform the use-value determined by directors and producers by accompanying what is on the screen.

Gender and Creativity

The proliferation of natural metaphors to describe creativity in the early Romantic era gave way to those concerning animals and birth. In this section I want to address this other aspect of this Western discourse of creativity, which likens it to a form of male motherhood.

Battersby (1989, 121–22) considers Nietzsche's writings on the subject, where he refers to cultural creators as "male mothers" engaged in "spiritual pregnancy." Men who fail to create are postmenopausal in Nietzsche's view: "Compared to a genius—that is, to one who either *begets* or *gives birth*, taking both terms in their most elevated sense—the scholar, the scientific average man, always rather resembles an old maid: like her he is not conversant with the two most valuable functions of man" (122, quoting Nietzsche [1886] 1966 § 206, 125, emphasis in Battersby). Battersby writes of Nietzsche's claim that artworks have their origins in "the cerebral system bursting with sexual energy," to wit, "physiologically: the creative instinct of the artist and the distribution of semen in his blood" (121, quoting Nietzsche [1883–88] 1968 § 805, 424). For him, woman's lot is biological reproduction; men's is cultural production. Men's labors are viewed as organic processes, so Nietzsche employs terms and metaphors appropriated from women's traditional roles. Such sentiments were the norm in the late nineteenth century, according to Battersby.

Conceptions of genius and creativity that took their cue from women's procreativity (Battersby 1989, 122) have persisted through the twentieth century. Carl Jung wrote in 1945 that "just as a man brings forth his work as a complete creation out of his inner feminine nature, so the inner masculine side of a woman brings forth creative seeds which have the power to fertilize the feminine side of the man" ([1966] 1981, 209). Men are creative; women's role is simply to support them. Such ideas still exist in various forms, one of the many ways that the cultural businesses are caught up in patriarchal cultures. David Hesmondhalgh and Sarah Baker (2015, 28) found in their study of gender segregation in the cultural businesses that this ideology persists, with women much more often employed as workers involved in organizing and handling the creative work of others.

Battersby (1989, 131) also cites academic and psychologist Frank Barron, an influential scholar of creativity, who writes, "The creative act is a kind of giving birth, and it is noteworthy that as an historical fact intellectual creativity has been conspicuously lacking in women, whose products are their children. At the risk of making too much of a linguistic parallel, it might be said that nature has literally arranged a division of labor. Men bring forth ideas, paintings, literary and musical compositions, organizations of states, inventions, new material structures, and the like, while women bring forth the new generation" (quoting Barron 1968, 221).[3] Women procreate, men create.

The qualities of the artist by the nineteenth century were culturally coded as feminine; as Rozsika Parker and Griselda Pollock (2013, 82) enumerate them, they are "strange, different, exotic, imaginative, eccentric, creative, unconventional, alone." Sean Nixon (2003, 100, drawing on Parker and Pollock) comments on this seeming paradox as an ambiguity. But it's not an ambiguity at all; it's a contradiction that is worked out, at least in the fields of cultural production considered here, as music moves through its supply chain. As I've written elsewhere (Taylor n.d.a), supply chains can perform all sorts of value work. The music supply chain in film and television production doesn't just purify or refine the products of the composers' labor; it defeminizes it (which is in patriarchal culture a form of purification). As music and other supply chains in the cultural businesses take the gift out of the commodity, as Anna Tsing (2015) so memorably theorized, they also excise the feminine. They do this through labor processes that "tame" the composer's work, rationalizing it for its function as use-value in the finished product. It is illustrative that a couple of the orchestrators I spoke to described their jobs as being akin to structural engineers—they receive a score from a composer and rationalize it, making sure it is structurally sound (see chapter 4).

The Creative Function and Group Production

The way I think of the creative function in what follows is not just as a discursive symptom of neoliberal capitalism (for good or ill), but as a discourse deeply shaped by its patriarchal roots that people believe to be real and whose behavior is influenced by these beliefs. Public discourses about creativity have exploded in the past couple of decades, just as there has been a veritable explosion of interest in the creative or cultural businesses. Hundreds of publications celebrate these businesses and unquestioningly adopt the creativity trope, whether these publications are by journalists, business school professors, other academics, or still others.

But what does it mean to be creative in group production?[4] The creative freedom that one can find in the cultural businesses is often elusive, dependent on frequently diffuse structures of power and authority, limited by time and sometimes technology, and is subjective, negotiated. Perhaps nowhere are the contestations between creative freedom and the money people more fraught or contested than in the film business, since budgets can get into the tens or even hundreds of millions and massive profits can be realized by a hit. It has become almost a cliché to read about a film director's battle to realize a particular creative vision against the budgetary and other constraints imposed by the money people. Feature film directors need to find ways to do what they desire, either within the Hollywood system (notorious for not letting most directors do what they want to do) or the independent film route, the latter involving a lot of time spent drumming up enough cash to make a film.

A quick example. The acclaimed director Steven Soderbergh announced in 2012 that he was through making films but returned after about five years with hopes that a new model of financing would permit him to make the sort of film he wanted with smaller budgets, which translates to less oversight and constraint by the money people. During the hiatus, he said, he was working on a new model of financing films, thinking about "what resources were required to put a movie into wide release, and whether or not I could help create a model that would be more efficient, while also allowing complete creative control over the process from beginning to end" (quoted in Norris 2017, 46). He went on to say that, for him, it is a question of attempting to learn, after a film has been released, about what worked and what didn't so that audiences could be better targeted and resources more effectively utilized. But he admitted it was a constant uphill battle with the money people: "Given my circumstances, it'd be hard for people to imagine I feel I'm pushing against forces bigger than myself. But I can tell you, if you're a creative person in a field that uses these kinds of resources, you always feel like that. If you're independent-minded and don't really like being controlled by other people, then yeah, you are constantly swimming upstream" (48).

These sorts of stories abound in the film literature, so there is no need to rehearse them anymore (see, instead, Ortner 2013). I recount this one story to demonstrate how entrenched the discourses of creativity are and how implacably opposed its brandishers are to money, even though the ideology and discourses of creativity emerged with the capitalist market for cultural goods. It's a question not of whether or not there is creativity, but of who is allowed access to the creative function and how people struggle with these constant constructions and negotiations.

A director such as Soderbergh can aspire to the creative function, which in these fields means drawing on the discourses of creativity to justify honoring their intuition, their instincts about what really matters in a film or episode—script, actors, and more. Composers, however, are below the line. They are hired to do a job, and they are afforded various degrees of creative license depending on the project, budget, and the management style of those above them. Directors and producers want to hire the best they can afford given their projects' budgets, but they know they are hiring someone to do a job. Famed director Michael Mann (2015), in answer to a question about how he chooses the composers for his films, compared choosing a composer to casting: He tries to hire whom he desires based on what he wants them for. Sometimes he'll hire a single composer to try to give the film a "unified sensibility"; other times he'll engage more than one composer for a single film to vary the emotional perspectives. "In the end," he said, "it's the film and my vision that dictate which music is used and how. If a composer wants to have his music stand alone, he should be a recording artist and let his work contest itself in that arena." Mann concluded by saying, "when it comes to the process, I'm very involved, and it's purely creative and highly intuitive."

The television producers I interviewed characterized the role of the composer in similar ways. Some will give more latitude, but the choice of composer and overall sound is still their prerogative. Producer Harvey Myman, who clearly affords composers more freedom than many producers, told me that he normally shows composers the pilot when it's complete or nearly complete to try to spur a composer's creativity; since composers, unlike producers and directors, don't normally have access the creative function, those who do must remember that composers are capable of performing creative work. Myman said, "It's really exciting when you don't forget that these are artists and give them room to try things." Myman said that the music shouldn't call attention to itself, it should support what's happening onscreen, but at the same time, he said, "I was always a supporter of bringing in people with surprising choices. I'll be reading résumés, and I'll think, 'Whoa, okay, this guy's pretty cool,' as opposed to the composer who's got ten comedies on the air." Myman likes to hire people and trust their creativity and specifically singled out composer Ben Vaughn, who, he said, has "never been a guy with such a specific sound that he was a prisoner of it." Myman's overall goal is "to find someone who wants to support what the creative vision is for the show but goes after it with that same creative drive, not just going into their files and saying, 'Yeah, I got that.'"[5] But Myman is something of an exception; musicians' creativity is normally viewed as servicing the agenda of those who employ them.

As implied above, in television, the first step toward the hiring of a composer is finding someone to write music for the pilot episode. Producer Kamran Pasha told me that this is an important moment in the development of a show because, as he said, "the music defines the feeling of the entire show"; the composer is "essentially creating a template for the music." It is in writing music for a pilot that the composer might be given the most creative freedom; once this template is established, anyone who writes music for a series needs to stick to it. Pasha said that the composer who writes the music for the pilot isn't necessarily the person who is going to provide the day-to-day composition for the program, but it is this founding composer who establishes the sound. Pasha said this composer might even receive a producer credit if they're powerful enough figures, which allows them to continue to have influence on the music.[6] (I'll speak more of the pilot process, from the composer's perspective, in the next chapter.)

Part of the decision-making process for a new program involves selecting a composer to write the theme song, though the composer might not be the same person writing the music for each episode. Alf Clausen, the longtime composer for *The Simpsons*, has described the importance of the theme song this way (though he didn't write it for that particular program):

The ideal for composing a theme song is that it's supposed to continually remind the viewer of the substance that's going on within the body of the episodes week after week after week. And it's supposed to be something that will ID for the listener when that program comes around—hopefully that the theme is recognizable. . . . If you're sitting in the kitchen having dinner and you hear this theme song come on, you know, immediately what the show is, which is the point, it's to get people to come in and watch because that's what keeps you on the air when people come in and watch, but they have to be told sometimes: "Well, should we leave our kitchen and our fabulous lasagna in there or go in and watch a show."[7]

Producers frequently hire people with whom they have worked in the past to write the music for their programs, but they also will seek out composers whose work they admire from other programs. Pasha told me, "They'll watch films and television shows and think, 'This person captured the feeling of that.'"[8] But, he said, conversations about hiring a composer can be heated. Discussions of music occur in postproduction meetings, where most people involved offer recommendations. The postproduction manager, the line producer, and others all advocate for their composer candidates. The showrunner and the creator of the show also champion their own vision and candidates. Then, Pasha said, it becomes a political discussion. Imitating one of these workers, Pasha said, "'Okay, you want me to work with this guy that's done three of your TV shows at the CW [cable network]? But I don't know that he can pull off my show.'" Then, Pasha said, "You have to have that political discussion, and you have wins and losses. And the next stage, if there's no one settled on, is that the showrunner watches the shows, views other samples of theirs that have not yet been released." Pasha said people will wonder about other music that composers might have on their computer in addition to the programs they have done: "They can be very, very intense discussions."[9]

Composers and Creative Freedom—Under Certain Conditions and with Constraints

Generally, film and television composers view their job as enhancing the emotional undercurrent of the action and dialogue onscreen. But they must accomplish this according to the desires of those for whom they work, producers and directors, those with access to the creative function. Composers find themselves having to negotiate orders and requests as a normal part of their job. They repeatedly told me that they can't have any ego in their jobs; they must do what is asked of them, and if something is criticized, they just come back with something they hope will be greeted with approval or at least a positive suggestion.

Miriam Mayer told me she thinks of herself as a decorator of a house, but not her own: "It's the director's house, and even though I might want to go edgy or crazy, if the director wants it in chintz, I'm going to do it in chintz because it's their house, and I'm going to use all my intelligence and creativity and experience to give them what they want."[10] Whatever creativity she is allowed must be put in the service of pleasing the bosses.

Several composers—from the most lauded, such as Mike Post, to lesser-known musicians—told me they could not have any ego about their work, which is how they described the process I have characterized as self-disciplining. Sharon Farber, like many composers I spoke to, said it's the composer's (and many others') job to give the director peace of mind, to assure them that everything will be done to their best abilities and on time. Being a composer, or almost any worker in the business, is about servicing the vision of the director or producer, those with the creative function. "Our job," Sharon told me, "is to take what we know—our inspiration, our talent and our skills, and use it all as a vehicle to bring the director's vision to life." Sometimes, she said, this can be difficult. Composers can feel that they have written great music that is perfect for the scene, while the directors feel it's not what they're looking for. But, Farber said, you can't let your ego get in the way. "You just say, 'Okay, let me rework it and send you a new version based on our discussion.' And you do. You recompose and make the director happy so that you can be happy as well."[11] Matt Hutchinson told me he felt that writing advertising music left him no opportunity to be creative, that he was just a hired gun. But he also felt that there was comparatively more creative opportunities in television and film, even as he nonetheless must to appeal to producers and directors.[12]

Mike Post was perhaps the pithiest and most realistic when describing the demands of television writing:

> Number one, it's got to go on the air at nine; or, whatever time it's going on the air, it's going on the air. So, you cannot spin yourself into some hole trying to make it better than perfect. You have to be able to say, "Hey, that's my best shot." And then, for me, the other prerequisites

are: I've got to like what I write, and they've gotta love it. If they don't love it, it isn't right. This is not a hit record. This is not stand-alone art. This is not concert music. This is music made to go with their picture and make their picture better for them. So, if it's not better for them and they don't love it, I'll do it again.[13]

Post thinks that many composers lose sight of this, fretting about "my music, my music!," an attitude for which he has no patience. "You've got to know the gig," he says. It's not art; it's going on the air. And if the bosses don't love it, it's no good. "And you can't get so hung up on what you wrote to not understand that it has to make them feel more about the picture they've written and directed and produced. And, so, you've got to leave your ego just way behind."[14]

Before the composer has been hired, or written the music, filmmakers, showrunners, or others in command will use recordings of previously recorded music as temporary placeholders for the custom music to be written later. David Schwartz said that the use of this music, referred to as temp music, has been a big change since he entered the business in the early 1990s; the trade press during this period frequently asked composers whether they liked it.[15] Established composers tended to claim to hate it. Elmer Bernstein said, "I think people who make temp-tracks should be *shot!*" (MacLean 1993b, 14). Temp music has also become more common as films are test-screened for audiences before the original music has been completed. If audiences liked the temp music, composers could be asked to emulate it (Eicke 2019, 14). Some better-known composers refuse to view a film with a temp track; Alexandre Desplat said that this allows him to be more creative in his scoring (Barth 2007, 14).

And sometimes directors and producers become so enamored of the temp music that they have a difficult time imagining their film or program with anything other than that music. Schwartz said that people producing the show have been listening to the temp music for a long time, and it's difficult for that music not to influence the requests and demands made of the composer. Schwartz thinks that the influence of temp music has "made a lot of projects sound like temp tracks, in which each song is from some different world, and there's not a lot of continuity. There doesn't have to be continuity, but it's nice when you have thematic stuff that pays off"— that is, themes that can be used to animate characters and create a sense of unity.[16] Composer Matt Hutchinson told me of a project in which the director used some temp music and became so attached to it that that was all he wanted. Hutchinson inquired if the director had tried to license the music because he couldn't copy it, legally or morally. And so, the director licensed the music. But most people, Hutchinson said, recognize that the composer is going to come in with new music and that they'll have to let go of the temp music they have become attached to.[17] Joey Newman has had similar experiences, though he said he can be more creative when there is no temp score. "Then I can just feel out something fresh and unique, but it takes time, and the problem is we don't have time." Sometimes, he said, you have to "navigate the temp," figuring out how to give clients what they want while still devising new sounds and fresh takes on it.[18]

Many composers spoke of the sorts of strictures and constraints under which they normally work, which speaks to the difficulties inherent in group production. Emmy-winning composer Ben Decter, who works mainly in television, said that in film and TV music one must please a lot of people. Decter said, "Sometimes it's hard making everyone happy. If you can make ninety percent of the people happy, that's pretty great. Then you have to move on to the next episode."[19] When asked about realizing his artistic vision in comparison to various producers, Decter said it's usually possible to exercise some degree of agency, "to sneak yourself in to a pretty good degree." Ideally, he said, everyone gets onto the same page. There are times when he has felt discouraged, giving an example of a big-budget network program he worked on that starred an Oscar-winning actor and was produced by a famous director. Decter hoped the show would feature an orchestral score but was surprised to learn from the showrunners that that wasn't in the budget. Decter felt conflicted when it became clear that the showrunner was using a lot of orchestra music in the temp score. "They wanted an orchestral score but apparently not enough to pay for it. So, you have to check your purely artistic self at the door." Decter said that one of the showrunners had become so attached to the temp music that he was continually asked to compare what he had written to the temp score—often his own music—and to emulate it closely. Decter said that, as a freelancer, he felt compelled to carry on but fantasized that, if the show had been renewed for another season, he could to sit down with the showrunners and say, "'Here's the score from the first season; you cut it together and come to us if you want anything changed.'"[20] Decter said he realized that this notion was a fantasy.

Some composers, however, said they liked the limitations placed on them by those above them and that they found having to work within clearly defined parameters creatively stimulating. Anne-Kathrin Dern said she prefers having the constraints both from the nature of the job itself—she knows she is writing music to order—and from the specific instructions for particular projects imposed by particular directors and producers. "The moment you give me a blank piece of paper and say, 'Do anything you want,' I actually have more trouble than when someone says, 'Here's a movie that already dictates the form of your compositions and the subject matter, and we really want orchestra, and we really like this and that soundtrack.'" She said that within the constraints and boundaries she is given, she still feels that she has a good deal of room to maneuver creatively: "I always manage to write what I want within the limitations I'm given, so it's perfectly fine for me."[21]

What really matters to composers is the relationship they have with their bosses; this is the only hope they have of being able to write what they want. Composer David Schwartz spoke highly of Mitch Hurwitz, his producer on the Fox television series *Arrested Development* (2000–2007). Hurwitz would have him write many cues and even request more on the sound recording stage. Schwartz said he didn't mind the last-minute requests and the sheer volume of cues he had to write because Hurwitz was so engaged in the music. Schwartz said he was willing to take a lot of direction but, at the same time, was also willing to push back a little and say, "'Can we just listen to what I wrote? We never really got to hear that,'" to which Hurwitz would say, "'Oh, yeah, you're totally right; just go back.'" Because he was able to have this sort of back-and-forth with Hurwitz, Schwartz said, "We have an unusually great relationship."[22]

John Nordstrom (who, since our interview, began working on *The Bold and the Beautiful*, for which he has won two Daytime Emmy awards) also spoke of the good working relationship he had with his producers and how they would generally react after viewing an episode containing his music before it was broadcast. His favorite projects were those in which he felt like he was on good terms with his bosses from the beginning. He was rarely asked to throw anything out and start all over again, the sort of scenario he has experienced before. He thinks that when working relationships are amicable, he produces better work. "It really spurs creativity, and you feel like you can do your best stuff when you know where they're coming from and they've been able to articulate what they want. Then you just think, 'Okay, cool, now I'm just going to go for it, because I know they're going to like it.'"[23]

Some composers told me they have learned to think of themselves as filmmakers as a way of attempting to adopt their bosses' perspectives.

Composer Christopher Wong said he thinks of himself as a filmmaker more than a composer when writing for films in order to try to see what his directors want and visualize himself as part of a team. He said it's important to consider himself to be part of a team that is making the film better. He doesn't think about the kind of music he would like to write; he can only do what he can do, saying he's not the person to write gangsta rap music. "But," he told me, "I think that it's more successful if you approach everything with the question 'How can I make this scene better?' and 'How do I make the characters and the performances and the story more believable to the audience?'" Wong said that when he thinks that way he's a filmmaker and that this is the difference between being a film composer and a composer for the concert stage.[24]

Kurt Farquhar articulated a similar strategy, telling me that he works closely with television showrunners in order to demonstrate that he is on their side, that he is thinking about the show the same way they are, not just as a composer, but as a filmmaker/composer. Farquhar said that many composers want to look at the project from their own standpoint, which "is the worst thing you can do." Farquhar thinks it is crucial to get in accord with the showrunner, making them realize that your vision of the project is the realization of their vision. "You start talking with the showrunner and get them on board with what it is that you want to achieve. I talk about the character, the inner workings of his mind, and there's some context to what's going on and say that we can exemplify it with music. These are things you have to think about, the story, not solely what's best for your music." Farquhar thinks that when a showrunner is convinced that he is as invested as they are in the story they have written, you have a partner: "Now it's no longer just you saying, 'I want this.' Now it's the creator of the show." Farquhar said it makes a big difference having the showrunner fight with him. "You have the showrunner come in to go over the music with you; you tell them what you did, what you're going to do, and why it works, so they are part of the whole ride with you."[25] In this way, Farquhar stands a chance of writing the music the way he feels works best.

Some composers attempt to mitigate the crushing schedules by working on teams or sometimes by hiring others to have additional music written for them. One how-to article recommends developing a formulaic way of working (Mollin 1992, 15). But working with others can help one realize how creative they are, even if they might not comprehend it at the time. Matt Hutchinson told me of working with Joey Newman and how much he enjoys the unexpected things that Newman will do with music Hutchinson has written. "It was my theme, but the rhythmic structures he chose to put underneath it and all these things were different than what I heard in my head. And that was what was so fun about it. I feel like that's the creativity and that is our stamp that's on things."[26] Following one's own intuition—sometimes stimulated by others—is what creative freedom means for these musicians.

While the demands of time can necessitate working in teams—whether as composers or orchestrators, as I will discuss—this sort of ideology of teamwork is another result of the shift toward neoliberal capitalism as manifested in these businesses. *Governance* (Foucault's term not just for the exercise of governmental power, but for conduct more generally, as discussed in chapter 1), as elaborated by Wendy Brown (2015, 131), displaces in the workplace "the lateral solidarities of unions and worker consciousness and the politics of struggle with hierarchically organized 'teams,' multiparty cooperation, individual responsibility, and antipolitics." Composers and orchestrators may turn to teamwork for reasons that appear practical and necessary to them but which are increasingly part of the culture of the neoliberal workplace. (I'll have more to say about neoliberalism and responsibility in chapter 7.)

One of the ways composers can attempt to exercise creative freedom is less through a particular job than through the sheer number and variety of gigs (as some advertising musicians told me in Taylor 2012). Those with training in writing for film and television are taught to write in a variety of styles, and they can be asked to write anything. Ryan Shore believes he can realize his creative ambitions because he often composes for a wide variety of genres (he listed comedy, action, horror, period drama, war, sci-fi, the Western), and he has been asked to compose music in many different media as well—film, television, and games. He told me, "I find there's a very large sandbox to play in creatively," and he enjoys the challenge of writing for different types of projects.[27]

Some composers enjoy writing in particular genres for the creative freedom they allow. Anne-Kathrin Dern told me she particularly likes writing for animation, fantasy, and science fiction because "they are so diverse in terms of what you can do musically. You can pretty much do anything, and it'll be okay; you can go extremely big, extremely small; there's always some kind of love thing going on, there's always adventure, there's always magic."[28] Dern said she is free to do whatever she wants in these genres, which is the most that composers can hope for.

While most of this book is focused on the more hidden musicians—those who make a living, and sometimes a good one, but who toil mostly in the shadows—I was nonetheless curious about those who have risen to the top of their fields. Do they face the same issues and problems as their lesser-known counterparts? Even famous composers are usually told what to do, such as Randy Newman in the epigraph to this book. Bruce Broughton, well known for many films and television programs, told me very clearly, "You have to work on it until the director gets what he or she wants."[29] And the legendary Lalo Schifrin, most famous for his theme to the original *Mission: Impossible* series on television in the 1960s, told me he recognized that he was working in a structure, that whatever project he was working on wasn't his own creation, that he understood that he was contributing to the totality of the work. He used the term *audio-visual counterpoint* to characterize the role played by music in film.[30]

Time

There are also constraints and compromises on composers' creative freedom because, as they see it, of the compressed schedules many are forced to adhere to, exacerbated by the rise of digital technology, which makes possible the sorts of last-minute editing and alternation that didn't happen in the analog era. Trevor Rabin, the composer for *Armageddon* (1998), recounted that producer Jerry Bruckheimer gave him a clock counting down to the day the score was due, "and that was in front of me at all times," he said.[31] A published interview with several composers in the late 1980s reveals that time pressures were extreme then, before digital technologies were widespread. Henry Mancini said that in the 1950s, when he began scoring for films, composers were given ten weeks, but the window by the late 1980s had shrunk to about four weeks (which is still the norm today). Alan Silvestri explained time pressures in that era as follows: "We're often scoring within a week of shipping. The way they presell films and buy time in theaters . . . it's very back-end. Everything slides their time. The shooting takes a little longer than planned, the cutting takes a little longer, but your back-end date stays the same. A film hasn't even started to shoot, and they've already got play-dates" (Zimmerman 1989, 3, ellipsis in original).

Orchestrator Tom Calderaro told me that there once was a six-week period during which the film was "locked," meaning it couldn't be changed, and the composer had those six weeks to write the score. Calderaro said the composer would start writing in the first couple of weeks, and the orchestrators would come on board after that. These days, everything must be done so quickly that probably more than one orchestrator is used. "Today," Calderaro said, "it's mostly music by the pound, and you'll do what you're told"; even famous composers must do what they're told, he said. They may complain about it afterward, but while they're working, they only have time to try to meet the deadline.[32] One composer told Stephan Eicke (2019, 15) that the constant reediting of films has changed the way he and others write since, if it's orchestral music, rewriting is a "nightmare," and he thinks this is why most film music today is simpler than in the past, making it easier to edit.

Since music is one of the last elements to be added to a film or program, the composer is always a victim of the schedule. Christopher Wong told me that official release dates can't be changed, that studios have a legal obligation to place films in theaters by agreed-upon dates. Wong said he's lucky to get four or five weeks but has written music for a few films where he was only given three and a half weeks. In such situations, he said, you just have to do the best you can. Wong said when these truncated periods of composition happen, it is difficult not to be angry about it, to worry that the quality of your work has been compromised. "But," he said, "it usually doesn't really hurt your career, and you just try to get over it. You just learn that these things happen. You just have to roll with the punches."[33] It is all part of the culture of these fields that everyone below the line must be a team player, must discipline themselves.

The increase in the number of managers has also added to time problems. Orchestrator Calderaro told me that, in the old days, it was a lot of work to edit a film, and there weren't multiple prints, only a single print and a safety, since more prints cost more money. Today, editing takes less time, but there are also more requests for changes, and there are more people empowered to request them. He told me, "Just think about the change from when it was a colossal undertaking to make a major cut in a film, but with digital technology that is so easy that sometimes you have to indulge these people."[34]

Since composers are pressed for time, so are those who work for them. Music editor Craig Pettigrew told me that there is much more music in the film and television businesses than there once was (because of the proliferation of cable and, now, streaming services), and so there is more music to write in less time. But, he said, that doesn't speed up the creative process for composers: "The time it takes to make a creative decision hasn't really changed. You still have to make that decision. That's creativity, and the computer doesn't do that for you. So that means there's more music to write in less amount of time." Pettigrew also told me, "They'll say, 'What you did in four days last time, we have to shave a day off the mix schedule.' And we talk among ourselves, and we swear that we won't do it because next time it'll be two days. They'll say, 'Well, you did it in three days last time. . . .'" But, he said, "We keep on doing it; we keep on meeting their demands."[35]

A music copyist gave me an example of what a schedule is like today for an animated film that was to start two weeks after we spoke. "Years ago, we would have been busily working on it right now, but in this era, I'm not going to see anything at least for another week, which means a week closer to the start of the recording sessions." This copyist said that the business hasn't started the process earlier and made it more leisurely. Instead, "we've compressed the schedule to the point that the director's not ready, the film's not ready, nothing is ready, so everything is squeezed into this much shorter amount of time to get it done." Less time, he said, means they need more people, especially people who work with the technology, people "to make all the checkpoints you need to make in the technology, which is temperamental. You have to make so many checks and double checks and triple checks to make sure you've accounted for every possible thing that could go wrong with computers."[36]

But, just as some composers welcomed the constraints placed on them by those above them, others said they feel that dealing with time pressures has helped them become more creative. Bear McCreary said that the time constraints for writing music for *Battlestar Galactica* on the Sci-Fi Channel forced him to delegate more, which helped him be more creative. He had a week to score each episode and was spending a couple of days orchestrating and writing parts, so he decided to get some help. He was reluctant at first, fearing it would compromise his self-expression, but he hired people he trusted and found the process to be liberating. He came to think that learning how to delegate has become an important part of his success, saying, "Anything that does not involve the most intimate creative process shouldn't be done by me." "Intimate creative process" for composers refers to fundamental decisions about style, instrumentation, honoring one's intuition. Making the decision to delegate has also allowed McCreary to be able to take on more projects (Schrader and Thompson 2017, 160–61).

In television, composers might have as many as two weeks or as few as one day. Or less. Alf Clausen, famous for writing the music for *The Simpsons* for many years, can, like all composers, face deadlines that are not for the faint of heart. He tells a story of beginning a 7 p.m. recording session with a thirty-five-piece orchestra for the latest episode of the series when he was approached by one of the program's producers, who asked him if he could write a song and record a demo for it that same night; the cast was scheduled to record it at 10 a.m. the next day. The producer gave Clausen the lyrics, and while conducting, Clausen read and reread them. The music librarian handed him some blank manuscript paper on which he wrote the melody of the song while still rehearsing and conducting. When the orchestra took a break, Clausen played for the producer what he had been able to write on the piano. He was given the go-ahead to continue, again while rehearsing the orchestra. He and the producer worked on the song some more during the next ten-minute break, and he then gave his sketch to the librarian, who made a readable version for the musicians. When the recording session ended, he retained a few musicians to work late, and they recorded the instrumental part of the song with one singer. The producer took the demo for the actors to sing the song the next day. "Talk about multitasking!" Clausen said (Barth 2004, 5).

Compressed schedules have changed every aspect of production. As music editor Kevin Crehan told me,

> There are a lot of technical innovations that have changed us and how we do business. For example, if a three-minute cue was requested, you would have to create a spotting note that, when printed, was a quarter of an inch thick. Every line of dialogue would be on it. Every timing, every cut was timed; any camera movement was timed. So, composers were used to getting this little document, and then they would plug the numbers into whatever system they were using. They'd figure out the BPM [beats per minute]; they'd start to compose, see what they wanted to hit. All of that has changed because we fly picture in and out so fast, there's no time. Spotting notes are pretty basic. You just basically give a start-and-stop and the scene description.[37]

Crehan said that music editors would sit for hours and speak into a dictaphone and that there were many extremely fast typists at their disposal. Then, if the composers weren't local, notes would need to be physically sent to them. Before spotting notes could be digitally distributed, Crehan said, part of his job was sending out the notes:

> One of my jobs was dashing to FedEx. If you had a composer in New York and you wanted to get three cues out late in the week, it would be a mad dash across Burbank to get to the FedEx office over in Toluca

Lake (because that was the last pickup) and get the notes in so that the composer would have them Monday morning to get going on the next set of cues. So that's a huge change. And we used to have couriers come on motorbikes and bring notes to composers in Malibu and Hollywood and all over LA.[38]

Media Variations

Degrees of creative freedom are determined not just by bosses, budgets, or time but also by the prestige of the medium. There is a clear hierarchy in this world: The greatest prestige is in composing for film, then television (and within television, streaming services are competing to be the most edgy and, therefore, prestigious, more so than network television), then advertising. These distinctions have blurred somewhat in the past few decades, as I noted earlier, but the amount of prestige that attaches to them has remained relatively intact. It may be that the prestige is related to the degree of creative freedom the composers are thought to be afforded. Joey Newman told me that there seems to be more creative freedom on streaming services than on network television, where he has had several shows over the years. Streaming sitcoms can be longer (thirty minutes compared to twenty-two minutes), as well as much edgier, including the use of profanity. Income still seems to be better on network programs (to be discussed in chapter 7), but even on a network program, "at some point a composer can feel stifled, and when he or she finds out that maybe this cable network, or streaming service, is interested in your creativity and musical risk-taking, maybe they won't constrain you as much."[39]

Composer Cindy O'Connor, who has done some work in the theater, said it was a very different experience for her. She echoed what everyone said about who's in charge in film and television but said that, in live theater, the writer is king, and the director oversees the production. O'Connor said she scored some nonmusical plays with a theater company in New York City and that, after having done so much film and television work, was shocked when the director gave her comments after she presented him with some cues. "He had some notes, but he prefaced it by saying, 'Now I have a few notes, but I don't want to compromise your vision.' A film composer's brain would explode: 'I get to have a vision? Somebody doesn't want to compromise it?'" O'Connor said it's a completely different world, in large part because there is no money in it, since theater composers aren't paid what film and television composers are.[40]

Penka Kouneva, mainly a writer of music for film and video games, finds that both afford creative outlets, saying that games "are always inspiring my creativity because I need to compose themes that support the game's aesthetics and brand, and then, compose music for all levels of gameplay." And the schedule isn't nearly as frenetic compared to TV scoring or feature film scoring.[41]

Technology

Musicians in film, television, and advertising (see Taylor 2012) who were working during the shift from analog to digital technologies profess great ambivalence about it (though those who entered the business after the advent of these technologies do not, since they haven't known anything else). Musicians who remember the transition tend to believe there has been a general decline in the quality of music used in film and television as a result of the de-skilling of their comrades, who may not know how to arrange or orchestrate or, sometimes, read and write music. I will discuss technological changes at greater length in chapter 7, so here, I will confine my discussion of technology to how it has, at least in the eyes of workers, affected their ability to be creative.

More than anything else, budgets determine the forces used in film and television scoring. Composer Bruce Broughton said he uses digital technology to synthesize a lot of the music he writes, depending on the budget; less money means fewer live musicians. Broughton told me it is common now to combine music by synthesizers with live musicians, just enough live musicians "to make it sound real, with a sense of a real performance and real humanity." Broughton said that having at least some musicians is essential, that it is "the human personality that makes all the difference. You can't get that off of a sampler, so if you get a real person to perform, like on this little film I did, it just makes the score bloom. If I do it on a synthesizer, it's emotionally flat. It sucks."[42] David Schwartz said much the same thing. He started in the early 1990s, when using live musicians was still common. He still tries to employ live musicians even though it costs him more. It's not just the superior sound he prefers, but the give-and-take with musicians. "I like them to give me their take on it and then say, 'You know, I like what you did here, but let's go back to the notes for this part.' So that can really help."[43]

For Broughton and others who remember the transition, technology has changed every aspect of film and television production. While digital technologies frequently replace live musicians, electronic instruments were at first viewed as adding to the color palette of the orchestra, which is still the case. Sharon Farber told me, "I think that technology is a great tool that really helps us create; it provides us with the opportunity to present the director with how the score will sound with a real orchestra, and many films are scored solely on the computers without any live musicians (although, in my opinion, there's nothing like the real thing!). Samples today are extremely well-made, and the music can sound extremely good if you know what you're doing. It also provides us with opportunities to create new and exciting sounds that can be intertwined with live musicians."[44] But, as Broughton told me, no one thought such instruments would take over.

Other Music Workers and Creative Freedom

Music workers' labor becomes increasingly technical as the music moves through the supply chain, to the extent that to characterize technical work as creative (or not) fails to capture the technical nature of the work. There are still plenty of decisions to be made, choices to make. But workers can still be afforded the opportunity to make decisions; they don't necessarily think of all these decisions as creative, but the choices they make nonetheless affect the music and its recording.

Orchestrators

Orchestrators, whose work mainly involves taking a handwritten or computer-generated score and arranging it for an orchestra, say that there is a good deal of craft in what they do. Today, it is increasingly common for a film score to be composed by a rock or pop musician who has no classical training, who might not read or write music. It is nonetheless possible with modern digital technology to produce all the film music on a computer (which, for many films and television programs, is how all the music is made) and, then, if there is to be an orchestra or other group of live musicians, to use software to produce a score and parts for those musicians to play. But without classical training, those making the score and parts don't really know if they will be legible to, or even playable by, live musicians. Orchestrators and arrangers can help at this point, refining the computer-generated scores for live musicians. Tom Calderaro also said that the craft of orchestration involves rebalancing things. There are many elements that are absent in the computer mockup of the score, which is how the notated music is usually generated. Orchestrators must understand what sort of sound the composer is seeking—a skill that requires familiarity with orchestral scores—in order to correct the score before the recording session.

In the old days, Calderaro said, the composers he worked for knew how to write for the orchestra themselves, and they would write suggestions in their scores for their orchestrators and trust them to execute them. Composers would annotate their scores with suggestions for orchestrating for woodwinds or strings, and there were shorthands those composers and orchestrators understood. "Now," Calderaro said, "the shorthands that we get are like Frankenstein. The electronics are making the stuff sound good, but they really aren't a good indicator of what you're supposed to do on the page."[45]

In the absence of live musicians, composers can use prerecorded music from a library of such recordings to employ in their scores to emulate the sound of live instruments. These snippets of sound can sound passable in a computer-generated demo—which is increasingly employed—but that doesn't mean it will still sound good once it has been orchestrated and played by live musicians. Calderaro said, "These mockups can sound very good, so composers really have to pay attention to realize that there is work to be done." Drawing on an analogy he credited to another orchestrator, Pete Anthony, Calderaro said that, before digital technologies, the role of the orchestrator was akin to that of being an architect, whereas today it's like being a structural engineer, someone who makes sure the edifice is sound. "The architect is thinking about the beauty of it and how it's going to look. The job today of an orchestrator is primarily a structural engineer; he's worried about if this thing is going to stand up." Continuing with the analogy, Calderaro told me, "You can see what the architect did; it's beautiful where the windows are, and how the thing flows and changes over time, and it's really a great vision, but you know what, you've got to put something more than a two-by-four in the middle of the house." So, he said, orchestrators must reevaluate all the structural components of the score to see if they work well, or work at all, employing their knowledge of orchestral music to try to understand what the composer was trying to achieve.[46] Edward Trybek employed the same architect/structural engineer analogy but said that because composers vary greatly, his job varies as well. He might simply be engaged in error correction and little more; or, he said, you can encounter an architect who says, "'I see a giant green egg; make that happen.' You have all sides of that. It can be a gray area of creativity and composition and orchestration."[47] Greater musical ignorance of composer-bosses can result in more creative freedom for orchestrators.

Trybek also told me that he can't possess his own agenda, that "it is still work, and it is ultimately music made to order. And it has a specific purpose, so I can't just say to myself, 'Well, I feel like doing this today, and I'm just going to do that.'" But Trybek, like some of the composers I spoke to, finds the constraints imposed on him to be part of the challenge. A blank page might be intimidating, but "if somebody gives you some sort of box to work in or some sort of box to be trying to push the boundaries on, it actually helps to some degree."[48]

Recording Engineers and Mixers

Some think that digital technologies have introduced opportunities for more technical music workers to be creative. They make more tracks available to be manipulated, and tracks can be combined into what are known as stems (to be discussed in greater depth in chapter 3), bundles of recorded tracks, such as all the strings or all the percussion, so that whoever performs the final mix can control the sounds of various parts of the recorded music. Recording engineer and mixer Alan Meyerson, best known for working with star composer Hans Zimmer, told me that it is possible to be creative in making stems, or constructing them in such a way that the person who receives the files can't mess them up. Meyerson said that stems can allow the next person in the supply chain to be more creative—or to really screw things up. "So, you have to be very careful who is downstream from you. You want to try to keep your team pretty solid." I asked him if he would make his stems differently if he didn't have a team he trusted, and he said he often does. "I give them less control so they can only get themselves in so much trouble. So instead of giving them nine stems, I might just give them three stems." Meyerson said all this can get political if the person receiving his stems realizes that he has curtailed their ability to make use of them as desired.[49] Creativity and the ability to make choices are about power all the way down.

Several people discussed the kinds of choices that enter into the making of stems. Dan Savant, a music contractor (the person who hires musicians to record scores), said that the choice of stems is "kind of an artistic decision," that is, choosing the best configuration of stems for a particular film's sound. He said there are also room microphones to capture the sound of a room the orchestra is in as well as microphones closer to instruments. Room microphones are assigned their own stems to emphasize the orchestral sound if desired. Savant gave as an example a pop-orchestral cue that is supposed to sound hip, for which a big, orchestral sound would be wrong. He told me, "They use the microphones that are right on the instruments, since you get a drier sound, and they can choose whatever reverb they want. All this gets into very kind of artistic questions, depending on what they're using this recording for."[50]

Most of the music creators who work below the composer told me that no matter how technical their jobs are, they still must possess musical knowledge. Score mixer Phil McGowan said that, even though his job is primarily technical, people who do it need to be musical: "You have to be a musical person, too. You can't just be all technical, or else you won't have any creativity or any sort of style in the work that you do."[51] Knowing music means that there might be opportunities to weigh in on musical matters, not just technical ones. McGowan said that the occasions he has to offer creative input depend on the nature of the score. Some scores, he said, are straightforward; there's not much room for him to opine.[52]

Another avenue for score mixers to have some creative input is with respect to the demo mix of the score, which is generated by the composers' computer software and has become a normal way to present the music to bosses. Score mixers can weigh in on the mix during the recording process. McGowan told me that most composers produce what is known as a reference mix that he refers to because usually it has been approved by the director and producers to whom the composer is reporting. McGowan said he must keep in mind that this mix has been approved, even if he hears things in it that are problematic, which can lead to a confrontation with the composer. He said it's always an open conversation with composers about how close he needs to keep his mix to the reference mix. This can vary a good deal depending on the composer.[53]

Mixing is both a craft and creative work, according to most who do it. Alan Meyerson, known for his skill at both recording orchestras and mixing the recorded music, said that the composer is an artist but that he is a craftsperson or artisan. He makes an analogy, saying that he perceives his job as "someone who can go in and take a sculptor's drawing and take the hammer and chisel and make the sculpture for him. It's very, very creative, but it's not a primary source type of creation. I can't make anything creative on my own, but I can take what you do and make it better."[54] Mixers and engineers must work with what they have, refining it, improving it.

Scoring mixer Oren Hadar was one of the few people I spoke to who said he viewed his work as strictly technical—he is there to achieve the composer's vision, he said—but he clearly takes pride in his work and said he loves it. He is empowered to offer his opinion, but he thinks there is more creative freedom in making records, where "there's a certain amount of creativity where you can say, 'Oh, I'm going to put this really cool vocal effect on the vocal,' and then the artist would come in and say, 'Oh, it's cool.'" But, he said, "I don't really have the ability to do that with film and television. There are exceptions, but for the most part it's really by the book. But that's fine because I'm not in this for the creativity." For him, the satisfaction of the job is that "I'm working on beautiful music that makes people feel stuff and working with incredibly talented, intelligent, interesting people, and it's the collaboration and the give-and-take that does it for me."[55]

Music Editors

Music editors have a number of responsibilities (to be discussed fully in chapter 4), including editing preexisting music when it is used in a film or episode and cutting and pasting original music so that it fits the scene and time. Andrés Locsey, one of the music editors I interviewed, spoke about the latitude he is afforded in music editing, saying that he is sometimes called upon to use preexisting music written by the composer to generate new music. Producers asking him to find music for a scene allows him the opportunity to be creative, almost writing music by editing audio "because they're letting me do my own thing to figure out what a scene needs. I'll look at a scene and listen to all the music that I have from that composer and try and edit something original to make it work." Locsey also said that the temp process can be creative because, as the music editor, he molds other people's music from many films to make it work in a particular project. "It's like sculpting music," he said. "It's recycling music for another purpose."[56]

Money, Power, and Creative Freedom

Part of the issue for some of these workers isn't simply that creative freedom is managed in a hierarchy of people who can access the creative function, but that people whose main concern is profit are allowed a seat at the table, sometimes the head. No matter how much creative freedom or agency music workers might believe themselves to be able to exercise, they know that, at some point, the money people are going to take over, perhaps even overruling the director. A film director might be endowed with more, or a stronger, creative function than anyone else, but their concerns can still be set aside. Orchestrator Tom Calderaro told me, "It's just known and understood that at some point, the Big-Name Producer's going to show up and finish the movie. There's really no pretense that the people directing a Big-Name Producer's film are in control." He said this wasn't true in the old days, when it was an Alfred Hitchcock or John Cassavetes film, though a few directors today, he said—such as Martin Scorsese and Woody Allen—are still allowed to make the films the way they want to make them. "When you see a Woody Allen film, you know that it's the best thing that Woody wants to put out there. There are no disclaimers, like, 'Oh, you should have seen what we had going in the fifth reel before the head of production came in.' That just happens all the time now." Calderaro said that film production will be moving along, "and then all of a sudden, the clowns show up, the guys that have no business weighing in creatively, and yet they do." Because there is thought to be a lot at stake in terms of careers, jobs, and money, the businesspeople feel they need to protect the studio's interests. But, Calderaro asked, "What does a head of marketing know about making a film?" Calderaro even wondered if it is time to stop thinking of filmmaking as a creative endeavor because of the dominance of the money people: "Maybe we need to let go a little bit of the notion that a film is a creative undertaking, that it should represent the creator's vision, that it should be the writer, first, then the director and the actors." Calderaro thinks that expensive blockbuster films are already not thought of as artistic or creative. "Certainly, with the big films that's the case, the big blockbusters that are made for a whole different kind of experience: it's an entertainment experience, it's a marketing experience." But, he said, this is coming to be true on smaller films as well.[57]

There is a fairly direct relationship between the size of the budget and the amount of creativity and latitude afforded musicians and everyone else. Flora, the composer's assistant who wished to remain anonymous, told me that a $200 million film produces a huge amount of pressure on everyone, whereas writing music for independent films is still demanding in terms of time, but "I'm given a lot more creativity, so it's more like my thing. I'm seen as the main composer, so it's quite nice to have my own direction; I'm not answering to anyone else except the editors."[58] But enjoying a big budget doesn't mean that the work environment is automatically better. Composer Joey Newman observed that more money means more responsibility, more scrutiny, and "more cooks in the kitchen because it's got to be perfect and fresh, and the music is the last creative part on it, and you can fuck it up or you can make it incredible, and it's always going to be eyes on you at that point."[59] Newman also contrasted the difference between television and film, saying it was possible to have things approved with less of a microscope on you in television because creating content is so much faster, which means there is less time for the producers to weigh in, whereas a film can take a good deal longer, comparatively. The beauty of television, he told me, "is that we come in, and every week we deliver and finalize the score, so producers will have a harder time sitting on it, and hit us with notes of minutiae every week, and in a strange way, it can afford a much more comfortable way to work: there will be a deadline, and the show will have to air!" Once the production of the show has become familiar and the early kinks have been worked out, it runs like a well-oiled machine.[60]

Extremely low-budget films seem to be their own genre, one that can put even more pressure on musicians. There is not only less money, but less time, sometimes less than a week. Scores in such films are mostly synthesized since there is no money and rarely time to hire and record live musicians. Composers of such films also say that they must write more music; one said he has never written less than fifty-five minutes for a low-budget film. And composers feel that it falls to them to make the film work, which is why such films require so much music. One composer, Peter Rotter, said, "A lot of times the music in a low-budget film is what saves its butt. At least in a couple I've done, the movie is so bad the music has to help the acting out and has to help everything out" ("Chuck Cirino, Peter Rotter" 1994, 8). Another composer, Chuck Cirino, agreed, saying, "You have to fill it with music because you can't depend on the actors to carry scenes. . . . Because the drama is supposed to carry the scene and sometimes it doesn't, your music has to carry that scene and create a sense of pace to a film . . . that has none" (8, second ellipsis in original). One composer, in discussing a "shitty horror movie" for which he wrote the music, said his experience in such a low-budget environment was to be told to "save my film," "save this film"; "this scene isn't scary, and it needs to be" ("Chris Lennertz" 1995, 10).

Creative Outlets

Some of the composers I spoke to, particularly those involved primarily with film (probably because it is the form with the greatest prestige in these fields), told me that they wrote concert music (music for the concert hall) on the side, occasionally accepting commissions.[61] For a few of these composers, this was where they felt they could truly be creative, without constraints. Published interviews with composers as well as my own interviews frequently feature composers talking about how much freedom they were afforded by the director or producer (with fewer complaints about constraints, but this is a world, as we have seen, where one's reputation and agreeableness is everything). Some established and famous as well as some up-and-coming composers discussed writing concert music. Among the former, Lalo Schifrin has long had a career as a concert music composer and seems to be mainly writing concert music these days; that seemed to be what he was most interested in talking about when I interviewed him in 2017. Danny Elfman told an interviewer in 2019 that he was accepting more orchestral commissions and fewer film scores because writing film scores comes with constraints, whereas writing concert music allows him to be "off the leash" (Kaplan 2019).

Many less-famous composers spoke about their concert music projects. As Sharon Farber told me, "With concert music, it's totally you—it's your imagination, your emotions, it's what you want to do, and nobody's vision conflicts with what you want to say as an artist." Farber said that commissions sometimes come with requests, but that is rare. "When someone commissions you, they know your style; they've listened to other things that you've done, so they know whom they've commissioned."[62] And Christopher Wong said that, while in film music one must remember that one is part of a group working on the film, that's not the case with concert music: "When you're writing concert music, there's you, there's the conductor, and for some people, there's the audience. There are just not that many pieces in the puzzle. You write the thing; they play your work; hopefully people like it."[63]

Penka Kouneva told me that she is at a stage in her career when she has the opportunity to do "artist growth" projects and, so, has begun releasing orchestral albums on her own initiative. She calls them "concept CDs," characterizing them as storytelling music. She told me, "I think of my concept albums as the equivalent of a symphonic poem of the nineteenth and early twentieth century. Now, in [the] twenty-first century, my albums continue this tradition." Kouneva pays to record the orchestra herself, though one recording, *The Woman Astronaut* (2015), was sponsored via a Kickstarter campaign through which she raised $35,000 from her community of mentees, friends, and fans. She views spending her own money as a vital investment in her artistic growth and in her career. "These albums are my legacy, in addition to my film and game soundtracks."[64]

Veteran television and film music composer Stu Phillips, like many composers, noted how, in film or television music, the composer is bringing someone else's vision to life. But with concert music, he said, "It's totally you; it's your imagination, your emotions; it's what you want to do, and nobody's breathing down your neck and saying, 'This is not what I want.'" Phillips not only writes concert music, he told me about the arrangements of piano works by Sergei Rachmaninoff, Richard Strauss, and Alexander Scriabin that he orchestrated, just to keep his hand in (since, at the time of our interview, he was in his late eighties), and that he hoped to have performed.[65]

Conclusions

In some ways, the discussion of creativity, creative freedom, and agency here resembles my discussion of the history of music in advertising (Taylor 2012); discourses about art and creativity don't dominate this field of cultural production (though it is always a little jarring to watch the Academy Awards broadcast and its presenters and commentators reverently refer to film as an art form and pretend that money has nothing to do with it), just as they were absent in the world of advertising. But no one denies that creativity is being exercised. I have sought in this chapter to show just how it is exercised, at least for composers and those who work with and for them; in group production, there are constant negotiations, ceaseless attempts to find ways to make what one thinks is the right decision, the right choice to make the music work with the picture, to make it sound professional.

It is interesting that for so many of these workers, the question of their own creative freedom isn't that much of an issue. The more technical workers were happy to work within the parameters of their fields, though they could speak of the creative aspects of what they do when asked but more in terms of the agency they were able to exercise in their work. None seemed to find their work unfulfilling, but those composers who had creative outlets in concert music do seem to find some degree of artistic creativity and autonomy that most didn't feel they had access to in film and television music. Yet these composers nonetheless seemed happy in their work and proud of its quality, even as it is managed by those purportedly possessing the creative function, which allows them to view composers' labor as raw material in need of refinement for their own purposes.

COMPOSERS' LABOR

Having laid the theoretical foundation, this chapter and the next are more empirical, since one of the main goals of this book is to discover and document what these working musicians do. In some respects, the labor of famous composers isn't much different from that of the (mostly) lesser-known composers chronicled here, though the big names can command higher fees and, perhaps, in a very few cases, notably John Williams, are permitted larger groups of musicians and more time to record their scores.

Nonetheless, as we know from previous chapters (and the epigraphs to this book), composers work at the pleasure of producers and directors. Some composers might enjoy special relationships with some directors (John Williams and Steven Spielberg being the most famous in recent years), but, nonetheless, composers must do what they're told. They are cogs in a wheel with many moving parts—as many as a few thousand workers in total—but some of them can enjoy a more collaborative relationship with their producers or directors. It's not easy. In a recent lecture, Randy Newman said about doing film music, "It's a real hard job, in my opinion. It's still show business, but just barely. It's like threading a pipe in a way. . . . It's difficult to do it right, do it well."[1]

In this chapter, I examine what these composers actually do, how they produce music that satisfies the desired use-value of their bosses—producers and directors. While a good deal has been written about how neoliberal capitalism has affected the cultural businesses in terms of takeovers, mega-mergers, and increased influence of the suits wielding more authority over creatives (see Taylor 2016), less is known about how neoliberal capitalist ideologies and practices have affected the everyday lives of everyday workers in these businesses. In fact, what film and television music workers actually do isn't well known outside these businesses, except for what a few star composers reveal in interviews. I have spoken with a number of different sorts of workers in these businesses, people who perform significantly different tasks but all of whom work on film, television, streaming, games, or some combination. At the top of the musical heap is the composer (though composers have their bosses, as I have said). Film composers, at least in bigger, more expensive productions, can be backed by a fairly large team of workers, such as arrangers, orchestrators, copyists, scoring mixers, music editors, additional composers, and more. These workers usually view their job as supporting the composer, trying to give them the maximum amount of time and space to write, since they typically have only four to six weeks to produce a score for a film and much less time for a television episode. Since writing the score is the last thing, or one of the last things, done in producing a film or episode, there is always immense pressure on the composer to finish on schedule. Time pressure is one of the biggest complaints of all music workers. That and the growing difficulty of making a living.

The overall argument of this chapter is that composers' labor is viewed as a kind of natural resource that is acquired through primitive accumulation, which David Harvey (2005) has theorized more broadly as "accumulation by dispossession" resulting in a product that is valued solely for its use to those above the composers in the supply chain. Harvey's term is meant to convey the many new means by which neoliberal capitalism has continued to accumulate value since Marx theorized primitive accumulation. For Harvey, accumulation by dispossession encompasses many current practices, the most relevant of which for my purposes concerns copyright ownership by producers, not musicians, the latter being increasingly deprived even of royalties by streaming services and who are paid less to work more.

While this sort of appropriation of labor in cultural production has been with us since the rise of the cultural businesses, the ways that neoliberal capitalism has increasingly infiltrated these businesses shed light on its operations. Among composers, there has been the rise of teams of composers managed by a composer-brand who acts as an entrepreneur and manager. At the same time, while in the past composers were thought to be interchangeable, with very few superstar exceptions, today some are less interchangeable, for example, when a director wants a particular indie rock band and not another to write music for their film. There has thus been growing nichification, pigeon-holing composers in a particular style or medium (network versus film or streaming).[2] Also, the use of digital technologies that were supposed to make things easier have actually increased time pressure on composers and thus everyone else, as schedules have been shortened, and bosses feel as though they can ask for last-minute changes, which wasn't possible to do before the advent of digital technologies. Almost everyone works harder, competes more, and earns less.

In film and television production, various supply chains are already in motion by the time the composer is hired at the beginning of the music supply chain. In concluding this introductory section, I want to examine the hiring process from the perspective of the (capitalist) studio, the purpose of which is profit but which also functions to service the needs of the director or producer. Film directors usually want to hire a particular composer, as producers and directors think in terms of concrete labor, that is, labor that results in the specific use-values they want for their films. Studio executives think of composers more in terms of providers of abstract labor (i.e., human labor in general that is economically valuable). I asked Robert Kraft, president of Fox Music from 1994 to 2012, how he handles producers and directors who want to hire a particular composer (using the well-known composer Danny Elfman as a hypothetical) whom he, as a music professional, thinks costs too much or isn't the best person for the job. Kraft said he must address their requests by engaging in a lot of patient explaining. Producers and directors always push back: "'But I think Danny will respond to this material,'" they say, as if, Kraft said, "Danny isn't doing anything else; he's just lying around waiting for their script."[3]

But it's part of Kraft's job to service the film and the director, so he will call the composer's representatives and mention the project and budget. "The response is almost always, 'Let us take a look,' because you never know, and they never know. They are duty bound to say, 'Danny, this came in. Here's the budget. Do you want to read it? Explore? Do you like the director?'" Kraft said that once in a great while something improbable will work out, but mostly, he said, "I go down the path of borderline reality." He offered a hypothetical example: "If it is a silly, low-budget family comedy, and they feel like John Williams is really the only one who can do it, I very patiently explain that Maestro Williams is so out of our budget, and is so engaged with whatever he is currently doing, that this will be a very fast 'no.' Why don't we look at somebody who's the junior version of John Williams? I suggest composers that I love who could do this, and I play them some things."[4]

Kraft said that the best situation from his perspective is to collaborate with a director who already has a good working relationship with a composer, so it's a simple matter of ensuring that the budget and scheduling are possible. The worst-case-scenario situations, Kraft said, are those involving someone who has never directed a feature in a major studio before and doesn't know how the system works and, so, can only think in pie-in-the-sky terms, hiring a famous composer for the score and a superstar pop star to write a song for the film. In such cases, Kraft's job is to educate the directors and counsel them that the advice they received from their partner or thirteen-year-old child about putting a favorite band in the film probably isn't feasible.[5]

This brief overview of the studio's perspective on the hiring of composers lays out the tensions and compromises that are made every day in these fields. Composers are hired to do a job and are viewed in terms of their concrete labor by their bosses, producers and directors, who nonetheless hope to have an artistically collaborative relationship (though one in which they have the last word), while studios view composers as purveyors of abstract labor. But, regardless of their positionality in the field, studios, producers, and directors view composers as providing a service, their creative, "natural" labor available to be obtained through accumulation by dispossession to be refined into use-value.

Accumulation of Creativity and Use-Value

Let me address first the issue of the accumulation by dispossession of the creativity represented by the composers' labor. Elsewhere (Taylor 2020), I have mentioned the primitive accumulation of musicians' work, so here I would like to flesh out this claim. The first thing to take care of is the objection that, since composers are paid, how can the products of their labor be captured through accumulation by dispossession? It's true that composers are paid (though generally not as much as they once were, as I will discuss in chapter 7). But: Composers do not own the copyrights to their own music (though in the world of independent film, they might be given their publishing rights since there is less money up front; see Gallo 1997). In an action by the Composers and Lyricists Guild of America (their union) in the 1970s, the composers and lyricists demanded of the Association of Motion Picture and Television Producers that they retain the rights to their music and lyrics, their argument being that the music and lyrics were only being used once (in a broadcast or film). This was their main demand. The producers failed to budge on this point, so the composers and lyricists went on strike late in 1971. The producers essentially waited them out, and in June 1982 the union was broken (for more, see Eicke 2019). The point here is that, while composers are indeed paid for their work as freelance contractors, they don't own it and are thus deprived from using it as they wish. Legally, the term is "work made for hire" or "work for hire"—composers (and everyone in the music supply chain) are paid by producers to do a particular job. Composers receive a fee and what is known as the writer's share of the royalties, but that's all. Composers have no control over what happens to their music after they finish it; producers are free to do whatever they want with it, which is usually nothing. Roy M. Prendergast recounts a story of Lalo Schifrin, who wanted to conduct a concert performance of some of his film music. He contacted the studio that produced the film and requested a score but was told it wasn't his music and that if he wanted to perform it, he would have to rent it from the studio, though the studio eventually lent him the music gratis (Prendergast 1992, 157). Veteran composer Lee Holdridge thinks that much of the music he wrote for Universal Studios in the 1970s (before the advent of digital technologies) has since been discarded by the studio.[6]

This is a much different situation from that of authors of books, who also usually surrender copyright ownership but in exchange for the production, distribution, and marketing of their books. A producer who owns a film or television music score can use it however the producer wishes, if at all. Richard Davis (2010) quotes a producer's lawyer, who said, "When we buy a score, it's as if we are buying a suit of clothes. If we want to hang it in the closet and just leave it there, that's our business" (201, 227, quoting Prendergast 1992, 157). This system is a vestige of the studio system era, when studios employed composers, orchestrators—everyone—but the demise of the studio system meant that composers and everyone in the music supply chain now works for hire as a freelancer.

In characterizing the capture of a composer's labor as something that is accumulated by dispossession, I am subscribing to the broader views of primitive accumulation theorized by Werner Bonefeld (2001) and Massimo De Angelis (2001, 2004, 2007) but especially by David Harvey's updating and retheorizing as "accumulation by dispossession" (2005, 2007). John T. Caldwell employs the term *harvested* to describe how film and television workers' creativity is acquired (in Caldwell et al. 2013). Some of these authors theorize primitive accumulation not just as a precapitalist phase, as did Marx, but as something that is foundational to capitalism itself (Bonefeld 2001, 1) as well as ongoing (De Angelis 2007).

Other authors have made similar arguments about recorded music. Matt Stahl (2011), for example, is concerned with musicians who make recordings and how the socio-legal apparatus of the music business has gradually encroached on musicians' profit margins in order to increase its profit, and Stahl characterizes this as primitive accumulation (as others have theorized uncompensated labor in the digital world; see Ekman 2012 and Fuchs 2010 and 2012, among others). Fair enough. I am interested in a different field of cultural production, one in which the legal apparatus hasn't changed much over the years: Composers are paid a fee to produce a score and/or set of digital files in a certain amount of time, with parameters determined by their bosses. Accumulation by dispossession here works this way: Composers are viewed as naturally musical, naturally creative, their work akin to a natural product acquired by dispossessing the composer of ownership of the work, which is viewed by bosses as requiring refinement through labor processes embedded in supply chains.

This revised conceptualization of primitive accumulation is another way of theorizing how capitalists locate value in noncapitalist arenas and incorporate it through processes of translation (Tsing 2009, 2013, 2015), a phenomenon of considerable interest that I have discussed elsewhere (Taylor n.d.a). Here, I am seeking something of a theoretical hybrid in the sense that I want to retain that aspect of the theory of primitive accumulation that assumes a natural sort of production (even by nature itself), which is important in the business' construction of creativity—the composer's and everyone else's; that is, creativity must be understood as natural in order to justify its accumulation by dispossession and transformation into the use-value of a commodity. But I am also drawn to Anna Tsing's arguments about the production of value outside of capitalism's reach, a production of value that nonetheless can be brought into a capitalist regime through processes of translation; supply chains are what she theorizes—a good starts outside of capitalism but is slowly brought into it and turned into a commodity as it moves through a supply chain. Unlike Tsing's inspiring book, I'm only examining a supply chain embedded in other supply chains. There is no commodity at the end of the music supply chain, so I'm really considering only use-value: How is what is construed by bosses as a raw product—a notated musical score and/or an audio file—refined to generate use-value?

So, let's consider the question of use-value for a moment. Marx's thinking about use-values itself undergoes something of a refinement as one traverses *Capital*. Marx at first seems to dismiss the diversity of use-values, moving quickly to his abstract concepts: A commodity satisfies some sort of need; "the nature of these needs, whether they arise, for example, from the stomach, or the imagination, makes no difference," he says (1990, 125). He acknowledges that things can be useful in many ways, but that is not his concern: "The discovery of these ways and hence of the manifold uses of things is the work of history" (125).

In volume 1 of *Capital*, a few pages after the passage cited above, Marx complicates his conception of use-value: In order to produce a commodity, a laborer "must not only produce use-values, but use-values for others" (1990, 131). A good becomes a commodity when, through the medium of exchange, it is transferred to another person who has a use-value for it (131). Marx writes in chapter 7 that for the laborer to embody his labor in a commodity, "he must above all embody it in use-values." Capitalists compel their workers to produce specific goods with particular use-values (283).

Marx writes in his consideration of use-value in chapter 1 that "use-values are combinations of two elements, the material provided by nature, and labour" (133), asserting (with a gendered metaphor that Harvey [2010, 28] writes can be traced at least to Francis Bacon) that "labour is therefore not the only source of material wealth, i.e., of the use-values it produces. As William Petty says, labour is the father of material wealth, the earth is its mother" (Marx 1990, 133–34). Marx later writes that the labor process "is an appropriation of what exists in nature for the requirements of man" (290). Marx goes on to characterize the labor process as one that occurs between man and nature, a process "by which man, through his own actions, mediates, regulates and controls the metabolism between himself and nature" (283). The point I would make here is that natural resources are characterized as feminine in the same era when creativity was being constructed as a feminized natural resource—but nonetheless as the province of men, as we saw in the previous chapter. Capitalists view the products of creativity as the results of "natural" talent or creativity, products that must be refined and rationalized through labor processes and supply chains. The products of creativity are also defeminized in these processes—whatever is culturally "feminine" about creativity is removed as it moves through the supply chain on its way to being pure use-value of a commodity.

Marx takes up the question of the labor process and the valorization process in chapter 7 of volume 1 of *Capital*, issues of central concern here since I am arguing, drawing on Tsing, that it is labor processes in supply chains that create use-value for capitalists out of the "raw" material supplied by composers. Marx argues that, unlike the spider weaving a web or a bee building a honeycomb, a human has a plan, a goal in mind, before beginning to work. In the labor process, the worker's activity with the instruments of labor changes the object of labor that was planned from the beginning by the capitalist, who has taken responsibility for the labor process (Braverman 1998, 39). The product of this process is use-value, "a piece of natural material adapted to human needs by means of a change in its form" (Marx 1990, 287). Marx offers a discussion of raw materials, and lights on the example of cotton thread or yarn, which is already a product but also raw material, "changing its shape constantly, until it is precipitated from the last process of the series in finished form, either as a means of substance or as an instrument of labour" (289). Composers may consider their work to be a finished product, but they also understand that it will be viewed and treated as raw material and subjected to many labor processes as it traverses the music supply chain and is finally integrated into the film, episode, or game.

Marx says that capitalists produce use-values only because they form the material basis of exchange-value; use-values are the bearers of exchange-value. "Our capitalist," he writes (in this context, the studio owner, with the cooperation of managers in the form of producers and directors), "has two objectives: in the first place, he wants to produce a use-value which has exchange-value, i.e., an article destined to be sold, a commodity; and secondly he wants to produce a commodity greater in value than the sum of the values of the commodities used to produce it, namely the means of production and the labour-power he purchased with his good money on the open market. His aim is to produce not only a use-value, but a commodity; not only use-value, but value; and not just value, but also surplus-value" (293).

Getting In, Getting Hired

Now let me turn to the more immediate issues that concern composers: getting into the business, getting gigs. One of the questions I asked every interviewee was how they entered the business. Most people had been musicians from a young age, and most had formal training as composers, though this varied somewhat. Most people offered stories about the amount of perseverance required and their willingness early in their career to work for little or nothing in order to get work.

Getting into the Business

I argued in the previous chapter that once one is in one of these fields of cultural production, cultural and economic capital don't much matter in getting work. But they do matter in the sense that they can help people get into the business in the first place. It is so difficult to earn a living in these fields, especially at the beginning of one's career, that it is necessary to enter them with some sort of support system of economic capital and, frequently, cultural capital. Plenty of composers I discuss here came from families wealthy enough to support them while they tried to establish themselves in the business. Others came from more modest backgrounds and started in a musical field other than composition but slowly worked their way more into the business and began to secure composing gigs. The point is that it is frequently necessary to possess economic capital (or its promise from one's parents) in order to have a cushion while attempting to establish oneself in the business, especially for composers. Workers below composers tend to have less economic and cultural capital.

We know from chapter 1 that getting into the business requires a good deal of perseverance, both to enter a network and to expand it, amassing social and symbolic capital. Before this can happen, though, composers need to learn their craft. Virtually every composer I spoke to has formal training in music and most in composition. Older composers tend to have been more extensively trained in a classical fashion, knowing how not just to compose, but to orchestrate (write for specific orchestral instruments), inasmuch as, since before the rise of digital technologies in the 1970s and 1980s, composers wrote exclusively for live musicians. Composers of the last living generation (those born between 1920 and 1940) attended a variety of institutions of higher learning, but people born in the 1950s and after are very likely to have studied at the Berklee College of Music in Boston, today the premier institution of higher learning in commercial music, as well as in jazz and other fields. They, too, are trained to compose for the orchestra, but they also receive a good deal of technical training in various digital technologies used in composition today, since most television shows, video games, streaming programs, and many films are composed solely, or mainly, with a computer; today, only bigger-budgeted films, and a few television programs, employ live musicians or even an orchestra. Berklee promises its film scoring undergraduate majors that when they complete the major, they will be able to

- sketch and compose stylistically appropriate music in a variety of dramatic styles;
- orchestrate dramatic music using appropriate instrumental tone colors and voicings;
- conduct to picture and to electronic metronome, conducting multiple meter and tempo changes;
- create and edit temporary and final sound track recordings to picture for a complete media work;
- create orchestral mockups and electronic scores using current sequencers and sample libraries;
- record and mix scores and music stems using current software and hardware;
- analyze the dramatic arc of a musical score for a film or other extended media work;
- apply legal knowledge, business acumen, and marketing techniques to the operation of a small business; and
- develop a concept for a score and create an appropriate musical form for it.[7]

For many composers in the business, as well as other workers, the entry-level position is that of the composer's assistant, who can perform all sorts of tasks, including nonmusical ones. Musical responsibilities might include proofreading scores, setting up for recording sessions, and more. Flora, the composer's assistant who wished to remain anonymous, said her job involved doing "pretty much all the crap that no one else wants to do. I really do a lot, everything from all the assistant stuff like dry cleaning, coffees." Flora told me that one of her jobs was to make musical notation intelligible and clear for the live musicians, since recording sessions are expensive and a lack of clarity can result in wasted time.[8] The composer's assistant has power. Andrés Locsey said that as a composer's assistant, which is how he got into the business, you have it in your hands to ruin a $200,000 recording session. "For about six months, every Friday night, I went to bed worried that on Saturday I would have done something wrong, and the recording session would be a disaster! But it all went fine, and I learned a lot through that job, a lot of technical stuff."[9]

Ryan Shore is a composer today but started out working for his uncle Howard Shore, a well-known film music composer, after graduating from Berklee. He said he wouldn't call the work he did as that of a composer's assistant, which he characterized as more general and producer-like—keeping the workflow moving; he said that his work consisted of real jobs, such as music copyist and orchestrator. Shore told me he would use Finale, a music software program, to prepare scores and parts for the recording session, and he would take his uncle's MIDI files (Musical Instrument Digital Interface audio files that can be converted into music notation) and prepare the basic score for Howard to orchestrate. Ryan would then input the orchestration into Finale, which would be revised by Howard. Ryan would then go back and forth with Howard until the score was ready, and Ryan would generate the score and parts for the recording session, at which he would be present. Ryan did this for around ten films, and then Howard asked him to do the orchestration, so he orchestrated a few films, went into music producing, and then started to get work in feature films.[10] This is a fairly typical trajectory, though not everyone has a relative in the business.

Getting Hired

Once they have a foothold in the business, most composers' main goal is to be hired on a film, television, or streaming series. Employment on a series guarantees a certain amount of work (though not as much as in the past, as series might not be renewed after only thirteen episodes, and streaming series can be a one-off package of only ten episodes, more or less).

Kurt Farquhar told me that the hardest part of the work was not getting the first job—even though he was homeless at the time—but sustaining a career for thirty years, in what I described in the first chapter as an ageist business, winning jobs again and again; a trade press article says that half of a composer's time is spent finding the next gig (Borum 2016; see also Foliart 2011). "It is a battle that you're going to have to do every day," Farquhar said. "There's never a day that I wake up when I got another job that I'm not jumping up and down like the Lucky Charms guy and then going into hand-to-hand combat."

Working on the music for a pilot is a process of trying to devise a unique sound for the show, something that helps identify it sonically in viewers' minds, an endeavor that has become increasingly important in an era when there are so many films and series (see Savas 2018b). Farquhar said that people who are vying for a show will tell him they've produced an amazing demo, saying, "'They've got to love this. This is fantastic; it's the baddest thing I ever did.'" His response is, "'You only sent *one*?'" Describing his method, Farquhar said, "I come in after a show, and I'm hitting them with six, seven, eight different versions of how to play that piece. I start with exactly what they've asked for, and I do something that's exactly the opposite of that. I shift it about ten degrees, and I do that, and I do the exact opposite. Then I shift it another ten degrees, and I do that, and I do the opposite. And I shift it another bit, and I do that, and I do the opposite." Then he said, "I think of stuff that just will get you kicked off TV. And then I do that just-because-I-can music. Just bizarre; you wouldn't have thought of this, I wouldn't have thought of this; I'm shocked at what I just did. And it has nothing to do with anything that any human being asked for, and I'm having a good-ass time, but I do make sure that I do believe that it works for the picture. That's the only criterion. But it can be wickedly weird and different." Farquhar told me that over 50 percent of his commissions for theme songs and programs have been versions buried in the alternate selections he has prepared.[11]

Veteran composer Jan Stevens, best known as the composer for the sitcom *Scrubs* (2001–10), described the pilot process from his perspective. Finding the unique sound is the most difficult aspect of writing music for a pilot. He told me, "The first thing a producer's going to say is, 'We want to hear something we've never heard before! You know when you hear the *Seinfeld* theme, you know that one! We've got to have something like that!'"[12] In Stevens's view, finding the sound of the show is the goal, and once it is accomplished, the composer is more than halfway there.

The pressure to devise a unique sound exists in the world of music for games as well. Penka Kouneva also remarked on the importance of creating that unique sound in composing for film and for video games, and she offered a helpful description of their similarities. She said that, in both cases, the music helps conjure a world, an atmosphere, an environment where the story happens. "You're creating the emotional depth, the emotional dimension of the characters and the story." The other similarity with games, she said (if it's a triple A game, meaning one from a major developer), is that the characters must have their own themes, which, she said, is the same in film: "The ability to compose a theme that captures a character is a skill that translates between both film and games."[13]

Stevens said that after the sound of the pilot has been determined in a television show, there is nonetheless a lot of scrutiny of composers at the beginning of the show's run: "I'd say for the first year they're going to watch everything you do." But, he added, if the program is successful, the pressure is lighter for everyone; the composer is usually given more autonomy after the first year or so. If it's not, "They sit on everybody: 'Make the music better! The music's not good enough; that's why nobody's watching! Make this better! Make that better!'"[14]

In film, as in television, there are debates and discussions about suitability, availability, and budget. Robert Kraft told me that he and his department would have long discussions with the producers, director, and studio about finding the right composer who is available and affordable (the budget having already been set), how soon the director wants the composer to start writing—all this long before the film has been completed. Even before shooting has begun, some directors want to hear something, so the composer puts together some themes. "That often gets a composer the gig," Kraft said: "'Play me something.' And that maybe becomes a part of the movie." Kraft told me that many composers now record suites of music that contain all the main themes. They play these for the director, either before shooting starts or during, in order to say, "'This is sort of the vibe we're thinking about' and 'Where does this fit?' and 'Where doesn't it fit?'"[15]

After that, the first edit of the movie arrives, and the composer starts scoring scenes. The role of the studio music department at this stage, Kraft said, is in part to reassure executives that the temp music, the temporary, placeholder music in the film that they have become accustomed or attached to, isn't superior to what has actually been composed for the film. The music department checks in to hear how things are going, meets with the studio executives to play them some samples of the music to make sure they're on board with the direction the composer is taking, which is, Kraft said, "somewhere between never and rarely" because the executives have been listening to the temp music throughout the process, so they have become accustomed to music by luminaries, such as John Williams or Thomas Newman. "And suddenly they hear a cue by our composer, and they freak out because it's different. So, we push toward getting an approved score." Once the score is approved, it's recorded and mixed, and the music is mixed into the film. "And then we see the film, and then we have a couple of beats where the studio executives hate the music. Then we'll go back and revise and tweak it. And then you go to the premiere."[16]

Much of the process of selecting a composer and advising the composer about what producers and directors want is the beginning of the refinement process, attempting to shape the composer's raw material into something that bosses recognize as delivering the use-value they seek. Composers are told from the start what to do (though this can create its own problems, as

I will discuss in chapter 5) and monitored to varying degrees, their music entering the supply chain and a series of labor processes.

Getting the Job Done

Once a composer has landed a gig on a film or survived the pilot process on television, there is a supply chain of production with various labor processes, which differs by budget and thus by medium (I'll flesh this out below). Most music for all of these media is produced by a composer in a home studio. Composers receive instructions about the music from the showrunner in television (usually credited as an executive producer) or a director in film during what is known as a spotting session, where the composer, music editor, music supervisor (if there is one), and showrunner/director watch the episode or film and discuss, scene by scene, where they want the composer to add music and where outside music (which is selected by the music supervisor) will be employed. Some television composers report that spotting sessions may not happen, for example, when it is obvious what the show needs (see Eskow 2002). Music editor Kevin Crehan said that spotting sessions are mostly conducted online today where several platforms are available; everyone involved can watch the film simultaneously and view the time codes and discuss where music should be placed.[17]

The television composer may hire a few live musicians—or play something live themselves—and record in their studio and incorporate their contributions into the recorded soundtrack they make. The composer produces the audio, a series of cues electronically generated, then sends it on to the scoring mixer, who improves the audio quality to make it sound as professional as possible. The scoring mixer sends the soundtrack to the music editor, who makes sure everything fits to picture and incorporates any music that has been selected by a music supervisor. Then the soundtrack goes to whoever is in charge of final approval or edits. Generally, all this has been accomplished digitally on the computer; no music has been written down unless the composer has been able to hire live musicians.

Emmy-winning composer Ben Decter describes the process this way as it unfolded for a Shonda Rhimes drama called *Off the Map* on ABC (2011). After the spotting session, he said, he would have about five days to write music for each episode, about twenty to twenty-five minutes of music, recorded with a forty-five-piece orchestra each week, which Decter felt lucky to have had the opportunity to employ. Decter said that, even with writing all that music, composers are often asked to rewrite some things multiple times. He said he would get up at 5:30 a.m. and work late into the night, but on that particular show he had the assistance of an arranger and an engineer. After his files were ready, he would send them to his orchestrator, who would occasionally offer suggestions like, "'How about we add a little countermelody for the French horn here?'" After the recording session, Decter said, "We'd stay around for a couple hours to mix. This was a luxury. Usually, I mix my own music. By the time I got home, the next episode would often be waiting."[18]

Today, in an era when music doesn't originate as a notated score nearly as much as in the past, composers are able to generate a synthesized mockup of their music, which they can use as a preview for their bosses. (In the old days, a composer would probably play the score on the piano for them.) Making such a mockup can require extra effort, but, as John Debney told an interviewer, it can be useful in confirming that the composer is producing what the bosses want. "It's helpful to both of us because if you're going down a path that isn't maybe what they want, you can find out rather quickly in sometimes in very colorful terms—if they hate it, you know right away. . . . In my case, I love it because it gives us a frame of reference. . . . But once we find that path, it's a helpful tool." Debney offered an example of a current project: "I'm working on a show right now where the director had not heard a lot of demos before; he loves it now, because he can actually audition the piece of music, give me notes, and then I fix it. We send it to him, and then he signs off, hopefully, and then we go to the scoring stage."[19]

Sometimes the executives want some music to be rewritten, as Decter said. Jan Stevens described the process of sending a television episode in. After he has finished the music to his satisfaction, an edited version of the episode goes to the network, where someone views and approves it or requires edits, which are given in the form of "notes." Stevens said that, on *Scrubs*, he would sometimes be asked to make some rewrites but that, in his case, only about ten cues per season needed adjustments. Stevens said that after getting into a rhythm and style of work with the editors and producers during the first season, "I knew what they wanted, I knew who I was answering to, and so I knew how to write for that person. I knew who was going to make the decisions—rewrite the cue, throw out the cue, find something else—so I knew what to do."[20] With film, the production chain can be much more complicated, as I will discuss later.

From Individual to Team Production

The rise of neoliberal capitalism has affected every corner of these businesses. I will explore the most significant of these neoliberal effects in detail in chapters 7 and 8, though here, I will discuss one aspect of this shift, in which the composer essentially becomes a capitalist entrepreneur and manager within this field of cultural production. While production in the music part of the supply chain remains artisanal, it has become increasingly organized as a capitalist form of production. The seemingly ever-compressed schedule has increased the likelihood that a composer will take on more than one show or film project and must hire out to get the work done on time. Composers hiring other composers to get the job done (once known as *ghosting*, about which more below) has become even more common and normalized as deadlines have gotten shorter and as some famous composers have become brands and accepted more and more work that is produced under their brand name.

What happened differs little from Max Weber's characterization of a traditionalistic peasant becoming a capitalist laborer in *The Protestant Ethic* (1905), which captures this shift from the "traditional" composer working in a traditionalistic way being transformed into a capitalist composer as entrepreneur-manager. The traditionalist worker, says Weber, labored in a fairly leisurely fashion, but the transition to capitalism could be as swift as it was subtle. "Now at some time this leisureliness was suddenly destroyed, and often entirely without any essential change in the form of organization, such as the transition to a unified factory, to mechanical weaving, etc. What happened was, on the contrary, often no more than this: some young man from one of the putting-out families went out into the country, carefully chose weavers for his employ, greatly increased the rigor of his supervision of their work, and thus turned them from peasants into laborers" (Weber [1905] 2001, 30).

Famed television composer Mike Post was one of the pioneers of this new mode of music production, according to composer Alan Elliott,[21] the result of Post's early adoption of what is known as the package deal, a pay structure in which the composer receives a fee out of which they pay for everything (music editing, live musicians, if any, and more), retaining the remainder for themselves (see chapter 7). Post's studio was described to me by Ben Decter, who had heard from a college friend who told him that Christophe Beck (now a well-known film composer) was leaving Post's company and that there was an opening. Post is a legend in the field, and his work was well known to Decter at the time; he told me that Post's theme music to *Hill Street Blues* was the only TV theme sheet music he'd ever purchased. Decter said he met with Post and played him a cassette of some his music. "In response," Decter said, "he took off his sunglasses, looked me in the eye and said, 'How'd you like to work on NYPD *Blue?*'"[22] Decter took the job and said that Post gave him a lot of responsibility. The deal, Decter said, was from Post's perspective: "'You get to hang out in my studio, make some money, and you'll have a week to produce my score for NYPD *Blue* and make it sound like it needs to sound. I'll see you each week for the mix.'" Post would write out the parts on staff paper, and Decter and a colleague would go into the next room, where the recording studio was, and "spend a week with the synths and samplers, making things sound great." Decter also worked with Post on *Law & Order*, which, he said, "was a simpler process: Mike would perform the score, and we would finesse it and add some minor enhancements."[23] Post, in an interview, described this process as "dealing" work to these composer/apprentices, having a "dealing session" in which he tells them "exactly what I'm looking for in the music for that episode and then they write it" (Fink 1998, 159). In our interview, he said that he and his composing partner, Pete Carpenter (1914–1997), would work on the music together and then give it to their protégés. This system grew out of necessity, he said, inasmuch as, in one year, he and Carpenter were responsible for the music for ten shows.

> Now, as fast as we were, nobody can write that much music every week. So, we had a whole army of guys, and each week we would write the lick of the week. So, there would be a, a new heavy, a new adversary; there would be a kid with cancer; there'd be a love interest; there'd be an old friend. There would be a new element that was the A story, and then there'd be another element that was the B story. That's the way network TV is done. So, we would write the lick for the A story and write the lick for the B story. Then we'd have all the guys come to Pete's house, and we'd hand out cue sheets and say, "Here's the lick. Here's what this thing is about in this tempo. Try doing this and this and this." And we would split it with them. Or, we'd say, "Base it on the theme, do it about in this tempo, make a big switch here, make a big switch there, turn it here, and then do this." And we would just tell them what to do, and then they'd go realize it.[24]

John Debney, now a well-known television and film composer, also got his start as one of Post's protégés. Post, he said, could be writing the music for eight shows at a time with the help of a highly competent core team. Debney described the process of receiving the lick of the week from Post's perspective. "Every week," he said, "we'd go to Mike's office, and he'd have the bad guy theme of the week. He'd write it out. And it was usually a really cool little clever thing: bad guy. And sometimes I'd get the bad guy cues; sometimes I'd get the big chase scenes, 'cause, you kind of graduated into doing the big chase scenes because they were of a kind. So, I kind of worked my way up with him a bit."[25]

Ben Decter later scored his own show under Post's supervision. A year after he had begun working for Post, the senior composer asked him to take over writing the music for a show called *Silk Stalkings* from another composer who was working with Post. Decter wrote the music for a year and a half (1996–97). Then, "another year later, Mike said, 'Okay, I'm going to have some other guys take that show over. Now I want you to do a new show with me.' Over the next two years, Mike and I shared screen and writing credits for multiple series. And then I started to get projects on my own."[26]

Post told me he was proud of the fact that he always shared credits with his protégés; he and Carpenter would take half the writer's credit and their assistants the other half. At the recording session, he and Carpenter would make sure that everyone knew who wrote what. "If it wasn't a Mike and Pete cue, we'd say, 'This is Frank Vincent's cue.' We'd tell the orchestra, the producer. We'd tell everybody, 'No ghosting—everything out in the open, cards on the table.'" Post said that the practice of ghosting was widespread within the field, that composers would take credit for music they hadn't written, and that "the thing I'm most proud of is that I never did what a lot of composers do, and a ton of them do it nowadays. I mean, it's just rampant, and it was pretty rampant in those days, but they kept it a big secret; it was a dirty secret in the old days, and we never did it. We gave everybody credit."[27]

In film, the scale of a famous composer's team can be even bigger, since live musicians are more likely to be employed, necessitating orchestrators and perhaps arrangers plus recording engineers. One composer's assistant worked at Remote Control, a large facility in Santa Monica owned by Hans Zimmer, one of the top composers in film. Remote Control housed its employees as well as freelancers who occasionally worked for Zimmer. These freelancers pay rent for studio space but work for Zimmer when he needs them. Zimmer writes a melody, or a motif, or a theme and distributes them to composers working there, "and then they'll come back, and he will structure them into one score, to be as congruous as possible." I asked how many people Zimmer employs; the composer's assistant didn't know but said that about 75 percent of the people working there are employed in some way on a Zimmer film (for a detailed treatment of Zimmer's working methods, see Eicke 2019).[28] Joey Newman described working with one composer—who had an office staff as well as multiple composers and orchestrator—as a "factory vibe."[29] Composers usually still compose, but a few of the high-profile composers who win a lot of jobs have hired other composers to do some of the work they once did themselves. This sort of arrangement has always existed in an ad hoc fashion but has become increasingly normalized, one of the ways that neoliberal capitalism has shaped these fields of cultural production.

Music production by such large groups is a fairly recent development. In the past, the practice of ghosting (composers hiring uncredited others to help) was generally frowned upon, even though everyone knew it was common and something of an open secret given the crushing deadlines composers usually face; orchestrator Tom Calderaro told me that it used to be a big secret that people went to great lengths to protect. The idea was that a director hired a particular composer and expected that composer to do the work. But ghosting has always been done, just on the sly until recently. The reasons haven't gone away—the composer is pressed for time, has taken on too many projects, doesn't want to do what was asked of them. In the past, ghost composers were never treated well, never given credit, Calderaro said.[30]

This is not the kind of secret that is easily maintained, since people who write music sign a certificate of authenticity attesting that they wrote the music, and music editors keep a list of all cues for bookkeeping purposes. Or, as Calderaro said, in the old days, if you were ghosting, you weren't named on the cue sheet in order to preserve the false secret that a single composer wrote the entire score. The only pay a ghost received was from the hiring composer. "If you were ghosting, you got your check, and then you went away," Calderaro said.[31] But, one could be well paid, as composer Shirley Walker told another interviewer: "I came into the business at a time when the nature of ghost writing was that you were paid big money not to talk about the fact that you were doing it and to support the illusion or delusion, whichever you prefer, that composer X was actually doing the work that they were being paid for" (quoted in Schelle 1999, 364). These days, composers who write extra music receive credit for having written "additional music." Composer Deborah Lurie has written additional music for the well-known composer Danny Elfman. She told me, "I got started because his schedule to complete the score was simply unrealistic without a bit of assistance. They calculated every day he had left before recording and how many minutes of music were realistic for him to write per day, and it was simply not possible for one person to do."[32] As Calderaro told me, "Composing a film score has become a team project now."[33]

Composers who write additional music study the existing cues and then attempt to emulate the style of the main composer. Lurie spoke about working on *Charlie and the Chocolate Factory* (2005) with music by Elfman: "I just wrote some of the cues that he didn't have time to do, using his themes. He oversaw what I was doing and coached me, gave me feedback, and honestly, he was a very good mentor. He had written a fair amount of the score by then, so I was able to study what he had done and write in that style."[34] Joey Newman said this sort of handoff works fairly well; once he has established a style for a particular show, the composers he hires to write additional music can copy it so that the final product is seamless.[35]

In such a system, there are plenty of opportunities to take advantage of younger composers who are eager to break into the field and work, at least at first, for little or no pay. This has always been true for people early in their careers, as we have seen, but has become more common with the overproduction of film and television music composers. Joey Newman told me, "The young guys can get very abused very easily, especially if they're really good and don't know how to negotiate and be confident in their worth. It can be a very manipulative, dangling-the-carrot, controlling situation, depending on your personality and how hungry you are."[36]

At the same time, established composers who take on jobs they don't actually do themselves disadvantage young people trying to get into the business, trying to make a name for themselves, make a living. According to Zach Robinson, who entered the business more recently than many of the people I spoke to (he was born in 1989, and his first music credit is from 2013), these composers accept more projects than they were able to handle in the past. Some composers are responsible for eight shows, he told me. "And it's quite obvious that they're not doing it, and a lot of them aren't even overseeing it; they just have someone who is doing it and delivering it, which is crazy, and that affects my career."[37] Robinson isn't opposed to composers hiring others to assist them, but he thinks that some composers go too far, barely writing anything themselves and not sharing royalties with the composers who actually do the work. He thinks that composers who receive payment for work they haven't done, or even supervised, are a problem, and he disapproves of those who take on projects they immediately pass on to their employees. "Projects that you're just literally giving to other people, but they have your name on them. And you might be giving them back end [royalties]; that's cool, but there are people who don't do that; there's something wrong with them."[38] Another composer said the well-known composers who take on a lot of shows don't do much of the work, that they show up for spotting sessions but that may be all. This composer told me, "I've done freelance work for other people, and they'll go into a spotting meeting and literally take a picture of their spotting notes and send it to me, and then I do it. And a lot of younger composers don't get paid well enough for that."[39]

Part of the problem today is that a few big-name composers have become brands that the studios want to be associated with their programs or films, even if studio executives or producers and directors know that the famous, branded composer isn't writing all, or even much, of the music. Robinson said he thought that if viewers were blind-tested and asked who wrote the best music, the big-name composer probably wouldn't be picked most of the time, so the appeal of famous composers is that producers and directors know that a big composer has a team that will get the job done on time.[40]

Sometimes, well-known composers accept more jobs not just for the money, but to be agreeable to those hiring them, not wanting to refuse a job for fear they won't be asked by that person again. Established composers might take a gig even if it doesn't pay well or doesn't offer much symbolic capital. Or perhaps they'll agree to write music for a cool indie production since that offers them the symbolic capital of hipness and coolness, if little money. According to Robinson, this sort of behavior also hurts him and other workers of his generation because it deprives them of opportunities. Even if composers writing additional music are well treated by the famous composers they work for, they're still being denied the ability to network, to accumulate social capital; they are not the composers who are meeting producers and directors face-to-face. Robinson said that getting the experience, even getting credit isn't enough. "The most important thing to have—and I'm still working on this—is to develop a personal connection with the creator. That is how you do it. You can't expect your agent to get you stuff; you can't expect knowing someone at a studio to get you something."[41] Developing one's social capital is constantly part of the work that most of these musicians do.

Video Games

Video game production is much slower than film and television production and thus hasn't, or hasn't yet, witnessed the rise of the sorts of group production of music just described. Composers have much more time and are involved from the beginning, instead of being brought on at the end of the production process. Also, budgets are better for games, sometimes giving the composer the opportunity to write for an orchestra; one composer refers to gaming as providing a "renaissance of modern orchestral music" (Muddiman 2019, 36). Alex Hackford, head of A&R at Sony Computer Entertainment America at the time of our interiew, told me that, while film production is usually twelve to eighteen months, the video game schedule is longer, from two to four years. He said it's a long and labor-intensive process that involves a lot of mockups: "We'll pull a composition apart to see whether it can work derivatively, whether we can pull a piece of music apart and use it for multiple different means," that is, functions within the game. "Sometimes, you're not left with much."[42]

Hackford described film and television as "linear media," that is, everything proceeds linearly, whereas in video games, users can find themselves progressing through the game in a very different way every time they play it. This means that a piece of music that lasts a certain amount of time won't suffice. Hackford told me that the sort of musical sequence that would function in a film won't work in a game because films are linear while games are not. Films have beginnings, middles, and ends; video games are different. Hackford said, "If you run a song linearly and something doesn't run through the course of the game—say, running down a hill or running through a hallway or driving around a racetrack—and users don't do it at the pace that you anticipate them doing, there has to be some allowance made for that." This nonlinearity presents unique challenges, Hackford said, "because how *you* play a game is going to be very different from how *I* play a game or how somebody else plays a game." It's not possible, Hackford said, to "hire somebody to just write for every possible action"; it's not practical.

Hackford emphasized that game music has to be flexible, composed so that it can accompany any number of events in the game convincingly. If, he said, the player is a character in a hallway that comes to a T, the character can go left or right. There is no way to the game designers to know which way a particular player is going to go. Offering a rudimentary example of a pot of gold at the left end of the hallway and a monster trying to kill the player on the right, Hackford said that, "musically, those are two very different experiences, and you have to find a way to conform, in a reasonable amount of music, to encompass both of those experiences."

Because it can take as much as sixty or seventy hours to play a game, it isn't possible to hire a composer to write that much music. Composers are therefore asked to write what are thought of as suites of music, "big, dense suites of melodic music or sort of packs or templates of sounds and mood pieces that can be extrapolated out based on the particular actions a player takes in the game." Hackford said that, in the example of choosing whether to go left or right, "say it's a sixty-four multitrack piece of orchestral material; if I decide to go left, stems 1 through 8, and 24 to 32 will play, and if I go to the right, a different subset of those same stems will play." Decisions about which stems are used when are made by the composer's team as well as the game developer's team as well as specialized software. Composers have to write about two hours of music that have to be able to cover sixty to seventy hours of game experience.

Hackford believes that gaming has opened up substantially over the past five years, that it is no longer seen as less prestigious than other sorts of commercial music composition. Now big-name composers are writing for games; Hackford named Howard Shore, Bear McCreary, and Henry Jackson. In Hackford's view, games are still in a kind of infant stage in terms of their embeddedness in the culture, but more and more people are growing up with them and learning them as a kind of language, and he thinks that, as they become more normalized in the culture, their importance will be increasingly recognized.[43]

In other respects, game music is similar to film and television music. Game companies use music contractors and record overseas, as with much film music. Planning the music for a game is much like it is for film, engaging in discussions about what producers want the overall sound to be, what do they want to evoke, though game development is kept much more secret than film development. Composer Ryan Shore said that getting a job writing a game can happen in a number of ways—he could be contacted by a game developer, a producer working on the game, or the game studio, depending on the game. He also said that his work depends on the playback device; if it's powerful, it's better able to play the music.

Shore also said that writing music for games is different from writing for film or television because you don't have to worry about your music competing with dialogue, a factor about video game music that Shore likes. Shore also discussed the nonlinearity of games compared to film or television:

The composer doesn't always know what's happening on the screen, since different players can take different paths through the game, unlike in a film or episode, where you know exactly what is happening when. Shore described the process of writing music for a game. For a console game, a "common request might be they need a three-minute piece of music which can loop. So, you have to ensure the end can seamlessly go back into the beginning. And then they may request the music to be in layers or stems. So, I would compose a piece of music where there's a melodic line playing on top, and an accompaniment playing below, a percussion element supporting that, and perhaps guitars and synth playing with that—and all to complement each other."

Shore said that because the composer's work is delivered as individual audio files, game developers enjoy a great deal of flexibility in incorporating them into the game; listeners have a personal musical experience while playing the game "because you delivered all the music in stems, and therefore elements can turn on and off as the game unfolds." Smartphones are not as capable at sophisticated playback, Shore said, so games designed for them are less demanding musically. But, normally, Shore said, he is asked to record "loopable pieces of music that speak to whatever the generalities of the scene might be—this scene is about action, this scene is about comedy, this scene is about heroism—and you write pieces of music that speak to that, and they just give you directions as to what they're looking for."[44]

Composer Penka Kouneva compared composing video game music to writing music for commercials, since the game music plays an important role in creating the game's brand. "The musical theme and the overall sound have to be so specific and so tied aesthetically to the vision of the game that they create a musical signature for the game, which serves as the branding for the game." Games, she said, need to use music as a branding device in order to distinguish themselves from each other: "In the same way that jingles brand a product and you always associate that musical theme with the product, similarly video game music brands the game and becomes inseparable." Kouneva said that this is difficult to do. "It's a mighty challenge to compose a theme that's such an earworm it becomes a signature."[45]

Kouneva also told me that game composing is very rigorous and based on formal rules and parameters. "For instance, the tempo is regimented: A certain tempo range is for chases, certain tempo range is for exploration, certain tempo is for boss battle, certain tempo is for level 1 combat." This is different from film scoring. Kouneva also said that "game scoring is interactive—it reacts dynamically to gameplay, whereas film scoring is either themes, variations, background music under dialog, or set pieces (e.g., chase, love scene, suspenseful anticipation, etc.)—always matching the film editing in a linear way. In this aspect, film and game scoring is different, and game scoring is harder." But, she said, writing music with such rigorous expectations has helped her improve: "I became a master composer after I became a game composer."[46]

Recent Changes

In recent years, there have been a number of major changes in these businesses, some of which I have discussed or will discuss elsewhere—including the outsourcing of recording sessions, the rise of streaming services, and more. Here I am concerned with less visible shifts in the businesses that composers raised. One of these shifts I would characterize as the decrease in importance of the skills of notated music, composing for acoustic instruments, orchestration, arranging; I have already discussed the rise the of composer as an entrepreneur-manager and composer teams.

Nichification

In the old days, composers mainly received training in jazz arranging or classical composition, the sort of foundational training that programs such as Berklee's built on in more recent years, programs that train composers to write in a number of styles; composers were generalists, all-purpose musicians, able to deliver whatever a director or producer might ask of them; if a boss told you to sound like Johann Sebastian Bach or John Sebastian, you did it. This, however, seems to be changing. Composers are increasingly expected to be specialists in particular genres. Deborah Lurie, whose first credit is from 1996, talked about this shift away from composers who could write for orchestra or almost anything: "When I was in school, we were all studying to be maestros, like Elmer Bernstein, Jerry Goldsmith, Marc Shaiman—all these people who could do anything you wanted. Kind of in the tradition of, say, Leonard Bernstein or Henry Mancini."[47]

Even though there has been a trend since at least the late 1980s to try to make television music sound more like popular music (see Trakin 1990), today, there is an increasing amount of existing popular music that has been imported into film and television, to the extent that it has become both producer and product of an overall nichification in these fields. Deborah Lurie told me, "I feel like many filmmakers don't necessarily want one of the old superstars as a composer anymore; they want someone who specializes in a specific sound or style. Often not from a scoring background specifically, but, like, a recording artist for example," Lurie said. "Nowadays, if you want a certain sound you get the person who does that in particular. The current technology and digital scoring process allows for a composer to potentially have less of a background in scoring and as a dramatist. If a composer simply writes great music, the modern technological process can often accommodate someone who is less versed in that kind of thing." She continued, "In fact, some scores are not even written to picture now. They are constructed using a sophisticated music editing process." Lurie said this has been a challenging time for composers trained in the more classic scoring tradition because if once you were a musical chameleon, you now "have to home in on a much more distinct signature sound. It's more important to be sort of an identifiable brand in a way."[48] The days of orchestral scores aren't what they used to be (though there was a brief renaissance early in this century; see Crisafulli 2000). Composers, it seems, now need to brand themselves as experts in a particular style. Being a stylistic chameleon isn't always necessary anymore. In Lurie's view, composing an orchestral score might still be required, but it is increasingly a specialty, its own niche. There is thus a growing division of labor among composers, accompanied by de-skilling, as composers are called upon less and less often to write in a variety of styles.

Unlike Harry Braverman's argument about the increased use of technology and the greater division of labor resulting from it, which destroyed craftsmanship (Braverman did not employ the term *de-skilling*, which came into use after the publication of his book), the transformation of what had been the composer's craft—writing for acoustic instruments, orchestras—is becoming a niche form of production, the result of the increasing division of labor in film, television, and video game fields of cultural production that, I would argue, stems largely from the rise of ideologies of hipness and coolness (see Taylor 2017). Producers and directors might not request an old-fashioned orchestral score; they increasingly want their favorite indie musician to provide a score. Or they desire existing songs by their favorite musicians, and they are aided in finding them by the relatively new worker known as a music supervisor (see Anderson 2013; Lewandowski 2010; Loraine 2020; Smith 2001; Taylor 2017).

But most composers don't think the orchestrated score is going away, even if it is becoming more of a specialized form of composition. Composer

Matt Hutchinson told me that he thought there would always be a desire for orchestral music in films and video games and mentioned the popularity of *Star Wars* as an example: "Those movies and those games are still some of the most popular out there. People love the scores. I just don't ever see it going away, I think it's just going to be part of the industry."[49]

A musical effect of the increased use of popular musics is not just the increased use of non-orchestral music, but that the music itself works in different ways. Tension isn't created through dissonance or harmony more generally—the stock-in-trade of composers with a classical background. The use of harmony for affective purposes is much diminished in most film and television music. It's striking to watch older films and television shows and hear how composers employed dissonance to create feelings of apprehension, danger, disturbed psychological states. Now this is all done by other means, with low-pitched sounds and loud drones seeming to be common these days, sounds of the sort that formerly were used to signal the arrival of a massive spacecraft.

Pop and Rock

One of the major effects of the shift to digital technologies has been the increased presence of pop and rock music in film and television music (see Bernstein 2019; Crisafulli 2008; Heine 2020a and 2020b) as well as in advertising music (see Taylor 2012).[50] Popular musicians, as earlier adopters of digital technologies than classical musicians, were in a better position to claim certain jobs so that popular musics have now become a significant niche in the business. This is part of a broader shift of the ubiquitization of popular musics and the decline of listeners to classical and some other musics. Also, the rise in prestige of pop and rock music as part of the hipping and cooling of the cultural businesses (see Taylor n.d.a) has meant that some producers and directors think it's cool to have a known rock artist or group listed as the composer for their films or programs, and maybe they'll get to hang out.

Composers recognize that producers and directors are going to hire how and whom they want and are mostly accepting of this practice. Ryan Shore said that, "for the most part, people often want to collaborate with creatives who are exciting to them." So, he said, a director might say, "'This is my favorite band or artist; I've loved them forever; they're part of the soundtrack of my life, and I'd like to collaborate with them on the film I'm making.'"[51]

Also, with the increased difficulty in making a living from sales of recordings and the tiny amounts paid by music streaming services, many popular musicians are seeking other ways of earning a living, especially if they aren't keen on touring more. And, so, as composer Matt Hutchinson told me, some popular musicians have begun to view film and television scoring as an option as well as advertising music.[52]

Yet another reason for the increasing use of pop and rock may well be the perception among filmmakers that schools such as Berklee are churning out too many graduates who produce music that isn't much different. Several of the older composers I spoke with complained about how today's film and television music all sounds the same and is emotionally unengaging, the result in part of standardized training and the common use of the same digital technologies (to be discussed in chapter 7). Rock music, especially indie rock music, is a good antidote to what is perceived as the sort of standardized training that is now the norm.

Musicians coming from a rock background might not know how to write music, or orchestrate it, or conduct it, however. Robert Kraft told me that he can think of successful collaborations between bands and directors—some that surprised him—but he usually counsels directors to hire a composer rather than a band or individual artist. He tells clients, "'Well, they don't score movies and are about to go on tour,'" so the idea that a band or an artist is going to spend the next six months focused solely on their film is not likely. "They might mail in some music and hope it works. And they'll be in Pittsburgh on Tuesday." Kraft thinks that directors and producers will not receive the same amount of attention from a recording artist or band that they would enjoy from a composer. Nonetheless, artists or bands are frequently hired. Kraft said that if a band is engaged to score a film but needs technical help, the studio will help find an orchestrator or whoever is needed; the studio's job is to facilitate.[53]

A couple of my interviewees described what happens when a band that doesn't know how to write music composes a film score. Recording engineer and mixer Alan Meyerson narrated the process as he witnessed it with the band Daft Punk. As he explained it, a fair amount of negotiation and mediation was required because "they're not really score guys." So, normally what you do in such a situation, he said, is to bring musicians together with someone who has "more traditional skill sets" in film and television scoring. Meyerson said that the band needs to have the right temperament, a certain amount of humility, for this to work, a process that varies and can be tricky. "There's always a technique, and it changes with every musician; if they're a DJ or a hip-hop artist or an R&B artist, there's always a way to mind meld the two shapes into something that works well together." But this requires a person with traditional skill sets to make it work: "If it's someone who's a big-idea person who really doesn't get into the minutiae, there might be a situation where the band might write themes, or they might come up with larger motifs, and then you have to get composers to go into rooms and actually carve cues out of it. That happens quite a bit."[54]

Flora, the composer's assistant who wished to remain anonymous and who worked for someone who had been in an indie band, told me of having to generate a score and parts from his Logic Pro sessions: "[My boss] will write the music on his computer, and then if the studio wants live musicians to come in, which is usually the case, then he'll give me his sessions, and then I'll put it out into sheet music form."[55] Flora described a recent project, a studio film, for which her boss shipped his music to six orchestrators to prepare the music to be recorded by Hollywood string players. In another recent film, the composer wrote all the music on his computer, and then the studio decided they wanted a live orchestra. Flora's boss is a band musician who wasn't trained in orchestration, so, the assistant told me, they orchestrated his sessions from Logic software, put them into sheet music, and then sent them out to the copyist, after which their boss checked them to make sure everything was acceptable.[56]

I asked orchestrators about this trend. David Krystal said he's happy to do it; that's his job. He said he has been surprised by the creativity he has encountered with these musicians, given that they haven't been (cons)trained by the same rules that composers and orchestrators follow. But, he said, "Sometimes their stuff is a bit crazy, and you do have to revise it and/or tell them, 'Hey, we are going to have to change some instruments here. It's great music, but it's just not going to play.' And usually they're pretty understanding of that."[57]

Sometimes an orchestrator might receive an audio file and is told to transcribe it. Edward Trybek told me of an instance where he received only an MP3 file that he was instructed to orchestrate. (He was cautious about not naming the project, so I don't know if this music was from a band or an MP3 generated by an individual with a computer.) Trybek said that normally he would receive a MIDI file (from which notation can be generated), not an MP3, which is an audio file that he would have to transcribe music from, and he gave an example. "They said, 'We have this eighteen- or twenty-one-piece band. Go watch the movie and just add orchestra to it— Go!' There were some stipulations about how it needs to be in a particular style, but it was really just about adding an orchestra, and that was more like arranging than orchestration." Trybek and his fellow orchestrators made an approximate transcription. He told me, "They essentially had a rhythm section playing, maybe a few synths. But they wanted us to add orchestra in addition to it. So, we did a rough take down, and then you're arranging an orchestra around it."[58]

Earlier generations of musicians, however, who are accustomed to orchestral work, have some issues with this trend. Orchestrator Tom Calderaro told me that there are a few famous composers who don't know how to read music, which was a well-kept secret: "You could be sitting at the scoring stage, and the guy can't read music; you're keeping the sham alive. As long as they believe he's a musical genius, we're all going to be working here next week." But, he said, everything has changed today. Bands are getting hired not only because directors and producers like their music, but for other qualities that Calderaro said he could only speculate about: "Maybe they don't see this guy as bringing a lot of baggage as a composer, or as a school-trained composer; maybe he's going to have some kind of fresh, unique, edgy aspect to what he does. There's some truth in that." Calderaro said that not only is the lack of musical reading skills not a problem these days, but that "in some circles you might be in as a composer, it might give you that little bit of edge, that cool, edgy thing."[59] Commissioning music for a film or television program from a known musician or band can also add value to the film or program. Composer Matt Hutchinson told me, referencing Netflix's *Stranger Things*, that "hiring a band does bring an intrinsic value to film because you not only have the built-in audience and fan base for that artist, but the unique voice of the band as well, so I get it."[60] But Hutchinson said he thought the world of film and television music was becoming compartmentalized.

A couple of composers, who said they didn't mind rock musicians entering the field, nonetheless offered critiques. My conversation with Ryan Shore about rock musicians in film and television produced an interesting discussion. Shore said that a big difference between a composer and a film composer is that the film composer needs to understand not only how to compose music but also the "language of storytelling, film, narrative, and how best to use music with picture and dialogue to tell a story." Shore said that some people might be great at composition, but that doesn't mean they know how to write music for storytelling.[61] Zach Robinson was equally accepting of rock musicians in film and television music but also emphasized that rock musicians don't necessarily know how to write to picture:

If you expect to hire a musician to come in and write twenty-five minutes of music and then you're going to place it wherever you want, you can cut it in wherever you want, and you say you want a sad piece and a happy piece; if you're expecting musicians to come in and—pardon my language—frame-fuck a scene, where you're going frame by frame, and you say, "Oh, I need it to hit this smile, and I need this to hit," a lot of them, but not all, are going to have a hard time with that.[62]

Another composer said it was common for a film composer to come in and assist many of these musicians. But most of today's composers, including Shore and Robinson, seem to be sanguine about the increased use of rock music in their world, espousing a kind of big-tent ideology: everyone is welcome.

I spoke to Trent Reznor of the band Nine Inch Nails about his experience as an artist entering the world of film music scoring, and he was candid about his lack of experience. Director David Fincher pursued Reznor for his film *The Social Network* (2010), and he initially refused but ultimately changed his mind; his musical partner, Atticus Ross, had some experience in film and television scoring. Soon after accepting, Reznor and Ross viewed some of the film, which was written by famed screenwriter Aaron Sorkin: "We're watching the film, and panic was setting in because I realized that I might know how to write music for sweeping over a landscape or for a serial killer attacking or something, but I don't know how to score a movie that's wall-to-wall dialogue: Sorkin, rapid-fire dialogue, no space."[63] There was no obvious place where a theme was going to play, he said. The film seemed impenetrable, and it wasn't clear what the role of music would be.

Reznor said that Fincher "can sometimes speak a little bit in riddles because he's trying not to tell you what to do; he's providing information that you need to interpret." So Reznor sought the advice of renowned film composer Hans Zimmer, and Reznor and his partner Ross began to think about the music. They had seen about twenty-five minutes of the first cut and had read the script and thought about what Fincher had said about the music. Reznor spoke of the kinds of musical ideas he considered. "Maybe," said Reznor, "it sounds propulsive—the sound of creativity and pursuing that idea, and that idea is writing code and trying to chase that idea." Reznor said he approached writing for the film as he approached writing songs for Nine Inch Nails: "Sometimes it starts with identifying what it is trying to say lyrically. What's the story I'm trying to tell? What feeling am I trying to get across?" Eventually, Reznor said, he took "those breadcrumbs of lyrics or concepts" and then tried to "dress the set with music." With songwriting, he said, "It's kind of like I've got a script. I'm now dressing the set like a set designer with sound, melody, and whatever other elements to reach for that goal: which is to emotionally affect you in some way that appeals and is sincere."

Reznor said that once he thinks he grasps the core of what the music is doing, "I can apply the skills that I have to this other medium by deconstructing it and bringing it down to its essence what it actually is rather than, 'Here's the scene of someone turning a corner and looking at somebody.' I don't know how to write that, but I know how to write the thing around it." Reznor and Ross began writing short compositions through which they "explored the range of variances of the set of feelings or an emotional tone." Then, "We extracted music for the scenes out of those pieces." In this way, he said, he and Ross were able to use the skills they already had to make their music conform "to this other medium/other process." Reznor said he could see how enthusiastic the filmmakers were, excellent people he and Ross had the good fortune to work with: a "supportive, encouraging, kind, and helpful environment" without interference from the studio. Reznor credited Fincher with having undergone the battles for creative freedom "so that you can come into the safe zone and do what you want to do in collaboration with him. You're not getting notes from the studio or any of the shit like that."

I asked Reznor what it was like for him as an artist having to work for someone else. He acknowledged that he wasn't in control, that he was in service to the picture and the creative, Fincher. However, Reznor said, "I had such an enormous amount of respect for him and learned so much from the experience. Although we didn't agree on everything, it was right. I'm in the weeds on this thing. He's thinking about the whole picture in ways I'm not. It was really interesting to watch his brain. He's able to get super micromanage-y, but at the same time, he's also thinking about how it all ties together. It was a great experience." Reznor said he actually enjoyed not being in charge on *The Social Network*. "It's fun to not be the boss. It was fun to work in service. It's something you believe in, people you respect, and you're learning from. It was kind of fun not calling the shots and thinking, 'Okay, they said no to that. All right, let's do it better then.'" In the end, Reznor told me, "What happened through that process was one of the best creative experiences I've had in my life."[64]

For others, collaboration can be more trying. Randy Newman said in a 1994 interview that working on the music for the film *Maverick* was difficult, that he wasn't used to collaborating:

> I've worked all my life and no one except my wife has told me what to do since school. When I make a record, no one tells me anything . . . and these are people whose picture it is, and you have to accommodate. It's difficult for me when I don't agree to change my music around. I had to do a bit of changing on the stand, to underline things that I didn't think needed underlining. It was mainly for the film editor, Stuart Baird, but that's part of the job, it's just the process of getting used to it. Essentially the score sounds like me. I'm happy with it. ("Randy Newman" 1994, 10)

The Urban Scoring Style

It's not just rock sounds that are increasingly employed in film and television music, but other kinds of popular music sounds. Kurt Farquhar told me that being Black in a white-dominated business worked both against him and for him—against him for obvious reasons of racism, especially perhaps, at major studios, but for him because sometimes it was felt that a Black composer was needed to write music that, in Farquhar's words, "felt more Black."[65] He also thought there were some Black showrunners who were reluctant to engage him for fear it would provoke yet another battle with their bosses, but he gives a lot of credit to Black producers who have hired him over the years. He was asked to write some hip-hop scores early in his career, even though, as he said, he'd never picked up a rap record in his life. But he is a quick study and ultimately introduced what he called the urban scoring style to television. Before this style, he said, "You couldn't have heard much difference between the scores of shows, for example, *The Jeffersons* as opposed to *Archie Bunker's Place*" (two well-known sitcoms of the late 1970s and early 1980s).

Farquhar defined the urban scoring style as based in part on European classical sounds, but weaving in elements of hip-hop and R&B. He recalled a scene in a dramatic series from years ago, a scene with a young Black girl who had dressed up and snuck out of the family home to go to a college fraternity party where she is nearly raped. She returns home, shaken, and is in the process of removing her makeup. Farquhar tried to imagine what she might be thinking. "I'm looking at this little girl looking at herself in the mirror, and the question I asked was, 'If she heard music in her head like I do, would it be a mournful English horn and oboe and clarinets? Or would it be something that was more indicative of the sounds that she listens to on the radio now?'"[66]

Farquhar told me he doesn't reject European sounds; he combines them. "I have some elements of sounds that are more urban in nature, from the type of music that contemporary people at the time are listening to." Farquhar also said that he doesn't write every score in this style "just because it's Black people's faces up on the screen." In scoring *Black Lightning* on the CW network, for example, he doesn't add hip-hop beats every time a Black person appears, or it would be nonstop. "But," he said, "I will do more subversive things with it." He will take a hip-hop beat and "span it out through the orchestra," having orchestral instruments mimic the sound of instruments from hip-hop and jazz. Farquhar described a scene from episode 112 of *Black Lightning* in which he took the "stylistic nature of a Miles Davis solo in the late eighties, when he was doing the funk stuff, and he'd do all these little broken phrases." Farquhar wrote a cue in which "the whole string section sounds like it's like a broken-up Miles Davis solo." Viewing the scene, it's possible to hear what Farquhar meant: unison strings playing a syncopated melody over an insistent beat. Farquhar summed up this approach by saying, "Urban scoring, the feel of it, how it's phrased, is more like the swagger of hip-hop or jazz."[67]

Multi-Camera, Single-Camera, and Back

Most of the composers I spoke to said that the biggest changes they have witnessed during their time in the business was the rise of digital technology and streaming. Kurt Farquhar mentioned something no one else did—the shift from multi-camera sitcoms to single-camera sitcoms, and back. The term *single camera* doesn't mean the use of only one camera, but rather denotes a style of production that is much more filmic, shot without a live audience. Multi-camera sitcoms are more like live theater, with stages in front of an audience, the characters moving from one set to another.

Farquhar told me that when he first entered the business in the late 1980s, most television programs were multi-cam sitcoms and constituted about 80 percent of his work. He said he could see the single-cam shift happening, which intensified after a couple of these shows became very successful. "And then the next thing you know," he said, "everybody wanted a single-cam sitcom." The difference, from his perspective, is the amount of music required: "The average multi-cam show has about a minute and ten seconds of music; they're basically transitionals and setups, act-ins and act-outs, very little underscore." But he went from that to a situation in which "you're underscoring the emotion of the scene just like an hour-long dramatic series."[68] Composer David Schwartz also said that single-camera comedies are a lot of work, "pretty much solid music" (quoted in Rhodes 2004, 11). Farquhar said that was a major change and that producers wanted different sorts of composers. "In the blink of an eye," he said, "most multi-cam sitcoms were gone." It was hard to get hired on a single-cam sitcom because "if you didn't have one on your résumé, you were seen as a multi-cam guy." Farquhar said he knew then that he had to reinvent himself as a dramatic composer.[69]

Now, Farquhar told me, multi-cam sitcoms are becoming popular again, even though there was a long period when there were virtually none, to the extent that there were very few people available who knew how to make them. "But," he said, "if you're one of the old guys who didn't fall out of the business, you're one of the people they could go to." So, he currently scores one of the biggest multi-cam hits on TV, CBS's *The Neighborhood*. Farquhar said he wasn't asked to audition for the show given his previous experience: "They called me up and said, 'Hey, please, can you do this show?' 'Yeah!' It was the shortest interview I ever had." He attended a very brief meeting and was told, "'Well, we really wanted to use you.' And we talked for about five minutes, and I said, 'So, I'm actually doing this show? We're actually going to work?' 'Oh, yeah, just have your people call me.'" And then, Farquhar said, "we went to work."[70]

Overproduction

Many composers, especially older musicians who have witnessed many changes in the business, complained that the field is oversaturated with composers. (Richard Bellis wrote in 2006 that the field had at least tripled in the previous fifteen years [132].) There are too many composers trying to gain a foothold, which means that some are willing to work for little or no pay, and the package deal system encourages a climate in which composers undercut each other (see Borum 2015a, xvii). The biggest problem, Joey Newman told me, "is that composers have been undercut, not just by production budgets, but also each other. We've lowered the bar so much that composers are willing to pay out of their own pockets to have the opportunity to secure a project."[71] Older composers placed the blame for this oversaturation on the Berklee College of Music, which they believe over-produces graduates. But, at the same time, some said, there is more and more content being produced. The overproduction of composers has resulted in depressed wages—or none—which makes these fields more likely to be peopled by those with economic capital to spare, another effect of neoliberalization.

Veteran television composer Stu Phillips also talked about the problem of overproduction. Professional schools such as Berklee are busy churning out graduates, he said, so that there are always two hundred new composers but not two hundred paying jobs. If four hundred people are vying for the same job—some of whom are willing to do it for nothing—and if the bosses don't like a particular candidate's music, there are always more people willing to compose music gratis. Phillips expressed impatience with young composers he encounters at meetings of film and television composers who take a job with no pay and then complain about the fact that they're not making any money. "I'll look at these kids, and I'll say, 'What are you complaining about? Nobody made you take the job. You need the money? Well, why did you take the job? If all four hundred of you wouldn't take the job, guess what? They'd have to pay somebody to do it! But as long as there's going to be one of you four hundred who says, "Yeah, I'll do it for nothing," why should they pay you? There's no reason!'"[72]

For Joey Newman, it's not just that composers are willing to work for little or nothing; factors other than the composer's work and track record also come into play. For example, Newman said he has heard of composers who, really desiring a particular job, will say, "'I will pay for the music budget' and undercut everybody." Noting the vast amount of content now being produced, Newman said that composers may have to score multiple projects at once just to make the same income they once made from one network show or studio film. And, affordable digital technologies have made it possible for anyone to be a filmmaker or a composer: "Nowadays," Newman said, "it may seem that if you've got a rig and you've got a buddy who's a filmmaker, you're set. And if your show or movie becomes huge, then you may be the new 'it' sound." But, he wondered, "What about the people who have studied the craft of syncing music to picture, delivering on budget and on time, and composing music in *support* of the drama and not just for music's sake? It's more about getting the gig now than it is even being able to write the music for it."[73]

Because of this overproduction, the sort of people skills necessary to build, maintain, and improve one's social capital, one's network, have become even more important. Newman thinks that the skill set today is more about landing a job than doing a good job. "Because," he said, "if you're going to hire me, I've got five other friends that are fabulous, great composers; we can all do the exact same thing, so why am I going to get the job? The only way that I'm going to get the job is because I've somehow attracted that showrunner more than the others." Newman said composers are a dime a dozen now, and showrunners realize that, so their thinking is, "'All of you guys can do the job, but who do I want to hang with? Who's cool?' And depending on who the showrunner is, they might have a big ego and want to hang with the big-ego guy."[74] According to Newman, getting a job today is all about the "gelling factor" plus trust and comfort—social capital.

To make ends meet, some composers are creating, or contributing to, music libraries, prerecorded music that is stored and licensed for use in various media platforms (see Waldman 1996). Ben Decter told me he knows composers who are scoring prime time programs but who are simultaneously creating music catalogs that are available for licensing. "I guess," he said, "it's just everyone trying to figure out how to make a living. But in some ways, it feels like we're shooting ourselves in the foot. It's helping create vast catalogs of music that potentially lower all the pricing. On the other hand, though, it's nice to have a part of it."[75]

Composer Kurt Farquhar mentioned the rise of reality television and the proliferation of cable channels, the latter of which, he said, do not pay very good royalties. In order to try to continue to make a living, he decided to start a library, hoping it would "supply some of the great wealth of music that they need for reality series. And maybe I could do deals later where I do a combination of library and some original music from me because the average reality show needs so much music that to sit there and write every week is too much."[76] The library is thriving and so is his original scoring career, he said.

Farquhar also said that the fees he receives these days are a third or a quarter of what they were in the 1990s. So, not wanting to rely only on his library as an extra income stream, Farquhar decided to start training and employing music supervisors and music editors, and people who can do music clearance (make licensing agreements to use preexisting music in films and television programs). In addition to hiring him as the composer, "We can package the whole thing. You can also use the library. You need a music supervisor on this dramatic series, so we'll supply you music supervision. You need a music editor; we can supply you with the music editor. By the end of the day, we've been able to hit them with fees in four to five different ways. And, therefore, now my company is making more than it was in the heyday of the highest-paid shows."[77] Farquhar is the only composer I interviewed who has diversified to this extent.

Conclusions

Composers, as the people who generate the musical raw material that enters the music supply chain in film, episode, and game production, are still artisans, writing music for a fee while not being permitted to own the products of their labor. In this sense, very little has changed over the years. But even long-standing practices of musical production and refinement have been affected by encroaching neoliberal capitalism, which has meant the rise of the composer as an entrepreneur-manager who supervises teams of musicians, as well as the nichification of the field of cultural production of music, both in terms of musical style and genre but also with respect to the visual genres—network sitcom (as we saw in the previous chapter), single-cam versus multi-cam, and more.

Capitalism, neoliberal or not, has proved to be consistently able to adapt to modes of producing value that might not have much to do with capitalist value. But the victorious capitalism theorized by Max Weber ([1905] 2001, 124), a form of capitalism that, he said, reached its apogee in the US, where it has taken on the character of sport, is increasingly evident in the world of film and television production. Composers outdo themselves to work harder, sleep less, win more jobs—even paying to work—their prizes taking the form not just of greater and better symbolic and social capital, but economic capital—when it hasn't been accumulated by those above them in the supply chain, that is.

THE MUSIC SUPPLY CHAIN AFTER THE COMPOSER

Adding Value

While not all the music workers who come after the composer that I interviewed characterized their work as creative—some said that it's not (as discussed in chapter 2)—what people told me about their work nonetheless reveals just how creative they can be, even if it's about seemingly technical matters. Some spoke eloquently, and proudly, about the contributions they make to a film or episode or game. Everyone described clever ways of dealing with tremendous time pressures, difficult assignments, or last-minute changes being asked of them. And we see even more clearly the self-disciplining practices that these workers engage in, making sure that their conduct is appropriate in group settings so that the composers' vision can be realized—and so that they themselves can get hired again.

These workers are also creative in the social relations of production, endlessly working out ways of getting along with other workers, forming teams, learning when they can contribute—and how—and when they should hold their tongue, supporting their composer-bosses, helping people get a foot in the door. With the term *social relations of production*, Marx was referring not to the relationships that develop in the workplace, but to the effects of the division of labor in any society and the sorts of power relationships present in such divisions. It is a question of who has control of the productive forces in the process of production. The social relations of production in any production process are deeply imbricated within their cultures, where different logics of power can operate. Anthropologist Donald Donham (2015, 716) writes that "relations of production, by definition, correspond to the basic structures of power in a society, however that power is constituted—whether by economic, coercive, or religious means (or some mix of these)." The fields of cultural production studied here exhibit several modalities of power, especially the economic and prestige as measured by symbolic and social capital. Either modality—economic or prestige—gives its possessor creative authority, which is also defined by a third modality, the hierarchical structure of the business.

What we see with the writing of scores, or the generation of computer audio files, is that, however finished they may appear to be to those who made them, refinement is always necessary. A composer produces one conception of a use-value, but others in the supply chain produce other use-values, employing tools with their own use-values. Marx (1990) examines the process of creating value (defined as the amount of socially necessary labor time in the production of a commodity, say, textiles), considering the wear and tear on the machinery and the labor time required to produce the material of the yarn, say, cotton. The various sorts of processes necessary to produce the cotton, and the machine, and then to spin the yarn "may together be looked on as different and successive phases of the same labour process" (294). Marx notes that the products used to make the yarn, cotton, and spindle "must genuinely have served to produce a use-value; they must in the present case become yarn. Value [as socially necessary labor time] is independent of the particular use-values by which it is borne, but a use-value of some kind has to act as its bearer" (295). Workers are constantly in motion, constantly drawing on, and producing, use-values.

This chapter considers those who take what the composer gives them and move it along the supply chain, refining the composer's "raw material" into something that fulfills the desire for use-value of producers and directors. I'm separating these production chains into two streams, one concerned with notated music, the other with digital production. Those who come after the composer include the composer's assistant, the orchestrator and/or arranger, the music copyist, and the contractor (the person who hires live musicians to record the score) and live musicians, recorded by a recording engineer. When the composer is writing for live musicians, the digital production chain begins with this recording. If live musicians are not being used, the chain starts with audio files generated by the composer, then continues to the scoring mixer and music editor. These streams eventually converge, of course, once there is a digital recording. But for the sake of analysis, I will separate them here.

Notes and Scores

As with composers, workers further down the music supply chain tend to have formal training as musicians or in more technical fields, such as sound recording. Some of them currently work in jobs for which they were not trained but have nonetheless found their way into. Many fell into doing what they are currently doing, telling me of having started on one educational or career path but then moving to another. Composers became orchestrators, performers became engineers or mixers, and so on. In many cases, people have relied on personal contacts, either to learn their trade outside of a formal educational setting or, sometimes, to land a job, utilizing whatever social capital they possess.

Winning a job isn't much different for these workers than for composers, though none of them can hope to achieve the public recognition a few elite composers enjoy. But some earn high reputations and are much sought after. Many of these workers are hired by the composers, and some develop close working relationships with their composer-bosses.

Orchestrators

Since most composers write at an electronic or acoustic keyboard or guitar, or at the computer, their music needs to be written out for whatever instruments and voices the producers or directors want, which is usually, of course, very much dependent on the budget. Normally, the composer writes the score (though fewer and fewer "write" the score; it's all on their computers), which may or may not include instructions or suggestions for the orchestrators. (And some scores go to a proofreader after they're orchestrated.)

Regardless, orchestration is more than just adding instruments; orchestrators need to make sure that a written score sounds the way the composer wants it to sound, which can involve a good deal of editing, rewriting, and tweaking—this is the first step in the supply chain, the process of refining and rationalizing composers' raw material when it originates as notation. Tom Calderaro, who has been in the business for decades, explained orchestration and arranging in terms of rebalancing things. The notated score that can be generated by music recording software is seldom legible to the musicians who are to record it, so orchestrators need to edit it into something playable.

Orchestrators face the same time pressure as composers, so today they tend to work in teams, like many composers, in order to meet deadlines. David Krystal told me that he usually receives little time, sometimes only two to three weeks before the recording session, which is pretty tight. This is why people tend to work in teams, he said, in order to get everything done on schedule: "You can kill yourself and get it all done potentially," he said, "but if it's a full-blown late Romantic-era style score, you're not going to be able to orchestrate two hours of music in three weeks. It's just too much."[1] Edward Trybek told me that this shift to working in teams has been one of the major transformations he has seen in the business. There are more and more, he said, and not just teams of composers. He himself works with two other orchestrators. Splitting the work means less money but, also, less time pressure—no one needs to stay up all night desperately trying to finish. "And," he said, "it makes it easier to say yes to work when you know that it's not all on you to get this out the door."[2] Composers—who hire their orchestrators—are mostly aware of this system; if not, Trybek said he informs them and that he hasn't encountered any problems.[3] Broadband internet hasn't just made it possible for music to be recorded in faraway (cheaper) places, one of the main effects of digital technology on performing musicians; orchestrators themselves can now work away from the major centers of film and television production, though, as Trybek said, "They're still working crazy hours, just somewhere else."[4]

Sometimes budgets can be changed, or miscalculations discovered, while an orchestrator is working, and alterations might be demanded in the middle of the orchestration process. In this case, the orchestrators are more than simply refining the composer's work; they are partly involved in creating it. David Krystal said it doesn't often occur, but it does happen. "I have found out days before a recording session that the client hadn't given me a 100 percent accurate lineup; for example, he had made a mistake in giving me the original brass numbers, or there were last-minute changes to the ensemble. So, I have to go through all the scores and change them. You just have to roll with it." Krystal said that truly major changes have never been asked of him at the last minute (his example was orchestrating for a full orchestra and then being told it was going to be a string quartet), but, he said, "I've had numbers move around on me a fair amount because they are trying to record on a certain budget, and sometimes they have to say, 'Okay, we can't have as many players here, but we want another session.'" Or sometimes the numbers go up and he is told, "'You know what? We really need more brass players to get the right sound, so we're just going to pay more out-of-pocket.'"[5]

The orchestrator's processes of refinement and rationalization have become more open-ended and less definitively finished than in the past. What determines that a score has been finished is not so much the composer or orchestrator (or proofreader), but bosses who can demand endless last-minute changes. Older workers told me that there used to be a period when a picture was declared "locked," meaning no edits could be made so that the composer could maximize composition time. But because digital technologies make edits comparatively easy, last-minute changes have become the norm, and pictures are never really locked anymore (music editor Andrés Locsey told me the current term is "latched").[6] Edits late in the game make more work, and added pressure, for everyone. New music isn't always being written, but existing music needs to be edited to fit the picture, which can involve reorchestrating it No one wants to do the same work twice, but they must proceed nonetheless. Edward Trybek told me, "Sometimes we'll be orchestrating something knowing that they're going to send an email later saying, 'Hey, you know, there's been some changes in measure ninety-three, and at this point the tempo changed, and these three bars we completely rewrote.' So, we'll have to go and change that to the new version."[7] Trybek said that television is even more tightly scheduled than film but that video game production is much slower.

Copyists

Once the notated music has been composed, orchestrated, and proofread, it proceeds to a copyist, whose job is to produce a readable score and parts for musicians. They are refining and rationalizing a product for its use-value not for consumers/viewers, but for the musicians who will record the score. In the old days, the copying process would be done by hand. Alf Clausen, who is best known for composing music for *The Simpsons* for many years, was a copyist early in his career; even back in the 1970s, people involved in music production were extremely pressed for time, so an assembly-line system was developed. Plywood tables would be set up against the wall, rounding the corners of the room, with a copyist at every position. "Each guy would copy four measures off of the score page. And then once he got his four measures done, he would pass the score page to the next guy. The next guy would copy four measures. They would pass it onto the next guy."

Clausen said that not only was he well paid, but that he learned a good deal from being able to work on the scores of established composers.[8]

Today, since almost everything is accomplished digitally, copying music is mainly a matter of making sure that the score and parts generated by computer software are legible and playable by human musicians. Musicians do not receive their parts in advance, since everything is done down to the wire, so they sight-read their parts at the recording session. I spoke to a supervisor of music preparation and director of the music library at a major studio, who told me that he and his team must make sure that the entire process goes as smoothly as possible. He said that preparing music for the performers to sight-read requires specific knowledge: "What the skill set of a copyist is, is to really understand and study the players and understand exactly how to write the music for sight-reading." The recording session will start, and the musicians are going to begin playing music they've never seen before. "That is a skill set," he said, "to figure out ways to warn musicians what is coming up, making sure that you space it, make sure every dot is in the perfect place, make sure it's something that they can look at and just read and they don't have to think about what's going on on the page, but they can just do what they really do well."[9]

Music copyists, who are something of a dying breed in this era of digital everything, also must make sure that there is music on the stands for musicians to play when the session starts. The copyist I interviewed told me he became a supervisor in 1997, so his job is to oversee the process of working with the composer and orchestrator to finish the musicians' parts, to make sure the orchestra players arrive with all their required instruments (more complicated than it sounds, since many people play more than one instrument), to organize the recording session, to make sure everyone knows what to bring, what music they're playing, who plays on what, which pieces they're playing, making sure that all the players have all their music, making sure that everything is written so that it's easy to read, that everyone can find their music easily, and in general ensuring that everything is ready so that the recording session can go as smoothly as possible.[10] Recording sessions can cost tens of thousands of dollars per day, so efficiency matters.

Contractors

In order to record the written music, the composer or orchestrator contacts a contractor, who engages the necessary musicians required for the recording session. The contractor's job is to hire the highest-quality musicians within the budget, around which there is usually some negotiation. Contractor Dan Savant of Savant Productions, Inc., explained it this way: The director talks to the composer, and they decide on the kind of music to be used. If it's orchestral, the composer generates a wish list of however many players and which instruments. Then they approach a contractor, such as Savant, and ask how much it will cost, and they try to budget what they desire. If they're unsuccessful, they contact the contractor and say that perhaps a smaller orchestra will suffice. More negotiations ensue until an agreement is reached on the number of players and the instrumentation. The contractor then hires the musicians and is present during the recording session; sometimes a contractor will also be a player.[11]

Music contractors keep lists of their preferred musicians; at the top of the list are the musicians known as "first call." Some contractors work hard to book the musicians they think are best for a job; one contractor said, "I will not only call the appropriate musicians, but I will cajole, beg, and barter to get the right musicians on the call for a given job" (Barth 2017, 1). Sometimes composers will want certain players, and whether or not they request them, contractors will try to populate recording sessions with familiar faces to put the composer at ease (Barth 2017).

Performers

After the bosses approve the score—which they listen to as a mockup generated by a computer—after the score is orchestrated, after the score goes to the music copyist, after the musicians are decided upon and hired, the musicians then assemble for the recording session. But the orchestra needs a conductor. Often the composer acts as the conductor; sometimes the orchestrator performs this role. Whoever isn't conducting is likely in the recording booth.

Most of the performers I talked to have less of a sense of where they are in the process than the other musicians I spoke to—they receive a call (it is everyone's desire to be a "first-call" player on a contractor's list), show up at the designated time and place with the instruments the contractor has told them to bring, play the score in front of them in a three-hour session, and, most of the time, that's it (sometimes there is more than one session; superstar composers such as John Williams can record for several days). Instrumentalists, like everyone else in this business, usually struggle to gain a foothold. Trumpet player Jeff Bunnell told me that one has not only to be an excellent player, but to possess a good deal of "seasoning and depth," which takes time to acquire; what he is really referring to is the sort of conduct already discussed: knowledge about how to comport oneself. One can learn a lot on the job from the older players, Bunnell said.

Bunnell also stressed the necessity of professionalism and flexibility; such conduct is at least as important for these musicians as it is for those ahead of them in the supply chain, since performers never work alone. Bunnell said he tries to arrive forty-five minutes before the scheduled start time of a recording session (the music is supposed to be on the stands a half-hour in advance). Trumpet players, like some other instrumentalists, might be asked to play in more than one style, so Bunnell needs to try to ascertain what style or styles are called for before he arrives. He said he brings a dolly full of instruments—trumpets in different keys, a piccolo trumpet, a cornet, a flugelhorn, different mutes—to be prepared to play whatever is in the score. He peruses the music as soon as he arrives. Since he can play in a number of styles, he isn't concerned about which might be required, but there are trumpet players who are strictly classical players. So, he said,

> if there's something that has chord changes, and they have to improvise a solo, they're in deep trouble; they don't know how to do that. So, they have to hope that someone else in the trumpet section can do that. So, they say, "Hey, I've got this little solo; would you mind doing this, because I can't do that." And, of course, you would say you could do it, and you help each other out, but if no one in the section can improvise, then there's a problem, and the composer should have told the contractor to make sure that someone can improvise in the trumpet section.[12]

Sometimes, Bunnell said, the music or a particular passage can be particularly difficult, in which case he practices quietly until he gets it.

Bunnell explained recording session conduct: Arrive early, keep your mouth shut at all times, and show respect for all the other players, especially the principal players (the ones in charge of each section). And there are lines of authority to be respected. These musicians are those who play in an established orchestra with a music director/conductor who would normally be in charge. In the world of film and television music (and studio recording more generally), musicians to a large extent discipline themselves. Bunnell told me that it's the principal players who are in charge; questions for the composer go through them. The person who runs the recording session is the contractor, who calls a ten-minute break every hour. And the composer is also in authority, whether or not they're in the control booth or conducting. It is the composer who decides what music the orchestra is going to record, the order, and how they're going to do it. Bunnell explained this last point: "If, for example, half the music doesn't have brass, then you want to record all the music that has brass; then you let them go so you don't have to pay them anymore. There are all sorts of financial things that affect sessions." Bunnell said that the bottom line is that the contractor is nominally the boss, as is the composer, but the contractor runs the session and advises the composer, along the lines of, " 'We're going to go into overtime, so let's finish this cue, and we'll call it a day, and we'll finish it tomorrow,' because they're thinking about budget." Or, he said, "If it's a big project and there's a huge budget they might say, 'Hey, you can go into overtime—finish this cue if you want to go into overtime,' and the composer makes that decision.' "[13]

As in everything in this business, social capital matters. Word-of-mouth recommendations, reputations, networks—all are important. Like composers and everyone else, getting ahead in the business is a practice of continually doing your best and demonstrating at recording sessions that you are paying attention by not talking, not reading a newspaper or a book, being totally focused. Bunnell emphasized that "you always want to play as musically as possible every time you pick up your horn, every note, it doesn't matter what it is, as musically as possible.[14] You just do well, and you play well, and when you get an opportunity to show what you can do, hopefully you do well, and you continue gaining a reputation." This is how performers find work, through the slow process of building a reputation. "If you do well every time, someone calls you; that's how you keep working."[15]

Some instrumentalists might need other skills than those described by Bunnell: They aren't just attempting to the best of their abilities to realize the use-value of the score; they are adding to its value, sometimes by contributing music. Carol Kaye, the legendary studio bassist, believes she became the most sought-after bassist for film scores because she could improvise bass lines. She credits her success to having come up through the ranks of jazz musicians before entering studio recording. She said the composers didn't mind that she was making up the bass lines, that's what she was hired to do. Composers run out of time, as we know, and sometimes they lack the time to write out the bass lines. Or they don't know what to write, she said. "They didn't know how to write a funky boogaloo bass line. We're talking about the finest composers in the world—they needed to be commercial. The music had to be commercial, and so they relied on the top players to invent some lines." Kaye told me that the renowned composer

Quincy Jones could be so busy that he sometimes didn't have time to write out all the bass parts, "so he counted on me to invent the lines. And I kind of knew what he wanted. You have to know what kind of lines that they want, for everybody you work for. That's what you always have to have in your mind. They want this; they want that. So, you do what they want."[16]

Other musicians can face the same sort of impromptu composition of their parts described by Kaye. Terry Wollman, guitarist, composer, and producer, talked about the speed with which producers and directors want music to be delivered, resulting in similar situations to those described by Kaye. "I've done sessions where the composer doesn't even have time to write it out; they just sing it to me, or we listen to it together, and they say, 'How about this?' or 'How about that?' We figure out a part right there because they're just keeping it moving. You memorize the cue, make a quick note, go in, and you record it and move on to the next cue."[17] Performing musicians might be afforded creative freedom in these sorts of cases, but they still must attempt to deliver what the composer desires.

With the rise of digital technologies, and especially broadband internet, which permits sending very large files, more and more recordings are being made overseas, usually in Eastern Europe, where fees are lower. Such outsourcing has been identified as a feature of today's neoliberal capitalism. It is also clear that some creative freedom has devolved from composers and toward the money people, as studios were increasingly bought up by multinational corporations and, thus, run more and more by MBAs instead of creative workers (see Hesmondhalgh 2019), another oft-remarked-upon trend in today's capitalism.

Composer Christopher Wong discussed the growing practice of outsourcing the recording of scores. Until the late 1990s, most film scores composed for Hollywood films were recorded in Los Angeles, but the rise of digital technologies made it possible to record in other locations, first by moving recordings around on hard drives and then, with greater bandwidth, by recording and monitoring recording sessions remotely. Seattle was the first American location to compete directly with Los Angeles in the 1990s, Wong says, "by allowing the recordings to be used with a one-time payment without back-end royalty payments, which is something the AFM [American Federation of Musicians] in Los Angeles would not allow at the time." At the same time, recording in Prague emerged as a cheaper option. Wong says that Seattle and Prague didn't take much business from Los Angeles at first, but then "London started becoming very competitive in getting work on Hollywood film scores, and since then they have become a preferred destination for recording the scores for the highest-budget movies." Other low-budget options then emerged in Europe, such as Bulgaria and Macedonia, and America, such as Nashville. "Over time," according to Wong, "the quality of the recordings at all these locations became more and more reliable. So, the reality today is that filmmakers and composers have a variety of different global options for recording orchestra on different budget levels."[18] Composers' access to the creative function has diminished, even in Wong's relatively short time in the industry (roughly twenty years at the time of our initial interview).

Performing musicians in the music supply chain do not participate in the process of refining the composer's raw material, but in realizing its value and, sometimes, adding value to it—up to a point. Producers and directors may desire the sound of an orchestra, but that doesn't mean they will pay for the best musicians to record it in Los Angeles. The ultimate aim of the producers and directors is maximizing surplus-value through the use-value they pay musicians to provide. Recording sessions with well-known composers motivate contractors to hire as many first-call musicians as they can, and musicians will even extricate themselves from prior recording commitments in order to play in a recording session with a famous composer. All this is part of the game of the acquisition of symbolic capital, as discussed in chapter 1, and it is also a means by which value is added to the music as it moves through the supply chain.

Recording Engineers

In a way, recording engineers are like composers: Their participation in the supply chain—the digital supply chain—is initiated when the music starts as notation. Their job is not one of refinement, but of creating the value of the recorded music, making live musicians sound as good as they can sound and producing digital files that allow mixers—the next step in the digital supply chain—the greatest flexibility (or not, as we saw in chapter 2). They work for and with composers, attempting to capture the sound the composers desire for their scores.

Alan Meyerson, best known for his work with the famed film music composer Hans Zimmer, told me that once he is called to record and has the schedule confirmed, there is usually a meeting at which he might see a little of the film or even view the entire film. Then, listening to the mockup, he will discuss with the composer how they envision the sound palette. Meyerson might be asked to take some of the composer's computer files and improve the sound. If it's an orchestral score, which is mostly what Meyerson works on, they'll talk about the size of the orchestra and what he calls its format—brass-heavy, or lots of strings, or something else; composers vary on this. Meyerson told me, "There are certain clients I work with where they like cellos, so there'll be a score with twenty-eight cellos and eight basses and no violins or violas, whatever it calls for." Meyerson said they try to make the sound unique. "You throw out ideas, and you brainstorm with the composer and his team to try to find an interesting way to do this."[19] Meyerson, like other composers and music workers interviewed for this book, hopes to be involved as early as possible in order to have as much input and control over the process as possible, though sometimes all he can do is appear at the recording session and record the orchestra with his own gear.

At a certain point, Meyerson will begin to record elements of the score, first, say, a rhythm section, and then take that recording and give it to the composer to use while continuing to write. Many composers today who work with orchestras record in a way that is referred to as *striping*. All the musicians may be present, but first, say, the strings will be recorded, then the woodwinds, then the brass, and so on. Scoring mixer Oren Hadar said there is often a read-through of the entire score with the orchestra so that the players have a chance to hear what the full score sounds like and get a sense of where their parts fit in. After that, they start striping. This could yield as many as three hundred tracks. Hadar told me, "It makes for a more complicated mix; it does give you a lot more control over the individual elements of the orchestra."[20] Striping is more expensive than recording the entire orchestra because not everyone plays at once, but it offers more control, as Hadar said, which is what directors want: It increases their creative freedom, even if it diminishes that of the musicians, who tend to prefer the synergy that occurs when everyone plays together (see Muddiman 2019 and chapter 7). Striping and the generation of stems (discussed next) represent an extreme rationalization of recorded music.

Music editor Kevin Crehan said that, today, so much of a score is generated using computers that the recording sessions with which he is familiar are often more for replacing certain parts of the computer-generated music with live musicians, what he referred to as "sweetening." Most composers, he said, "will be keeping major elements of what they've mocked up in the demo process," and at the scoring session they will record real strings or horns. Some composers, he said, will record live percussion in a couple of recording sessions and use that throughout their score. Crehan also said that there are now specialists who can make mocked-up recordings sound better; "they're really good at controlling the velocities and creating all the flourishes, crescendos, and subtleties."[21]

Bits and Pieces (of Music)

Music can start either as notation or as digital files created by the composer, but, either way, a recording generates digital files, and at this point, the analog and digital supply chains converge. It becomes clearer in this part of the supply chain the extent to which the social relations of production in these fields are shaped not just by hierarchies and by control of access to creative freedom, but by the various actors' estimations of the skills of other workers in the supply chain. Workers need to evaluate whatever situation in which they find themselves and assess if their input would be welcome, or heeded, which can vary based not only on the situation but also on the personalities involved.

Mixers

After the recording session, the music is mixed; the mixer could be the same person as the recording engineer, though not always. Mixers are akin to orchestrators in a way: They take raw material (in this case, recorded music as digital files rather than a score) and improve it, rationalizing it; theirs is also a job of refinement, though it is more than that, for mixers also do work that prepares the sound files for those after them in the music supply chain.

Contractor Dan Savant told me that the mixer needs to ascertain the format in which the music directors and/or music editors want the sound files. Pro Tools (recording software that many use) can create what are called stems, groups of audio tracks that can be prepared before the final mix. Stems can be as simple as just strings, just brass, just woodwinds, or they can be much more complicated. Recording engineer and mixer Meyerson defined stems this way: "Stems are different parts of music that have been separated out for control at a later point."[22] If the strings are thought to be too loud in the final mix, they can be lowered without affecting the other instruments. This is another way in which the composer—or producer or director—can invoke their creative function through controlling the sound of the mix.

Scoring mixer Oren Hadar said there are two reasons to make stems. One is editorial. "If there is a picture change, or if they just decide to reedit a cue for whatever reason, being able to do it in the stems and make the edits in the stems gives them more control over how they can edit." The other is so that the dubbing mixer (the person who makes the final mix) has more control over the elements of the mix. "If I didn't give them stems," Hadar said, "they would just turn down the whole cue, and now the composer's screwed because all of his music is so quiet. The stems give them the ability to manipulate individual elements more, and that gives the composer more of a chance for the cue to actually live, not just get turned down or deleted"—by someone above them in the hierarchy.[23]

But, Hadar said, sometimes if the dubbing mixer has a lot of control with stems, they can make many changes in the levels and the placement of the sound in particular speakers. Hadar told me that sometimes some negotiation is involved, for example, the composer saying they don't want a lot of stems for a particular project. Hadar gave an example of a recent project being dubbed outside of Los Angeles. "So, then the composer can't go to the dub, there's no music editor, or they don't have a representative there, so they have no way of knowing if the music is going to be played back the way it's meant to be played back." Hadar added, "I think I ended up sending only four stems, even though it's a feature film with seventy minutes of music."[24]

Recording today can result in many dozens of tracks combined into stems in all sorts of ways. Creating stems can be a massive undertaking—the engineer can end up trying to mix 150 tracks and 24 stems. In addition, when a mix to surround sound is made (known in the business as 5.1), the mixer can position stems spatially as desired; percussion stems could be placed in the speakers in the back of the theater, other instruments in the front. "Fortunately, or unfortunately," contractor Savant said, "sometimes you're giving them a lot of stems. So, the mix that you do in the studio might sound fantastic to you, but it might sound a lot different when you hear it in the movie."[25]

Mixers are also tasked with improving the sound of the recording, which is another sort of refinement and rationalization performed at their point in the supply chain. Oren Hadar described this part of his job this way: "Mixing is what I like to call audio Photoshop"; in the same way that a photo retoucher can take a raw photograph and adjust colors, shadows, Hadar can execute with audio. He told me, "I take a piece of music that's given to me, and I make sure that it achieves professional standards. And there are all kind of special effects I can do, same as you can do in Photoshop. But, really, ninety-nine times out of a hundred, I'm just making it sound professional."[26]

Other aspects of the mixer's job include what one could characterize as a process of standardization, another function performed by supply chains. In mixing, this occurs in a couple of ways. One is to ensure that the music isn't noticed where it isn't supposed to be so that there isn't a booming bass or some other disruptive sound. Hadar identified another aspect of his job, which is to make sure that, in a film or television show, the music he is responsible for is mixed to the same standard as the source music (previously recorded music). "If the score isn't mixed to a similar standard, it sounds like crap next to the source. So, you have to make sure that you're giving the composer the same shot on the scene as these songs; otherwise, you're just making the composer look terrible, so I'm trying to put the composer's best foot forward." Hadar also said it is his job to make sure that the volume levels of the various instruments are properly adjusted "so that the loudest thing is what it's supposed to be. So, if the most important thing is the oboe melody, then you make sure that people can hear the oboe melody." A lot of what he does, Hadar said, is "balancing the relative levels of the different instruments."[27]

Hadar was exceptionally insightful about his work, not just the technical nature of it, but how he interacts with others in the social relations of production. He said that a good deal of his job involves just critical listening "and being able to say, 'Oh, I think the strings are too bright here' or 'The horns have more reverb than that' and just being able to listen to a piece of music and really pick out all of the detail and then being able to implement what you hear." Hadar's work isn't just technical; scoring mixers need to know how to read music; at recording sessions, he said, "I'm following along all the bar numbers, reading with everyone, and I'm calling out, 'Oh, clam,' 'Oh, pitchy,' 'Bad entrance,' and I'll even turn to the orchestrator and say something like, 'Hey, did you intend to put that in? It sounds like that D is clashing with that E-flat; is that intentional?'" Hadar said that since he mainly works in television, there might not even be an orchestrator present at the recording session, which means he probably has the best ears in the room. Hadar said that the compliments he receives from composers make him "feel like I'm part of the musical team. I'm not writing the music, though once in a while I might make a suggestion, but that's rare; it's more just about being able to contribute to making the highest-quality recording, and that includes making sure that the playing is of the highest quality."[28]

Even though Hadar works mostly alone in his home studio, there are none-theless moments when he is able to realize that he is part of a collective process.

The last step in the music and sound process is on the dub stage, which Hadar described as resembling a movie theater but functioning as a recording studio. It's the site where the final sound mix occurs—music, dialogue, and sound effects. Hadar has the music mix but does not determine how long that mix is played in the program; this is determined by the dubbing mixer. Hadar himself makes sure that the dialogue can be heard, but final decisions about that are made by the dubbing mixer.

Music Editors

Whether a digital file has been generated by a composer in studio or by a recording engineer, the file eventually finds its way to a music editor, sometimes without making any other stops but sometimes first going through a scoring mixer. Music editors are the last link in the music supply chain, refining the recorded music so that it does what it is supposed to do when it is supposed to do it—maximizing its use-value for those at the top of the hierarchy.

The music editor is the middle person between the composer and film editors. Their job is to make sure that the music is always in sync with what is happening onscreen. It's also the music editor's job to place temporary music in a film so that while it's being shot and edited, the filmmakers have an idea of what it looks like with music. This is important, Andrés Locsey told me, "because almost all scenes need some sort of rhythm. If you're talking about action or drama or something else, you need a rhythm. So, you need to get the music that makes the film work." Locsey said that either he is free to choose the temp music or he is told what to do. "So, it's either, 'Just listen to anything you would like and give us your idea of what this should sound like,' or 'Do only Thomas Newman,' so that you would listen to only Thomas Newman and find what tracks work with specific scenes." After that, Locsey said, he views each scene to determine what moments need what, what kind of emotions are needed, when to start and end, and then begins to edit. "Just drop in the track and chop it up and make it work, almost like composing with existing music by editing it. That's the whole temping process," he said. Then, he told me, he presents this to the composer so that he knows what has worked for the filmmakers. Or, if it hasn't worked, he finds something different from the temp.[29]

Normally present at the spotting session with the composer and others, the music editor takes detailed notes about where in the film or program there is to be music, when it starts and stops, what sort of music, where there might be a popular song that is licensed for use in the film or broadcast, and so forth. From this session, the music editor will generate the spotting notes, which keep track of each cue. Craig Pettigrew told me that each cue gets a number and a start time and end time, along with creative comments. This list is sent to the composer, producer, and whoever else among the bosses wants it.

Once the temp music has been agreed on and the spotting session completed, the composer becomes involved and starts writing music. Locsey said that sometimes the composer will give him "suites" of cues that the director and producers like, and he'll start placing them in the film. "For example," he said, "if you have a main character, and they write their theme and they love the theme, then maybe they'll give me that theme and I can start cutting it in other scenes of the movie where we have the same character." Locsey takes the stems, which he said gives him freedom, explaining how he uses stems with this example of the main character: If the character appears in an intimate setting, Locsey might play the theme only on piano; or, if it's a dramatic setting, he can use the orchestral stem.

It's the music editor's job not just to keep everything in sync, but to shorten or expand where necessary. Locsey told me, "If a scene was two minutes long and they say, 'This scene is kind of slow. We need to make it one minute. Let's shorten it,' I have to shorten that music musically, edit it so that it still feels like music and natural and it doesn't feel edited."[30] Craig Pettigrew also talked about the revision process, saying that if a producer doesn't like a particular cue, "I can pull another cue in—it's almost like cutting and pasting in a Word document. I'll edit it, save it as a new session."[31] Pettigrew is being modest, as this sort of cutting and pasting demands a good deal of musicality.

The music editor can also reuse music from the same series, in which case they receive from the composer a list of cues to track. "Track," explained Pettigrew, "means to take music from the library of music from previous seasons or episodes that already exists and create the cues." Using tracked music relies on the social relations of production to run smoothly. Pettigrew said he receives a list of cues to track and gives them to the showrunner, who approves or disapproves them, sometimes with comments and suggestions. After that, Pettigrew passes them on to the producers, and then the composer will give them his cues. Because the composer hired to write the music might not actually be writing the music if tracked music is employed, the music editor has become more important in shows that have been on the air for a long time and for which there is already a good deal of recorded music.[32] At the end of the process before the final dubbing, Locsey said he hopes that all the music is in sync from start to finish once they have a full score. Sometimes, though, the schedule is too compressed, and the composer will simply say to Locsey, "'You take care of this one.'" Then, he said, it's rather like the temping process where he tries to figure out what works.

On the dub stage, music editors are present representing the composer; Kevin Crehan said that by the time the film is being dubbed, the composer is done with the project.[33] Along with the music editor is a two-person mix crew, one of whom works with dialogue and music while the other is in charge of sound effects, plus the sound supervisor and, perhaps, if it's a film, the director as well as a producer or two and a studio executive. Locsey told me that he must be present in case there are any changes because at that point in the process, the composer can't go back and write something new, especially if the score involves live musicians, who can't be rerecorded on short notice. It is Locsey's job to fix things at that point: the "last tweaks and adjustments while we're mixing the movie."[34] The last bits of refinement.

Music editors are also responsible for what is known as a cue sheet, which Locsey described as the legal part of his job; it's a log listing who wrote what and what performance rights association they are affiliated with (which is how composers receive their royalties, mainly from the American Society of Composers, Authors, and Publishers [ASCAP] or Broadcast Music, Inc.). In an environment where the ownership of intellectual property is an important source of income for copyright owners, such work is significant. Locsey gave an example from the YouTube series *Cobra Kai*. "I wrote '1-M-1' (which is music 'one' from reel 'one') written by Zach Robinson and Leo Birenberg, and it started in hour one, minute one, second five, frame twenty-two, and it ended at minute whatever, and it's one minute and twenty-five seconds long, and it's by these two guys—he is affiliated with ASCAP, and he is affiliated with BMI."[35] Locsey does this for every cue, whether it was newly composed for the particular program or film or whether it is a song that has been licensed. He sends the cue sheet in with the pieces of music for the purposes of archiving.

Music editors, like many music workers, see as part of their job protecting the composer's time. Their self-conduct is not just directed toward behaving properly in groups and respecting those above them in the hierarchy, but, in the case of the composer, providing backup protection. Craig Pettigrew said that one of his duties involves giving the composer as much time to write and relieving them of having to worry about the details. "The easier I make the composer's life," he said, "the more he or she will call me and have me on a job because I make his or her life easier. That's kind of the biggest part of my job, making the composer's life less hectic." This is another way that workers can build up social capital. Pettigrew said that even though computers make his work easier in many respects, for example, by speeding up the process, it also makes the work more pressurized, as we have seen.[36]

Conclusions

While in some respects workers in these fields of cultural production do what they have always done—provide music for film and television— the world has shifted around them, as it has for many workers. They are paid less to do more, in the same amount of time or less, with new digital tools that allow their bosses to demand more at the last minute and to facilitate the outsourcing of some of their labor. But they work it out, managing the social relations of production to get work done on time. The work they do serves the same purpose as before, adding value to music in the supply chain by refining what composers and recording engineers give them or creating value from the performance and recording so that the music fulfills the use-value desired of those above these workers in the hierarchy of these fields of cultural production. Workers also find ways to be creative, to honor their intuition, even if the work they do is frequently technical.

CHALLENGES

This chapter tackles what are perhaps the two biggest issues for composers and other musicians that arise from the nature of group production and collective labor: authority and communication, especially communication about music and sound. Group production in cultural fields—especially in a supply chain hierarchy, with its participants' conceptions of conduct (their own but also that of others)—can result in communications problems that are sometimes comical, when they are not frustrating. Such a structure brings with it inevitable problems of communication, perhaps especially concerning music, when people in charge might not possess much musical knowledge (though frequently holding strong opinions about their musical tastes), bosses who must nonetheless tell composers what they want. And there are problems of authority: It's not always clear who is in charge, so another issue for composers is simply ascertaining whom it is they must please. These issues have been around as long as there has been group production. (Robert Faulkner's interlocutors complained about the same issues in the 1970s, when he conducted his research; see Faulkner 1983.) Although they did not arise with neoliberal capitalism, the increase in the number of managers has been a neoliberal effect. All of the problems and negotiations surrounding communication and authority are part of the process of refining the raw material of the composer in order to ready it for its use-value in supporting a film or episode or game.

There were significant growing pains during the transition from radio to television, and questions of who was in charge were part of these problems. Perhaps not coincidentally, it was in the same period that, in film production, the director emerged as the person in charge. According to Raymond Williams (1981, 114), the producer, director, or manager type arose in the world of the theater, where managing actors was not the only issue. New staging techniques, new kinds of design and lighting, that were believed to be not only necessary, but desirable, began to be employed and had to be managed. Actors and writers assumed these managerial roles first, but by the mid-twentieth century, the director had become the central figure of authority. New reproduction technologies complicated matters further, since they required even more professional specialization (with respect to music, recording engineers, sound mixers, mixing engineers) as well as people to install, maintain, and repair equipment. With this, Williams argues, class lines were drawn, "often with continuing argument about jobs at or near the point of division" (115).

The quintessential case, according to Williams, is that of writing and printing. The former is seen as productive of content, the latter as "merely instrumental" (115). This divide has been reproduced repeatedly with the introduction of newer technologies, even those that make this division of labor unnecessary or redundant. "But whatever happens to particular processes," Williams writes, "it remains a general condition of modern cultural technology that it both requires social forms of production and yet, within this, under specific economic conditions, imposes not only a professional but a class division of labor" (115–16). The issue, I would say, is one of the safeguarding and apportioning of the creative function.

Who's in Charge?

Today, the increase of bureaucratization and managerialism in everyday life (see chapter 2) has affected film and television production as well. In the world of big-budget films (not the focus of this book), Stephan Eicke (2019, 29) interviewed film composers who have been in the business for many years who told him that the number of opinions they have to weigh now is greater than in the past, the result of bloated film budgets, which has increased the number of producers who have either invested in the film themselves or have brought investors to it. Actor John Cusack said in a recent interview, "Hollywood has changed a lot. When I was first coming up, it was connected to '60s, '70s filmmaking. The film companies weren't part of megacorporations where the film division was nothing compared with their vast holdings. There were *people* who ran studios. You can deal with one personality, but dealing with this veil of 25 junior vice presidents?" (Marchese 2020). Joey Newman told me that there has also been an increase in the number of managers in television.[1]

In the realm of independent and low-budget films, Miriam Mayer said that it's usually clear who's in charge—the person paying her.[2] But for most of the people I interviewed, one of the most frustrating and challenging issues is that it is not always evident who has authority. Workers with access to the creative function may nonetheless be curbed by the money people. This seems to be a long-standing problem that has worsened in recent years, in part because of the proliferation of managers. There are known hierarchies—the director in a film, the showrunner (credited as an executive producer) in television—but an outsize personality can skew the normal chain of authority, or a superstar actor or their spouse can wield authority, or there can be discord or lack of agreement among the bosses. Questions of authority perhaps matter more in the realm of music production because it comes so late in the process that film directors or television program showrunners often fear that the composer can come along and ruin their film or episode (see Faulkner 1983).

Composers understand that it is their job to fulfill the director's vision, but since ascertaining who is in charge is difficult, developing an understanding of the power dynamics is crucial. As Penka Kouneva told me, "The composer's first job is to understand who has the creative vision, who has the monetary control, and what's the dynamic between all the creatives. What's the dynamic between the creators, the producers, and the publishers? If you don't understand this, your job is jeopardized because you can get into situations where you're following the direction of somebody who's about to get fired, and you get fired next."[3] Kouneva said she has seen this happen. She had worked as an orchestrator for other composers and witnessed these dynamics and, as a result, has become politically savvy, learning how to conduct herself. Joey Newman discussed the same issue, saying he learned early in his career that it's important to find out who is in charge. "It's not always clear," he said, "but most of the time it should be because that person will have the strongest opinion and usually be the chosen one to take charge of music decisions. In television it tends to be easier because it is usually the producer, but the question is, which one?"[4]

Some composers told me they had to learn how to become almost ethnographic (not their term) in their interactions with their bosses in order to attempt to ascertain who it is they actually had to please. Or, sometimes, no one seems to be paying much attention, and it's difficult for musicians to receive any direction or approval. Or, the production staff isn't well organized, or someone quits or is fired. All these conditions can make it difficult for composers and other music workers to find out what is wanted of them so that they can do their jobs. Many people I spoke to had devised strategies of attempting to deal with this problem, which I will discuss below.

Questions of authority are particularly fraught, and important, at the beginning of the process of creating a new television show, discussed in chapter 3 in the consideration of the pilot process. John Nordstrom told me that at the beginning of the work on a television program, the composer meets with the showrunner; Nordstrom said he always hopes that only one person is in charge "because if there's somebody who says they're in charge, but there are actually four guys, then you know that you're going to be stuck in the middle of all these different opinions, and most of the time, it's just not a fun situation to be in. They end up using the composer to win arguments with each other."[5] Joey Newman said figuring out who's in charge when working on a television pilot can be difficult because there are many people involved, including those at the studio, but, he said, once you're past the pilot process, "you get used to it; once a nice pace is set, then maybe there's one or two voices." Newman also spoke of the necessity of dealing with difficult personalities and their changing moods, saying there is a language, a shorthand, between composers and showrunners that they use to understand what is going on psychologically. In short, they have to know how to read people. Newman said he will ask producers' assistants, "'How are they? How is the day going?' 'Oh, they're having a rough day.' So, I prepare for some things that on normal days might go off fine but might not go off well today. It is really helpful to be pre-warned!" And when the bosses arrive, Newman can evaluate them: "They might be tired, they might be stressed, they might be complaining, and that changes the whole thing. The dialogue between producer and the editor could be different that day." Newman concluded, "On a daily basis, it's very much based on personalities and moods, and that part can be the hardest to navigate because then you have to decide, 'How am I going to talk about something? Will I have to reframe the conversation?'"[6]

But the person in charge doesn't necessarily have the biggest presence, which makes it more difficult to discern who has authority. Ryan Shore told me, "If there were a Ten Commandments of the business side of film scoring, one of them should be to 'know who may have the final creative say on the music you are creating.'" Shore said that "each project is different. Sometimes the studio has the final word; sometimes it may be the studio, and sometimes it may be the producer."[7] Another composer said that sometimes he's not told who is in charge. Occasionally someone will just lean in close and say something like, "'Look, I'm the person you need to please.' Sometimes you just receive your direction, and you start figuring it out when other people start chiming in, and sometimes it's difficult to tell."[8]

Almost all the composers I spoke with offered some sort of anecdote meant to illustrate the difficulty of determining who is in charge. Shore's involved working on a pilot for a television show. He met with the show's two writers, each of whom gave him an idea of what they were seeking in the music. "One of them would say they wanted X, and then the next person would chime in and say, 'Yeah, yeah, yeah,' affirming what the last person just said, and then they would say something completely different." Shore said they were acting as though they were in agreement, but they were not. "I remember leaving one of those meetings feeling lost, thinking, 'OK, I think they're asking for two different things entirely; now what am I going to do?'"[9] It occurred to Shore to look at the script and see whose name was listed first, and that's how he decided whom to follow in that instance.

When composers are working on a project for a studio, they are technically working for the studio music department, whose workers, Shore said, "have their finger on the pulse of what the studio is looking for." Or perhaps someone higher up is overseeing things, such as the vice president of programming, but whoever it is, the composer must figure it out. The person they're actually working for might not be a creative type, but even if they are, if they're high up the chain of authority, they could be overseeing many projects. So, Shore said, there are music executives "who just concentrate on music, and you hope that the proper flow of information is coming through the studio from higher-ups through the department and on to you."[10]

Composers have different strategies for dealing with questions of authority and what people want. Zach Robinson said he doesn't need to be given free rein; he likes guidance. He simply hopes to be able to work for people who are open to his suggestions and who aren't wedded to particular musical ideas or styles. And he doesn't mind if his bosses are picky, since such people can be constructive. "The worst sort of situation is when you have someone that just can't make a decision, and it comes from their insecurities. It's one thing to not be able to communicate what type of music you want, but it's another thing to have zero direction to give." Robinson thinks this is what separates great directors from not-so-great directors. He said that a lot of people don't know how to talk about music, but directors should nonetheless offer some sort of guidance. Robinson said that every client is different, so he must undergo the process of learning who is in charge with every job.[11]

There is also what Joey Newman referred to as the "babysitting component" of a composer's job. He told me that he tries to make all of the people he deals with feel as though he has heard them out. Newman thinks that many people just want to talk; some feel as though they must weigh in. And among all the voices, he tries to pinpoint just who it is he must appease. In the end, he said, it's just one person with whom he must deal, the person who works with him specifically, and once he pleases that person, the others usually follow.[12]

Sometimes composers have to deal with bosses who are stars or outsized personalizes of another sort. For Penka Kouneva, the scoring business is about navigating minefields; it's not only about writing great music but also about collaborating with people and their egos, visions, expectations, and tastes. Kouneva told me, "Sometimes I joke about certain demands by the creatives falling in the 'Department of Impossible Expectations.' And I have to navigate out of an impossible expectation."[13] One composer for a successful television sitcom, who had written the music for every episode of the program's many years of broadcast, told me of a scene in which the actor/star had also become an executive producer. The composer said that during a visit to the studio to meet with the executive producer who was the showrunner, the star issued a number of instructions to the showrunner to be relayed to the composer while the three of them were standing together. And there are others who can weigh in. Orchestrator Tom Calderaro told me that there are always wars between the creative people involved and relayed an anecdote about a film he worked on starring Tom Cruise. Cruise's wife didn't like the score, he told me, so they had to replace the whole thing in only a few weeks.[14]

Is Anyone in Charge?

Occasionally, even when it is clear who the boss is, situations can get murky. Composer Matt Hutchinson, who echoed the importance of ascertaining whom you're writing for, said that things can quickly change. In film, the director is usually in charge, but, Hutchinson said, "I've also had films where all of a sudden the director is AWOL and the producer is the person taking the lead." Hutchinson said that at the beginning of one project he had a long conversation with the director, "and then suddenly the producer is the only person responding to any of my questions and giving me notes. So, is it coming from the director through the producer? I don't know." Hutchinson said you can sometimes figure out who is in charge based on who is getting back to you. But, he said, "There is no real way to know for sure at the beginning without flat out asking, which sometimes can feel a little bit odd," since this would defy the deferential conduct below-the-line workers are expected to exercise. "So, you have to feel out the room, and sometimes I have asked, 'So, ultimately who am I going to be interfacing with about the music?'" Hutchinson said he usually receives some sort of an answer to that question, but sometimes he finds that he must wait and see. Hutchinson thought that "there is a lot of psychology to all of it, and ultimately it is making sure that everyone feels like they've been heard. And that's kind of tricky."[15]

When it's not clear who's in charge, composers are frustrated. Jan Stevens told me about the process of auditioning for a particular television pilot for which he was told, "'We don't know what we want; we'll know it when we hear it.'" At this stage, he wasn't getting paid, but it was a good gig, so Stevens was willing to throw his hat into the ring without any compensation, which is common in this situation because the stakes are high and the payoff can be worth it. "So," he said, "I scored the whole show with what I thought was wanted and what I thought the audience might want to hear. I knocked myself out on it. I called a whole bunch of players—I only bring in the best because I want this to be my best stuff going out." Then he waited. In the third week he called the producers and asked if anyone had listened to what he had submitted and was told, "'We're not sure.'" More weeks passed. Stevens then asked what was happening and was told, "'We heard that one of the producers is listening to a Tex-Mex band. They're listening to this song and this other song.'" So, Stevens offered to write something like that, which was difficult to emulate. Stevens, like most composers, made more than one recording in order to have options. He made four demos, synced them with the picture, and sent videos of the scenes. Then he waited again. Stevens thought he was out of the running but finally received an email: "'The guy who had the power to make the decision liked it but is at the moment no longer with the show.'" Stevens decided at that point to cut his losses and move on to the next pilot.[16] This sort of extreme prevarication isn't that unusual in group production, where people not only vie with each other to be in charge, but people endowed with access to the creative function come and go.

Being Left Alone

Many composers told me that, in the old days, they would meet regularly with those in charge. Showrunners or directors once visited composers' studios, or composers would go to the studio, but this is less frequent today; composers are increasingly left to their own devices. David Schwartz told me that he likes being in the room with people in charge, but on one project, the showrunner stopped appearing. "People would sit there," Schwartz said, "but they didn't really want to express an opinion, so it'd be me, the music editor, and we were on the same page." But Schwartz said he prefers to work with the creative people: "You come up with different stuff if you can have a little back-and-forth conversation about it. And then, temp is great, because you can think, 'Well, I don't think this is really helping this here; there, I see what you're going for, but here, you know maybe we can do something like this.'"[17]

Deborah Lurie told me she very much missed the creative synergies that occurred when she would meet with producers and directors face-to-face. In the communications she would receive via email, and not always from a director, there could be "a chain to get feedback." In Lurie's view, conversations with other creative workers elicited "an artistic process that could not be replaced with more convenient technological methods." Lurie believes she is good at what she calls "musical empathy," which became "so much harder when I was just getting scenes without the actual creator of the scenes." This mode of communication and labor has resulted in more fragmented scores "because everything was taken on a scene-by-scene or moment-by-moment basis as opposed to a cohesive storytelling approach."[18]

Other music workers don't see their composer clients as much as in the past. Scoring mixer Phil McGowan said that composers themselves don't usually visit his studio and participate in the mixing process anymore either. He said that not long ago, the composer would come to his studio and listen to the mix; they would work on it together, and the composer would present him with notes. He would make adjustments to the satisfaction of the composer so that he could then finalize the mix and move on to the next cue. But today, said McGowan, "a lot of times I'm by myself completely, and I will crash down my surround mix into a stereo file and put that on Dropbox, and they'll listen to that in their studio and email me notes. I'll do the notes, send in the new version, and we have a back-and-forth." McGowan said about 90 percent or more of his projects are done this way now, mainly because composers have become so busy that they don't have time for studio visits. Sometimes they'll come over for a pilot or at the beginning of a film project in order to establish an overall sound, especially with an orchestra. But then, McGowan said, "Once we get some of the important ones done, then the rest of the mix, most of the time, they'll just stay in their studio, and I'll send them versions over the internet, and they'll approve them that way."[19]

Yet, I did not detect any sense that the workers I spoke to felt themselves to be alienated from their labor (see Hesmondhalgh and Baker 2011 on this point). Marx famously discussed how in the capitalist labor process the product of the worker's labor does not belong to the worker, as is true for composers, whose music is owned by producers. "From the instant he steps into the workshop," writes Marx (1990, 292), "the use-value of his labour-power and therefore also its use, which is labour, belongs to the capitalist." Even composers who have taken on so much work that they must subcontract some of it to other composers nonetheless feel that it is somehow their product and that they are proud of it. Any sense of alienation that people described to me concerned the solitude of working alone, which has been made possible with digital technologies and smaller budgets—social alienation, not alienated labor.

Authority below the Composer

Even when it's clear who's in charge, the diffusion of authority in group production can create problems not just for composers, who have their bosses, but for those further along the music supply chain who frequently answer to people other than the composers. Everyone I spoke with in music production under the composer said it was their job to support the composer; most employed the language of teams and teamwork. Music editor Andrés Locsey told me that, as the music editor, he always has to be the composer's best friend, make his life easier. But, he said, he also must do what the studio, director, and producer want him to do, keeping everyone happy. Locsey said, "Many times it's finding a balance of what everybody needs. If somebody wants something with a lot of action, but somebody wants something with not so much action, sometimes you have to do ten tries at something until everybody signs off." He said there are scenes for which he has made twenty versions "because people weren't happy, or one person was very happy, but another person wasn't, so you have to keep editing and editing and editing until you arrive at that specific place where everybody likes it. You can't really pick a favorite. You have to make things work."[20]

Locsey, like many composers I spoke to, often has contingency plans, other versions of cues on hand in case a boss doesn't like the first one. Oftentimes, he told me, "if I feel something works really, really well, I will do that, and I will just keep it in my back pocket. You can always keep working on multiple other options." Locsey tries many versions, "and then they'll say something like, 'Oh, yeah, of course that doesn't work. That's fine; let's try this other thing again.' And then everybody comes to a decision." Sometimes Locsey is asked to do something he knows is not going to work, but "if they sign off on it, I would say, 'Yes, okay. It's fine.' It's their project; it's not mine. I'm a part of this bigger thing, movie work—hundreds of people working there."[21] Locsey realizes that he's not the person in charge; it's the producers or executives or the studio.

Ultimately, the director in film or a producer in television will prevail. Scoring mixer Oren Hadar told me that sometimes there's a higher-up, such as a film director, who is focused on music and whom he will speak to with along with the composer, in which case, he said, "There can be a question of whose opinion wins the day, but nine out of ten times, it's the director, and so sometimes there's some sensitivity around that."[22] In film, it is the director who is the person who is allowed to think of the big picture, to enjoy the creative function. At a recording session, though, the person in charge is the composer. Sometimes, Alan Meyerson told me, the composer relinquishes that position to him as the recording engineer, or to the orchestrator, so Meyerson is free to speak up and ask questions. "Wouldn't it be better if we did x, y, and z?" The composer would say, "'Just tell them.' Or there are times when there are composers who don't care about talking that much, or I'll just take charge. I'll just do all the legwork until someone says, 'No, no, we're going to do this.'" Meyerson said that the hierarchy at the recording session is the composer, the recording engineer, and then the orchestrator. But even at his position in the chain of command, Meyerson sees part of the job as ascertaining who is in charge. In his studio, though, he's the boss. "Even when a composer comes in here, he's going to want me to run the show, unless it's someone like Hans [Zimmer], who really just does his thing, but other than that, they really want me to be driving the bus."[23]

Meyerson, unlike most others, discussed the necessity for being something of a therapist or psychologist for his composer clients. The kinds of technical concerns he works with (types of microphones, microphone placement, mixing) are opaque to some composers and perhaps even more mysterious to composers' bosses; so, he told me, "You have to be a bit of a therapist and get in there and make sure everything is going to be okay, that we're all going to be done on time; we might even be done early; it's going to sound great, and if we're not early, it's still going to sound great, and the world's not coming to an end." Meyerson said he always must deal with the personality side of the people he works with and make sacrifices for his clients. "It's a constant, day-to-day maintenance of your clientele," he told me. "It's a big one for me."[24] This is all part of the dynamics of group production and the preservation, or enhancement, of social capital.

The one event that might bring together everyone—those in charge and those who follow—is the recording session, where not just the performing musicians are present, but the conductor (usually the composer or orchestrator), the recording engineer, the music editor, as well as, frequently, producers and the director. There, the well-known hierarchies are in effect, but there are a number of music workers who have the authority to weigh in, even stop the recording process—not just the composer, but the recording engineer, the mixer, and the music editor.

Communication about Music and Sound

The problem of employing language to communicate about music has bedeviled musicians and nonmusicians alike and is a perennial issue in the academic music fields, especially ethnomusicology (see, among other works, Seeger 1977 and Feld 1984). Musicians in the fields of cultural production studied here encounter this problem daily. Composers frequently complained about problems dealing with their bosses, when they knew nothing of music or when they thought they knew something. Once in a while, a composer's boss might have musical knowledge, and composers considered this sort of relationship as more of a partnership (as with David Schwartz in the production of *Arrested Development*, as discussed in chapter 2). But this is more the exception than the norm.

Determining, and working with, the level of musical knowledge of one's bosses is one of the major challenges that composers face. For some, this is frustrating; for others, it's part of the challenge of what they do and why they like it. Some of my interviewees discussed this perennial problem. Composer Matt Hutchinson told me that the communication issue is interesting to him, even though it's difficult. And if the people he's dealing with possess musical knowledge, it can be even more challenging. "Sometimes," he said, "I've found that it's almost harder to talk to directors or producers who are very musical and have knowledge about music composition and theory because they may want to be more involved in the composition process." Hutchinson said he would almost rather work with a director who spoke in terms of emotions: "'For this scene the character is feeling this, and I want the audience to feel this.' And that would be perfect, because I'll turn that into music the way that I imagine it." Hutchinson gave an example of an unnamed orchestral project:

> When we got on the call for the first client review, they said, "Yeah, this is really cool, but we really aren't loving the flutes in this piece. There's something about this that just doesn't feel right." And I'm thinking, "Okay . . . ," and I'm racking my brain because there are no flutes in the music! So, I'm trying to figure out what it is that they're talking about. I didn't want to hurt anybody's feelings. So, you're trying to walk that line. I remember saying, "Okay, so what section exactly? Let's go here; let's break this down. Here you've got the strings coming in and have this happening." And then they said, "There, right there at that moment the flutes come in. It's just all off!" And what they meant by that was a cello. It was a cello, not a flute. It was the completely other end of the sonic spectrum of what I thought they meant. So, to try to make sense of all that is really, really hard sometimes.[25]

But Hutchinson and others can't break protocol; they must continue to conduct themselves in a manner expected of them given their position within the hierarchy.

Mike Post described the process as code breaking: figuring out what bosses want. "All the great producers," he said, "don't know what to say, musically—if they did, they'd write it themselves. They say English words to me and make descriptions of stuff. And you have to break the code. You have to listen to what they're saying and have it inspire you." Post described the conversation he had with producer Stephen J. Cannell about *The Rockford Files* (1974–80). The series star, James Garner, was a southerner, though the series was set in Los Angeles, so that had to be reflected in the music as well. Cannell described Rockford as someone who wasn't eager to get into a fight, was "clumsy with the girls," had a shady best friend and a father who was a trucker, and was mostly interested in his $200 per day plus expenses. "'He's Steve McQueen with humor. He lives in a trailer in Paradise

Cove [Malibu], and he drives a Firebird,'" Post relayed. Post and Carpenter's music employed a dobro, Allman Brothers' guitar sound, a blues harmonica, as well as eight violins, two cellos, four woodwinds, two trombones, two French horns, and a Minimoog synthesizer.[26]

Many composers relayed anecdotes that illustrate the lack of knowledge on the part of their bosses and that showed how they had to creatively discern what the bosses wanted. Post's story concerned the theme music for NYPD *Blue* (1993–2005). He met with producer Steven Bochco and co-executive producer Greg Hoblit at a Los Angeles restaurant to discuss the theme music. Bochco's question was, "'Has there ever been a main title that was just drums?'" Post replied that you couldn't do that. Bochco said that's all he had. Hoblit made an analogy between New York City and the human body with connective arteries—the subway. Those were the only two ideas he was given. Post worked with his then-engineer, Danny Lux (now a composer himself), to devise a compelling drum sound that outdid what Post thought was the greatest drum fill in popular music, from Phil Collins's "In the Air Tonight." And he researched the New York City subway and learned that much of it was constructed by Irish people, so he wanted a sound that evoked Irish pipes. "Everything was made off of that: 'drums,' 'subway.'" Post said that being a code breaker involved asking questions: "Well, what is it? What does he want? What do they want? And, what were they trying for? What was their idea, and how do I make it? How do I encapsulate it in forty-five seconds or in thirty seconds or a minute? And have it be memorable, have the audience walk out humming?"[27]

Hutchinson said he always asks for musical references to help him understand what his bosses are seeking musically. If a client requests a dance track, he'll ask for an example, which may or may not be what he thinks of as a dance track, but the sample he is given is helpful in beginning to calibrate what the client means. He said it is his job to deduce what the client intends and what they want musically. "I can't hold it against them if they aren't communicating it in a musical way or aren't communicating it a way I can understand right off the bat," he said. "That's my problem to solve, but it is sometimes humorous dealing with like someone trying to talk about something that's hard for them to talk about."[28] Miriam Mayer said that directors sometimes apologize for not knowing musical terminology, but she doesn't expect them to know it. Often, she said, "I'm into the weeds if they use a certain type of terminology and they're using it wrong; I get so confused that I can't see the forest for the trees. And I'm thinking, 'What do I do?'"[29] Like most of the composers I spoke to, Mayer said she preferred directors who speak in emotional terms, since that is what she tries to evoke musically.

It's not always a problem of communication, though; sometimes those hiring (or seeking to hire) a composer don't know what they want. Jan Stevens offered a story about a pilot he had worked on. He was told by a producer, "'I want an old-fashioned rock 'n' roll sound; I want this to be like Chuck Berry crossed with Springsteen crossed with . . . ,' and he gave me a whole bunch of stuff. And then he said, 'I love The Who!,' and in my mind, I'm thinking, 'Oh, this is going to be fun, but I wonder if the network's going to like this.'" Stevens made several demos, which they used, and the show then went up to the network executive, who asked, "'What's this old-fashioned music?'" Stevens said that at that point they only had about three days before the program was to air, and they called in ten more people to compose music for it. He didn't end up writing the music, and he thought that the music that was used wasn't great given the limited amount of time to write it. And the show only lasted four episodes.[30]

Some composers think that attempting to discern what nonmusical bosses want can stifle what creative freedom they might enjoy. Joey Newman told me he thinks that talking about emotion, character, story, pacing, is comparatively easy, but talking about sound can be frustratingly difficult. "What does she mean when she says, 'This is the wrong sound'?" For Newman, "The hardest part is when they're so adamant because they think that's what it is, but they're really talking about the wrong instrument or sound. Then I think, 'No, I don't have any of that in my score; there's no oboe in there; I don't have a bell. What are you talking about?'" Newman told me that while working on *The Middle* he joked about needing a "producer dictionary" because the showrunner employed such phrases as "plunkety-plunks" or "rinky-tinky," all sorts of onomatopoeic phrases meant to convey what she was trying to say. Or the producer would offer suggestions, such as recommending that the music should "end up on an up instead of a down" or a "sting-y out" or that it was too "twangy," though Newman notes that *twangy* can mean many different things, so it's necessary to dig in and figure out what is meant. Newman said that project became a course in how to interpret a showrunner's language. If things really weren't clear, Newman would say, "'Just talk to me about emotion, and let's go from there,' and then I'll figure out at my end what needs to change, and if I can't change that—and generally I'm able to figure it out—but if I can't, we go into a deeper conversation if something is definitely wrong," and perhaps they will refer back to the temp score.[31]

It's not just languages of affect or adjectives describing musical references that the bosses use. Engineer and mixer Alan Meyerson said that directors don't like to be in charge when it comes to mixing; they want him to do it (probably since it is mainly technical), but they also want to give directions, which they do in metaphorical lexicons of color and affect. This requires some interpretation or calibration of language as well: "They'd ask me, 'Do you think the strings could be warmer here?,' and then I have to figure out what they mean by 'warmer.' Is 'warmer' louder? Is 'warmer' more low-end? Is 'warmer' more reverb? And I have to get inside their head." Meyerson said that he has some clients with their own language and that "you have your little lexicons in your head: What does 'Henry Jackman–bright' mean compared to 'Matt Margeson–bright'? People talk in colors: 'Can it be more yellow?' 'Can it be more red?' 'Can it be more blue?' So, you have to learn everyone's language."[32]

If some composers are frustrated by their bosses' unfamiliarity with musical or other technical terminologies about sound, others told me they enjoyed the challenge of communication in the context of group production. Deborah Lurie said she loves the collaborative aspect of writing music for film. "Working with the director and fulfilling the musical aspect of their vision, so to speak, is really why I do this," she told me. "I love the combining of ideas among artists of different types, from acting to costume design, visual effects, etc., all unified by one main artistic leader and the coming together to build something that no individual could build themselves. That's the whole point to me." If someone told her to "'express your heart and soul in a thirty-minute concert piece,' I would probably enjoy that, but it would be more of like a departure from my thing." Lurie describes herself as a very empathetic person and said that one of the reasons for her success is that "I think I can see in an intense way where other people are coming from." She said that the experience of people understanding each other and learning from each other is infinitely fascinating. She "loves working with directors who don't necessarily speak in musical terms but who aren't afraid to express what they want with any way they can." The translation into music of what they express is what she truly enjoys, she said.[33] "When they speak in emotional terms and in the terms of characters' motivations and in underlying energies that we might not even see on screen, but the director wants to convey to the audience—that's what it's all about for me." She admits that the process can be challenging, "but the idea of writing the music for a story that the director's telling in their own unique way is so interesting to me."[34]

It's not just composers who have difficulties communicating with their bosses about music. When asked if he encountered the same problems that composers did in communicating with nonmusicians, Robert Kraft, president of Fox Music from 1994 to 2012, replied by asking, "Is there a percentage that's more than 100 percent?"[35] Kraft said that the main difficulty for him is not becoming impatient with those who don't know music. "The real challenge as a musician—which I am from top to bottom—is not having any kind of hubris or attitude about people that aren't musicians who are filmmakers. When someone turns to you and says, 'I don't like this; what's that noise?,' you say, 'That's a clarinet.' You could say, 'Geez, you should know that.'" But, Kraft said, he recognizes that there are plenty of technical aspects of filmmaking with which he is unfamiliar.

A recurring problem, Kraft told me, is that everyone listens to music and has an opinion about it whether or not they possess any technical knowledge. "I had a quote on my desk from Alfred Newman, the great first head of music at Fox and in some ways considered to be the godfather of the modern film score. I sat in his office and in his chair and had a quote of his framed on my desk. Alfred Newman said: 'Everyone on a studio lot has two jobs: their own, and music.'" Kraft said that he received an immense amount of advice about where music should go, how it should sound, what should be done musically.

Kraft also told me that as much as the great film music composers would complain to him privately, he learned from them how to handle executives' negative reactions to their music, another revelation of how even well-known composers must conduct themselves. "They'd say, 'That's a really interesting idea; let me think about that.' And I would be so impressed by that because I would want to jump out of my chair and say, 'You're kidding, right? That's the most brilliant thing this guy's ever written. And you're saying you're not sure if it works?' But I learned to say, 'I think this is a wonderful piece of music. I can see your point. We should talk to the composer a little more about ways that it could be maybe restructured.'" Ultimately, Kraft said, it's their movie, not his movie, and they might have particular ideas about how music should be used. Kraft told me that, after such exchanges, and while driving home after work, he would think, "'What an idiot. How could they not love that? This is brilliant. How in the world do they want to throw that cue out or that song out?' But I had to keep it to myself because it's their movie." Kraft summed up this problem by relaying the following anecdote:

I sat in a playback once of a kid's movie where the senior executive on the movie turned to me at the end and said, "I'm very concerned about something." And I said, "Wow, that sounds dramatic." And he said, "The family's collie in that one scene in the kitchen; I'm not sure about the music. I think the collie needs more irony." And I thought, "This one remark will be tough to beat for film executives' anxiety levels about things that just are not in their wheelhouse." But I said, "Interesting. Let me see what we can do."[36]

Filmmakers themselves say they share the same problems attempting to communicate with musicians. When asked about their greatest frustration when working with composers, communication was cited as the main issue, whether articulating what was in one's head or realizing that the words they are using do not convey the complexities of what they are thinking (Thomas 2007).

Working for Musically Informed Bosses

Some composers spoke of their good fortune in working with bosses who possess musical knowledge. Jan Stevens told me that for *Samantha Who?*, a program he worked on from 2007 to 2009, he was approached to replace another composer who wasn't working out on the pilot. Stevens spoke to the producers, who needed music that same day. After a quick reading of the script, he began composing; after two hours, he had developed a musical idea and sent it over. It was approved immediately, and he was hired. Because the main character had amnesia, the idea was to create something "unbalanced," so Stevens put together an odd combination of instruments: trombone, pedal steel guitar, electric and acoustic guitars, bass, and quirky percussion, including an assortment of exotic bells, instruments he used to add to the comedy and emphasize the off-balance personality of the lead character. "Every five or six cues," he said, "I'd throw in some bells at the end of the cue, which became the signature sound of the series. I got these bells that kind of warbled a little bit, and I got a boat bell, and I hit that every once in a while. And, a lot of times when a cue was ending, I would hit it with a tiny little glockenspiel or a little bell like that."[37]

Sometimes composers will be largely left alone by their musically conversant supervisors who know their music and trust them. David Schwartz told me he feels fortunate for many of the shows he has worked on with people who have given him total autonomy. He describes the showrunner

Mitch Hurwitz as a genius who "remembers more of my music than I ever will, and he'll say, 'Can we use two bars of this from last year, and six bars of this?' And the music editor will give me a look, until he got to know him. I'd say, 'No, it's probably going to work; you should try it!' And then they'll try it, and it will match in tempo, and they'll find a way to match the keys."[38] Schwartz said that on the last few projects they have worked on, Hurwitz had been too busy to go to the spotting sessions, so Schwartz would spot it himself, or along with the music editor, and press forward. Hurwitz would hear it for the first time on the way to the dubbing stage, having requested a CD from Schwartz so that he could listen to it in his car on the way over. On the dubbing stage Hurwitz would offer many suggestions about the music.[39]

Conclusions

Group production brings with it problems of authority—competition over it as well as the lack of clarity for workers. And, perhaps especially for musicians and other music workers, there are inevitable problems of communication with nonmusicians attempting to explain to musicians what they want and musicians continually attempting to decipher instructions that can be vague and subjective or coping with nonmusicians' descriptions of sounds, styles, and genres that can be almost comically—but frustratingly—inept. Some musicians relish these challenges; some don't. But directions are imparted, compromises are sometimes reached, and the work gets done. Most of the time.

IT'S A MAN'S, MAN'S, MAN'S, MAN'S WORLD

Most of the people I spoke to in these businesses are white men. The numbers of women and BIPOC people are increasing, though a good deal of bias against them remains, less in the form of overt racism and sexism and more the result of the nature of this closed world and the importance of social capital. According to the annual *Celluloid Ceiling* report on women in the film business, of the 250 top-grossing films of 2021, only 7 percent were scored by women (Lauzen 2022, 9), an increase of 2 percent from the previous year. Women made up 25 percent of all laborers in above-the-line work, 2 percent more than the previous year (Lauzen 2022, 1). Even in the most prestigious category, that of directors, the figure is better than for composers: Women made up 12 percent of directors working on the 100 top-grossing films in 2020, a decrease from 16 percent in 2019 (Lauzen 2022, 3).

Male or female, most people did not address the gender (or race or ethnicity) issue in our interviews unless I asked explicitly. Some of the women with whom I discussed gender concerns seemed to be eager to broach the subject; others were more reluctant or didn't think it was much of an issue at all. It may be that the reluctance to mention gender is common across the cultural businesses. It is certainly the case that many of the writings about the cultural businesses don't consider it most of the time—the *Oxford Handbook of Creative Industries* (Jones, Lorenzen, and Sapsed 2015) barely mentions it; *The Routledge Companion to the Cultural Industries* (Oakley and O'Connor 2015) has one short article (Milestone 2015). And gender is similarly absent or hardly mentioned in many other general treatments of the cultural businesses (with the notable exceptions of Carter, Steiner, and

McLaughlin 2014; McRobbie 2016; and Meehan and Riordan 2002; see also Hesmondhalgh 2019 and Hesmondhalgh and Baker 2015).

But gender and diversity in general did seem to be something of a generational issue. Older composers told me they just did their work, no matter the conditions; Penka Kouneva (born in 1967) told me she was "oblivious" to the issue.[1] Academy Award–winning composer Rachel Portman (born in 1960) said she doesn't worry about her gender at all (Schrader and Thompson 2017, 78). Another slightly younger composer who didn't want to be identified told me, "I was always just hired regardless of gender. Honestly, there weren't a lot of gender dynamics; I think it was an understanding that you don't bring that up necessarily."[2] Nan Schwartz, who scored her first television episode in 1982, said she just had to prove she could do the job:

> When I started, if you could write the kind of music the producers were looking for, you would be hired. They might have had initial reservations about me as a woman, since that was a rarity, but once they heard the music, that spoke for itself. I had to be able to show up for the spotting and then show up five days later and conduct the orchestra, and the music had better be right because they couldn't spend the money to start fixing it. And so, the fact that I could deliver, I was able to be employable in such a competitive field.[3]

The younger women I spoke to were more concerned about gender than were those ahead of them, and the youngest of all the composers I interviewed, male or female, raised the issue without my prompting. Zach Robinson (born in 1989) commented that the business isn't very diverse, that "it's a lot of white guys." He said he is seeing more women and people of color, but statistics show that, as a group, composers are the least diverse. He thinks things are changing, however: "What I'm starting to see now with more content and more opportunities is exciting, and I think that's just going to be good for music in general."[4]

There are deep and long-standing issues here of the conception of creativity as something possessed by men, not women, as we saw in chapter 2, a prejudice that has until fairly recently largely excluded women from the world of composition and most of the realm of performance. Women musicians face centuries of assumptions that their ability to procreate obviates their ability to create, and with procreation comes the responsibility of childcare. But while the Western conceptualizations of genius and creativity as male domains are powerful and durable, there are more parochial—and patriarchal—reasons for the male domination of these businesses. The deadlines, as many people repeatedly emphasized, can be crushing, which means that, if one has children, one also has obligations. This is also an extremely competitive business, toxically so for some. And the patriarchal association of men with tools—in this case, digital ones—also works against women in these fields.

Time and Family

The management of time has played a major role in making this a culture of men. None of the men I spoke to talked explicitly about how they rely on their wives or partners, though many clearly do (see Greiving 2011a and 2011b). But I did notice a shift from the first round of interviews (mostly in 2012) and the second (beginning in 2017). Many of the people I interviewed in the first round talked about how demanding it was to do what they do, how digital technologies meant that changes to the music could be required of them at the last minute and that they had to be prepared to make them, sometimes working all night. Many relied on spouses to take care of the children when they had to be absent for hours at a time. The later interviews, however, revealed a greater consciousness about trying to balance work and life. This is partly generational, since the first group of people I interviewed was, on average, older than the second. But, also, I think there has been a shift in these fields, or at least the beginning of a shift, in which there is greater tolerance of workers who don't want to be on call virtually all the time and who want to spend time with their families.

The Bad Old Days

Let me be clear: This is still an incredibly demanding business. But since a number of workers today are trying to work less and spend more time with their families, their efforts create a contrast with how people worked before—and how many still work today. Composer John Nordstrom told me a story that captures the sometimes-extreme pressure that composers face; it was about the time he was brought in at the last minute to compose the theme music for the television show *Models, Inc.* (which aired in 1994–95). Nordstrom recalled that only about four days before the program was to premiere he received a panicked phone call from the person in charge of advertising and promotion at Fox who said, "'Oh, my God, we can't get a theme that works for this show! You've got to help us out. Can you write something tonight because we have to get a piece of music and cut the whole opening?'" In that era, Nordstrom said, the opening main title for a show was about forty-five seconds, and it set the tone for the entire series, so this is an important piece of music to write on such short notice. He was told, "'If you can get us something by 8 a.m. tomorrow morning, if we like it, we're going to use it.'" Nordstrom said, "Of course, I can! I'm on my way home, and I'm going to start working right away." So, I just hauled ass home and told my wife, Jennifer, "Turn off the phones, I am locked in here until this thing is done." The following night, my first series theme aired on network television."[5]

Composer Matt Hutchinson also talked about the lack of sleep: It is sleep that is sacrificed, he said. "I frankly used to worry because I would think, 'Dude, you're up all night, and then you're up all day working; you know, when are you sleeping? Oh, well, I slept for three hours.' This is not healthy."[6] Because of the intense time pressure, it has become more common for composers to work in teams, as I have noted. Hutchinson said he is working more and more this way and enjoys it, saying that it isn't much fun to work by oneself all the time. Even so, he finds himself up late. "It's like this weird camaraderie of being in the trenches together when it's two in the morning and you've been working for eighteen hours and you're exhausted and you call the other composer: 'Hey, man, what cue are you on? Oh, yeah, I like what you did on this. Oh, cool.'" Hutchinson said he can't really talk to anyone else about this; they don't know or care. But he enjoys the companionship of teaming up, clearly a kind of homosociality. He described a film he scored a few months before our interview that was, as he put it, "a hybrid of indie rock, orchestral, and some Latin jazz." He said they had three weeks to write eighty minutes of music, the sort of time pressure that frequently happens to everyone in the business and that now necessitates teams much of the time. Hutchinson cited an example of once needing a singer, "and my friend Jordan came over and sang on this project. And the next day he's calling me: 'Hey, I need some guitar; can you help me out?'" Hutchinson said that everyone has the immediate sense of community, and everyone helps each other: "I think the idea is we all rise up together. And I've seen that to be true."[7]

Composer Jan Stevens said that his first job writing music for a television series, a sitcom, was extremely demanding, that he'd never worked so hard in his life. Stevens said he would attend the spotting sessions for his show with the director, producer, and the show's creator, and they would demand about seventeen minutes of music, which he described as "wall-to-wall." Stevens said he would try to be cool during the spotting session, but he would leave and ask himself, "'How am I going to do this?'" He'd go to a restaurant and have a bite and then, "I'd get on the phone with my best friend, and I'd be shaking, and I'd say, 'I don't even know how I'm going to do this.' But somehow it got done." Stevens said he was sleeping about four hours per night and barely making it.[8]

It's not just composers who face extreme time pressures: Everyone at each step in the music supply chain experiences them since they follow the composer. Orchestrator Tom Calderaro told me that when he was working on *Armageddon* (1998), his wife was working on a project that was keeping her up all night. "She came home at about 2 o'clock in the morning while I was getting close to finishing up something for the next day, and she comes and she says, 'What are you doing?' I said, 'I'm orchestrating a cue.'" Calderaro told me that on this particular film, they were even recording at night. At one point, he said, he had worked for two days with only a couple of hours of sleep. He conducted at the recording session and "was there all day, came home to just take a shower and get a little something to eat, and maybe get a five-to-ten-minute nap before going back to sessions." But he fell asleep and didn't return.[9]

Because of the hours, one must love what one does, according to recording engineer and mixer Michael Stern, who said, "It's not uncommon to work twelve to sixteen hours a day, and there are times when you go to work in the morning, and you drive back home at the same time the next day. If you don't love it, the process can kill you." But, Stern added, it's worth it, even though "there are times when I don't get to see my family because of it, and it's hard, because I have two young daughters." Sometimes he misses things in his family's life because of the demands of his job, "but the bottom line is, it needs to get done, it's what you've chosen to do, and it's the nature of the beast, so you either embrace it or you should find something else to do."[10]

Some people were frank about the toll such hours take on their family lives. Recording engineer and mixer Alan Meyerson told me that he knows people who have been divorced multiple times, though he also knows people in the business who have successful marriages, describing the demands of the business as very tough. He said there were periods earlier in his career when he was in the studio for three or four days. When you're in deadline mode, he said, "It isn't possible to respond to, 'Oh, come home for dinner; the kid needs something.' You have to understand this is where I have to be right now.'" Meyerson said that giving so much time is not about the money, but developing and maintaining relationships with clients. "It's always about that. I can't tell you how many free days I've given in my career."[11] Meyerson also said he tries to decompress when not working by playing golf and meditating.

Balancing Work and Life

Since in these businesses everyone, at least in the music supply chain, is thought of as replaceable (with very few exceptions), bosses show very little sympathy for the working lives of those they employ. Composer Ryan Shore succinctly summed up the conundrum of balancing work and life by noting that "the people hiring you most likely aren't often thinking about your own work-life balance since their priority is ensuring the music will be great and delivered on time and on budget."[12] But composers and other musicians are increasingly attempting to find more of a balance. Composer Anne-Kathrin Dern (born in 1987) told me that she thinks there has been a change in the business, that people in the younger generation are more concerned than the older generation with work-life balance. The older generation, she said, mostly had stay-at-home wives who took care of the children, noting that many of these composers don't have the closest relationships with their children because of the demands of their work. She said that her generation of composers came up working for these older composers as their assistants and have seen the toll such schedules take. "So, a lot of people now that are in my position, where we start to build up our own studio and we think, 'Maybe we should have more balance? Maybe we should figure this out in a different way.'"[13]

It is clear that many of the music workers featured here who are under age fifty want to spend more time with their families and are able to do so. Many spoke of how they attempt to balance work and life. Composer Joey Newman (born in 1976), who has three young children, told me that in every interview, every lecture he's done at a school, he has always spoken about work-life balance. He said he knows people who have completely left the business "because it's too time-grueling; execs don't give a shit; they don't value music, so they don't value your time; you're working nonstop hours, all hours of the day and night."[14] Newman said that a composer who is writing music for multiple shows needs a "music management system" to control everything and that this can put even greater demands on one's time. "If you have a family, or children, a boyfriend or girlfriend, do you want them to wonder if they're ever going to see you?" And, he continued, "Are you going to be the type of dad that doesn't show up?" He told me that the composers of his generation "are very aware of trying to spend time with their family; that's a very important thing. You just can't do four shows at twenty to forty minutes of music per week on each show; it's just not humanly possible; the math is not going to work."

Newman thinks that the male music workers with young children need to support each other. He told me of a friend who had just had a baby who said to him, "'I wish we had a dad's club for composers. It's really hard to be able to do both of these things.'" Newman said all fathers in the business have been through this and that he couldn't imagine how difficult it would be trying to do his work as a single parent. Newman said that for all of the men with families: "How is that even possible?" Newman said that their children are the focus for all of the men with families, but a demanding, creative, and isolated job doesn't coincide well with being a good parent. "But there's a way to make it all work and to get them to inspire each other."

Newman also believes that having children might have affected the decisions he has made in his career, saying, "I made different choices. I don't regret them, but I sometimes wish that I could have taken a little more risk earlier on, that I could've tried something truly out of my comfort zone. It's hard, though, when you have a family." Newman thinks he could do things other than composing if life demanded it, believing his family to be more important. "But," he said, "when you're trying to make a living in music and also need to be an active and present family member, friend, husband, or whatever, it all must coexist. All of it is a part of me, no matter what, both the work and family. It has to be; I can't exist as I am without one or the other." Newman also thinks that one's parental status can affect the music they write and the choices they make. "It shows in people's music if you think about it. Maybe it's just the life experience creating a richer musical atmosphere and palette. Connections to your kids may create a different musical flow: You're not the most important person in the room anymore!" Newman said he likes writing for comedies, in particular, because his kids can watch them but wondered how it would be possible to "go from writing a gory slasher scene and then having a nice calm dinner with your family and being a dad. That is a compartmentalization that composers are really good at doing because otherwise it seeps into your life, every little aspect of it."[15]

Some people I spoke with felt that there is a greater tolerance today for workers who attempt to balance work and life. Zach Robinson, one of the youngest people I interviewed, also thinks that the question of work-life balance has been shifting. He said he works hard but doesn't "kill myself" and isn't unhappy. He also thinks that many businesses today have more respect for the boundaries between work and home, believing that in the end, this will result in a better product. Sometimes clients can be extremely demanding, "but if you're working with people that are on the same wavelength as you and the vibe is similar, then it can be a good thing." Robinson said he has no patience for those who say, " 'You've got to stay up for thirty-six hours straight because that's the business, that's how you get things done; it's the hustle.' I think that's total bullshit. I think there are ways to succeed and time manage effectively."[16] Scoring mixer Oren Hadar, who is married, said he protects his evenings and weekends. "I'm lucky in that most of my clients have families, and so they understand having a family, and so they understand that, and, so, most of my clients are pretty good about not asking me to work on weekends or late unless it's really crunch time and it's really necessary." In general, he thinks he has a healthy work-life balance, better than most composers. Hadar said he rarely works on a project for more than a week, so even if one project is particularly demanding, it doesn't last long, unlike a composer who might be working for weeks on a film. Hadar said he has one client from whom he gets a lot of work who "will apologize profusely when I have to go late on a day because people have families themselves, and so they respect it." Hadar said he doesn't usually have to fight about this, and when he is asked to work longer hours, he knows it's serious. He has a couple of clients who are more demanding, he told me, so "I just set expectations with them, and I say this is when I'm available, this is when I'm not, and they can go to somebody else next time if they want to."[17]

Whether or not they have families, many of my interviewees pointed out that, early in their careers, they faced extreme time pressures since they were also scrambling to find work, taking whatever they could find even if they weren't paid. Composer Ryan Shore told me that there was almost no work-life balance when he began his career, since attempting to start a career in music requires vast amounts of time, and that composers on low-budget films often must do everything themselves: not just composing, but orchestrating, conducting, music copying, using Pro Tools, and mixing. There is often no budget to hire others to do these tasks. Shore wore all of these hats for many years, but, "Years later I started making efforts to have better work-life balance. I wanted to have a relationship in my life, and I wanted to do things outside of music." In particular, he said, "I wanted to make sure that how I was working was sustainable." It's not sustainable, he told me, to do all-nighters all the time, and he doesn't think that people can do their best work when they're so short of sleep. Shore said that he has given a good deal of thought about how to achieve a good work-life balance and that it has taken time to figure it out. Shore hires assistants and other professionals to lessen his load by asking them to perform such tasks as organization, file management, coordination of the flow of music, creation of spotting notes and cue sheets, all of which allows him to concentrate on the creative aspects of his work. Now, he said, he enjoys a great work-life balance, working typically from 9 a.m. to 7 p.m., Monday through Friday. He is mostly able to take evenings and weekends off, though he admits he's almost always thinking about music.[18]

If one becomes successful, there is greater ability to negotiate schedules. As an orchestrator, Edward Trybek said he has little control over the sched-ule, since it is tied to the composer's, but being successful gives workers more flexibility. One can then fashion a work-life balance by being able to turn down gigs. "The more successful people are in a position to be able to say, 'I work nine to five, Monday through Friday, and I'm not working on the weekends,'" Trybek said, giving the example of John Williams, who, he has heard, is golfing or walking by 3 p.m. every day. Even some people who are not as successful, Trybek told me, make a decision to balance suc-cess and their private life. "They say, 'Look, I'm fine with not trying to be on the A-list; you know, I'm happy being a comfortable B-list composer, hav-ing these stipulations.'" But, according to Trybek, the composers he knows who are on the A-list don't typically have a good work-life balance. "Actually, they work a lot, and sometimes their family life suffers for it."[19] Composer Anne-Kathrin Dern said she knows several men who turned down higher-paying, "next-level" gigs because they thought they'd never see their fami-lies. Dern said she doesn't have children, so it's not an issue for her, but "I've definitely seen this happen a lot more now in my generation and the generation above mine, where people are scaling back a little bit and are prioritizing. We don't want to be those kinds of parents. And in many cases both parents now work and share responsibilities. The days of one parent being able to spend sixteen-hour days at the studio while the other stays home are over."[20]

Other music workers employed by composers said they too face the same deadlines and time pressures. Music editor Andrés Locsey worked as a composer's assistant, and his hours were essentially those of the com-poser. The hours of composers and composers' assistants are more flexible, but they don't leave until the work is done: "You leave when the cue is ready to go for the session. If I'm getting ready to deliver for the dub, and it's midnight and it's still not done, I'm not going to think, 'Oh, I'm done because my day is done.' No, you keep working until you finish." When Locsey became a music editor, it was a night-and-day difference: "For the first time I was able to start at nine and leave at six or seven." Having a union helps a music editor a lot, he said; his work hours are more manageable, unlike those of composers, who no longer have a union. He witnessed the pace of nonstop work when he was a composer's assistant and still sees it among his friends who are composers. With the union, Locsey said, "It doesn't mean you don't work a lot. If you have to work a lot you'll work a lot, but someone will pay you for those extra hours. And the longer they have you there, the deeper into the overtime pocket they're going to have to reach."[21] This acts as something of a deterrent to being asked to work too much.

In seeking more time or flexibility, some composers have changed media. Composer Penka Kouneva told me she decided to write more music for video games after her daughter was born in 2006 because the schedule isn't as frenetic and because it is exceptionally difficult to work in television or film if one has a family. "This is another reason I became a game composer, because I wanted to be a good parent and stay home with my child and raise her." Kouneva told me that, in film, "toward the end there's always a crunch, but usually [in games] the schedule's nice and well-paced. And that's one reason why I'll always be writing games, because the schedule allows for having a life. In film and TV scoring, composers often work sixteen hours straight for days, pull all-nighters, which is detrimental to one's health."[22]

Demanding, even crushing, schedules are not a necessity of the business, as is clear from those who have managed to work out a more livable work-life balance, but such schedules are still common. Alf Clausen, composer for *The Simpsons* for many years, reports working twelve hours a day, Sunday to Thursday, spotting the next episode on Friday and scoring that night—to such an extent that the biggest challenge he faces is staying awake.[23] Such work hours result in large part from the toxic competitiveness that suffuses the business, especially since there seem to be more and more young composers who, trying to gain a foothold, are willing to work for little or nothing. They are also due to a greater demand for more content thanks to the rise of streaming services. Composer Sharon Farber addressed the issue of competitiveness and the toll it takes on people in the business, saying that she remembers to enjoy the journey and not only the end result.

She also thinks it's important to recognize others' successes, saying, "If you want others to be happy for you when you succeed, you need to be happy for others when they do. It's all about energy and mutual support. Not always easy to do in this very competitive field, but living with gratitude and walking your own path without comparing yourself to others is a key to living a life that is creative and emotionally happy."[24]

Farber thinks that being happy also means recognizing where you are and where you want to be in your life. "Thriving for the stars," she said, "doesn't mean always being dissatisfied with where you currently are; it simply means that you acknowledge where you are and that you make plans to go further." Farber remembers having a conversation with a composer who said he's never happy. She was surprised to learn that and replied, "'How can you not be happy? You're scoring big features, making tons of money; people respect you, people really think so highly of you, and you're really not happy?' And he said, 'Well, I'm not one of the five or six.'" To which she replied, "Yes, you are." But he kept on saying "No, no, I'm not." Farber remembers thinking, "When are you going to be happy? If you win an Oscar tomorrow, you're still going to be unemployed the next day and [have to] compete to get the next film. When are you going to be content? Never, ever? Is it worth it?"[25]

Home Studios

Almost everyone I interviewed told me they work at home in their own studio, what could be considered a man cave. Some of these studios are housed in former garages (many older homes in Los Angeles feature detached garages that are frequently converted to studios, offices, or guest spaces); trade press articles occasionally talk about setting up one's home studio (e.g., Rodd 2011). A few people said that, when they could afford it, they rented space outside of where they lived, though this made it difficult to work whenever they felt like it. And a few people, such as composer Ryan Shore, said he has been told by his friends who have children that it can become very difficult to write music at home, so it often helps to have a studio located outside the home.[26]

A few of the more successful composers I met had spacious studios in the house or in separate buildings. Such studies are impressive to the composers' bosses, though, in fact, with today's technology, a sophisticated studio doesn't require much space. Joey Newman told me, however, that some composers' bosses might expect a grand studio. "I can work on a $200 million movie from my converted-garage studio, and that's the reality of it," he said, but the bosses "might feel more comfortable and confident in you if you have the beautiful, big studio in Malibu."[27]

Part of the reason so much work is performed at home is because of decreasing budgets: Studios don't want to pay to have work done in professional studios. Mixer Michael Stern told me that because budgets aren't what they used to be, more of the final mixing is done in home studios rather than a commercial studio. The time pressures are intense, as we have seen. "We can be doing what we call 'chasing the dub'—delivering music cues a reel at a time while they are already on the dub stage—and a director can demand a change of something musically, which might involve getting musicians back to record or massive editing." All these issues, Stern said, can be more efficiently dealt with in a composer's home studio than in a commercial studio, where the composer might not have access to the necessary software, their own instruments, their own samples; commercial studios don't have to provide these things and probably wouldn't be able to since a composer's instruments and samples and other tools are quite personal.[28] The bottom line is that composers spend more time in their home studios than they once did, and more time alone.

Women's Experiences

In this final section, I want to focus on the experiences of women in these fields. Miriam Mayer thinks there is a lot of unconscious bias against women in the business and that if most people in the business were asked to judge a piece after having been told it was by a man, would evaluate it more positively than if they were told the music was by a woman.[29] While a growing number of women are scoring in film, television, and games, the mere fact of their existence isn't well known in the business, a source of considerable frustration for some (see Rose 2014) and which in part prompted the formation of the Alliance for Women Film Composers in 2014. Having read the trade press going back decades, I find it striking how few interviews with women composers there are and how infrequently gender is mentioned when a woman is interviewed; the same could be said about musicians of color, of any gender. The indie film world may be much more populated by women and people of color, but as Anne-Kathrin Dern told me, "The moment serious money is involved it just gets very political, and the people in charge default back to those they've always worked with and whom they trust. That trust has not historically been extended to women, especially when it comes to leadership positions, so we're not part of that pool they draw from, and it's very difficult for us to enter into that pool so late in the game."[30] Women composers are largely shut out from big-budget productions.

One exception is Sharon Farber's mentor, Shirley Walker (1945–2006), who died before this study began. I will spend a little time with her here, as she was indeed a pioneer. Walker said in 2000, "I am encouraged to see the film-scoring door open to women. There are so few women composers; we have a visibility that men have to work harder to achieve. Any successful career is based on whom you know. I don't think changes in the industry have brought this about. I think women now place more emphasis on building a solid relationship base. As my director friends' careers evolve, mine goes along with them" (quoted in Goldwasser 2000). Walker entered the business in 1979 and won her first major studio film scoring job writing for John Carpenter's *Memoirs of an Invisible Man* (1992). She recounted that "the biggest thrill for me was the people, the old timers who worked on the motion picture lots who heard about this score, that there was one woman in Hollywood who was doing the score 'just like the guys did,' that I'd actually written all the music myself, and I was going to conduct the orchestra, and that I was given the same level of support by the studio that a man's score would be given with no kind of special treatment, no orchestrator/guy who was going to 'help me out'" (quoted in Larson 1998). Walker observed that while other women composers, such as Carly Simon and Carole King, had received credit for writing a film score, they did not orchestrate their own scores. Walker was the first to write and record a major film score herself ("Walker on Walker" 2007).

Walker said that everyone knew history was in the making and spoke movingly of the experience of recording her score for Carpenter's film:

The first two days of that score, there were a lot of people who had come to visit the scoring stage because they were here to witness this event. I was almost in tears about that. I had to ask somebody why all those people were here, and when they told me it was just incredible. It's because there's a real tradition of oral history in this business. There are so many things that have happened in this business, that will never be written down by anybody, and it's private—it's for the people who work in this business, and that was their honor to be there and support me in that, and I was just incredibly touched by that. (Quoted in Larson 1998)

For Walker, it was a personal and musical arrival. "This is the first score where I can say 'This is what Shirley Walker's musical voice is.' Now I can show my full sense of adventure and humor, because most of the time you're being asked to do something that's like John Williams or James Newton Howard. But because *Memoirs* is my breakout project, I don't have to emulate the 'hot' style of the time" ("Walker on Walker" 2007).

Walker was part of composer Danny Elfman's team that produced the music for Tim Burton's *Batman* (1989), which led to her being hired as the supervising composer for *Batman: The Animated Series* (1992–95), a job she got through Doug Frank at Warner Bros. "And he had basically allowed me to do *The Flash* [television series, 1990–91]. He had supported the idea that I could do a series. Because even then, women weren't—they were afraid to give a woman a television series, for that same reason that we'd choke and die and not finish, or something. I don't know what it was" (quoted in Takis 2006).[31]

Pioneers, role models, and mentors like Walker, as well as supportive men (several interviewees named male mentors in the course of our interviews; see also Romanelli 2014), were important for many women composers. Several spoke of the importance of role models and mentors in learning how to make one's way in the business. Composer Cindy O'Connor told me she thought that one of the reasons there haven't been many women film music composers is that there weren't any role models. She said she was lucky with her mentor, Mark Isham, "who didn't care if I was male, female, what color. He didn't assume that I wouldn't be able to learn anything because of my gender, which was great, which is the way that the world should be. And because of that I was able to just learn and flourish." But when trying to get gigs, O'Connor was faced with peoples' expectations that composers are men, "or they call one of these five guys who have teams that produce a lot of music because they're the tried-and-true product that they want to hire again."[32] Germaine Franco praised her mentor, John Powell, saying that "having a mentor changes lives" (quoted in Savas 2018a, 16). Other women composers lauded their male mentors for not caring about their gender, only their abilities.

Nan Schwartz had a particularly telling story about how she began writing television episodes in the mid-1980s, when there were almost no women in the business, except for Shirley Walker. Schwartz was orchestrating scores by Pat Williams (1939–2018) for a program called *The Devlin Connection* starring Rock Hudson. Early on, Williams asked her if she was ready to start writing episodes herself, and she agreed. By that point, she said, she had been studying what he had been doing musically on the program.

Schwartz didn't conduct her first score; Williams did, after which there was the following exchange: The producer said, "Wow, Pat, that's really, that was really one of your better scores." And he said, "Well, I didn't write it—*she* did." Schwartz said, "That was a great way to introduce me to them because they probably wouldn't have hired me cold." But after first hearing her music and then realizing she could do it, they gave her more episodes to compose. Soon Williams turned the series over to her, leading to the first of her seven Emmy nominations.[33]

Sharon Farber told me that after she graduated from the Berklee College of Music she won an internship to the Academy of Television Arts and Sciences in Los Angeles. One of her mentors asked her whom she would like to meet, and she said, unhesitatingly, Shirley Walker because when she was still in college she would go up to watch *Batman and Superman* because she thought the music was so good and that she had always wanted to meet its composer. Walker took her under her wing. Farber orchestrated for her, then wrote for the show, but then it was decided that there was to be no more orchestra, only synthesized music, thus ending Farber's time with Walker.[34] Nowadays, Farber serves as a role model herself, aware of her status in the field as a successful woman composer. She said that many young women view her as a pioneer, and she hopes she can give them the help they need.

While Walker worked her way up, a composer of a later generation told me that she felt as though she was the token woman on some projects. She told me, "Those things are a little bit uncomfortable. I tried to just accept them as gifts and just say, 'Hey it's a weird time; this time needs to happen.' And what am I going to say? 'No, thanks?'"[35] Laura Karpman (born in 1959), one of the founders of the Alliance for Women Film Composers, entered the business in the late 1980s and thinks that being a woman has actually helped her: "I think I was able to get started easily, actually, *because* I was a woman—I was able to get an agent and start working in movies of the week." She also said, though, that she has benefited from working on "female-skewed projects," the sort of projects that, she said, "don't make anyone nervous that a woman is doing it" (quoted in Bond 2003b, 31). Lolita Ritmanis also believes she has benefited from being a woman by winning jobs from women producers and directors (Davis 2010, 349).

Shirley Walker's ascendance, followed by that of Nan Schwartz and later composers, has not changed the culture of film and television production, however. Sharon Farber (who is currently vice president of the Alliance for

Women Film Composers) told me frankly in 2012 that film and television music production was still a boys' club. A decade later, she said that producers, directors, and studios are all looking to hire women and people of color.[36] She remembers that one of her first agents told her at one point, "'We will take your name out, and we will just say S. Farber, so nobody knows you're a woman.'" Farber said that when she worked with Shirley Walker, she never noticed this kind of sexism and different treatment of women, though Walker never got to be one of the A-list composers due to her gender. "But then," Farber said, after she stopped working with Walker, "I started receiving weird statements, like a director who said, 'You look too young,' and I said, 'Well, look at my credits,' and he said, 'No, no, you're too young to do this film.'" Farber also faced directors who demanded sexual relationships in exchange for work: "One of the directors I worked with said, 'If you move in with me, I'll give you all my films to score.' Just like that. Just like that," adding that this was a long time ago.[37]

Other composers offered similar stories. Anne-Kathrin Dern told me of an incident when she was invited to what she thought was a business meeting but turned out to be a one-on-one in a private side room of a restaurant where she was essentially trapped, having taken a taxi there (this was in the era before ride-share apps). She also told me about a colleague who was working on a film with her and that after she refused to date the director, he and the other workers never spoke to her again. Miriam Mayer told me a more graphic story:

> When I was younger, around twenty-five, I worked for a guy who was my dad's age, a composer who was scoring soap operas, which is a gig I really wanted. I was ghostwriting for him, and I would bring music to him in his studio, which was in the basement of his beautiful house in Brentwood [a wealthy Los Angeles neighborhood]. His wife was upstairs, and one day he just grabbed me by the shoulders and stuck his tongue in my mouth apropos of nothing; there was no discussion or flirting or anything. I was really, really shocked and horrified.[38]

Mayer said she felt there was nothing she could do—she wanted the job. "I didn't know who his boss was. I had no recourse at all. So, I quit the job rather than be harassed like that. It was awful."[39] Dern told me she thinks such behaviors are common.[40]

Women musicians also have faced many derogatory remarks and sexist treatment. Sharon Farber recounted an incident that demonstrates the double bind women composers can find themselves in, telling me of a director who made an ugly remark on the recording stage, where she was the only woman present:

> So, I'm in this situation, thinking to myself, "If I say something now, they'll say, 'Oh, she's making a scene because she's a woman.' If I don't say anything, they think they can do this again, to other women." So, I took the director aside and said, "You hired me to score this film because of my skills, talent, and professionalism, what I can give to you, and you love what I've done. But here I am, having to listen to something so insulting—why?" He said, "Oh, I'm sorry; did you get hurt?" I said, "No, it's not about that; it's about respect. You want me to respect you, you have to respect me!" And then he got it, truly apologized, and never said anything like that again. You have to stand up for yourself.[41]

Farber also told me a story about when she was pregnant. When she informed a leading executive of that fact he said, "'OK, see you in eighteen years.'" "In fact," she said, "nobody knew I was pregnant. I didn't show until I was around seven months; nobody knew. And even after that I didn't post photos of my baby because I know this industry, because people will think, 'Oh, she can't do that because she has to take care of her baby.'" But, she said, "Women are strong. We can handle kids, career, responsibilities, deadlines, and many other challenges." Farber said it is possible to work even with a newborn, and she has been working nonstop. "You can do it. It's a little more challenging, but you learn when to work, and you are more focused when you do work. Just trust yourself, be strong, and make sure that you're always professional and deliver on time, no matter what."[42] Lolita Ritmanis spoke of the challenges of being in the business with young children, saying, "Who wants to take a breast pump to Warner Bros. for a session? And tell people you need to pump your milk during a ten-minute break?" But, she said, the work gets done, particularly if one is in a healthy marriage (quoted in Davis 2010, 349).

Anne-Kathrin Dern also witnessed discussions of hiring composers where women, and women with children, were not given the consideration she thought they merited. When she spoke in their defense, she wasn't invited back to participate in such discussions. "There are still a lot of gatekeepers that are keeping us out," she told me. "And if one of us makes it into the room, then we just have to play along in order to not be kicked out of the room."[43]

Men are also given more chances to rewrite something, when, in many instances, Dern wasn't granted a second opportunity. She told me of a case when her boss didn't like a cue and gave it to a male composer. "But then, after a week he was at a version twelve, so I thought, 'Why does he get twelve chances and I get one?' If I don't nail it, it's taken away from me."[44] Dern also told me of women musicians not being hired because the wife of the composer was jealous and didn't want her husband to hire young, attractive women.

Women musicians are also constantly faced with assumptions of a lack of knowledge or experience or authority. Dern told me, "I'd be in a room with a bunch of guys, and it's everybody's first day, but only I get the tech stuff explained extra, because they just assume that I don't know tech or software, even though I was working in music tech as my very first job."[45] Dern told me about the experiences of a woman engineer friend who also is a mixing and recording engineer. Every time there's a recording session, Dern said, even when it's obvious that her friend is in charge, the male clients will direct questions toward a man and not her, which Dern characterized as a subtle power play. Dern also conducts, and told me that some older men in the orchestra have told her that she shouldn't wear skirts or dresses and instead dress more like a man "to be more respected." Dern asked, "What does that have anything to do with my conducting? Here's the stick; look at it! You can't even see me from the waist down, so what are you even complaining about?"[46]

Women composers might also face expectations that they are unable to write music that is sufficiently masculine or violent when the film demands it. Laura Karpman said that she wrote music for a film that was rejected, and she was fired because the music wasn't viewed as masculine or muscular enough, so she used the music "in a violent, massive multiplayer online game and it was approved on first hearing" (quoted in Romanelli 2014).

Sharon Farber said that such incidents once made her angry but that she has since come to terms with the sexism of the business, realizing that that's the reality and that she just has to do the best work she can. "You can't take everything so seriously. It's a music business, after all; it's not life and death. We have to live in perspective, so, it's good; it's good."[47] Despite their past experiences, Farber, Mayer, and others think that conditions are improving. "I think it's really getting better," Farber told me. "I think people are more open; there are a few women that are getting in that are making it now, and it's really nice to see, and it's part of life; it's the challenges of life, and eventually you work with the people who really don't care."[48]

More recently than my first interviews in 2012, the #MeToo and Time's Up movements have shaken the film and television businesses. Dern thinks these movements have had a positive effect by helping to build a community of women composers and other music workers. Women in the business are talking to each other more about these issues. They have established help lines and other channels because sexual harassment often isn't reported or because smaller studios don't have human resources departments to which to report such events. Dern said there is now a private Facebook group where members can share stories, and some of the big studios have launched initiatives about inclusion and diversity. And there are the Future Is Female concert series and the Alliance for Women Film Composers, which has hundreds of members (see Romanelli 2014). Now, Dern said, if an executive says something like, "We would hire a woman composer, but there aren't any," there is a directory the composers can send. These women composers have also been attempting to change the hiring culture so that it's not just the same established composers who win jobs; if you look at the indie film world, she said, there are plenty of women and people of color. Women composers have also been more proactive in getting themselves on television and movie panel discussions to make sure there is more of a gender balance. Dern thinks more women composers are coming up through the ranks now and that there have been some older composers who have traditionally been supportive of women composers, such as her mentor, Klaus Badelt.

Even so, according to Dern, only 3 percent of women composers win jobs, and even when they do, there is a huge pay gap between women and men workers in the business. She told me of a friend, a senior assistant to a major composer in Los Angeles, who had recently learned what her predecessors had made, having viewed the most recent one's contract. She thought she should be making the same amount. "So she went to her boss," Dern told me, "and said, 'Hey, can I get a raise to this amount?' And they said, 'Are you crazy?' She said, 'Well, the guy before me got exactly that amount, and he had less experience and was doing less than I am, and I've been here longer now. So, what gives?'"[49]

The #MeToo movement has also meant that the landscape of social capital in these fields has become destabilized, with one result that some established people with reliable and strong networks have had to work to rebuild their network and regenerate their social capital. One composer, who has been in the business for a couple of decades and is well established, told me that networking has become relevant again. For twenty years, she said, one project would lead to the next. But now, she told me, she finds herself interested in meeting new people, in part because so many of the old bosses are gone. "Obviously," she said, "half of the most powerful people in the business have been overthrown in a very dramatic way. So, everybody—it doesn't matter how old you are—everybody knows that they have to meet new people" in order to manage their social capital. She said that the big-name composers have no problem getting gigs, "But if you're interested in the hottest, best shows and best movies, you've got to always be seeing what's out there."[50]

Penka Kouneva has thought a good deal about women composers and has embarked on a project of reimagining the music of past women com-posers whose voices she believes were silenced or marginalized. "The deep-est motivation for me right now," she told me, "is the unwritten music by women composers. I see this as a loss to culture." So, on her third album, *Rebirth of Id* (2017), Kouneva tells four stories, including one about the nineteenth-century pianist-composer Clara Schumann. Kouneva is fasci-nated by Schumann because "she was exceptionally talented, exceptionally well-educated by her father, and then she was distracted by her love for Johannes Brahms, her eight children (one of them was also mentally ill, and some died). Life's distractions made Clara quit composing." Kouneva said she grieves for the music Clara didn't write and that her response to that grief was to write an orchestrated suite of four compositions as if a lost sketchbook of Schumann's orchestra music had been found; it's entitled *Claire Vick's Sketchbook* (Kouneva disguises Clara's name; Wieck was her un-married name). "I am inspired by reimagining and 'writing' the music of other women composers because they didn't write it, and I feel compelled to fill this gap." Another work on the album was inspired by Alma Mahler, also a complicated figure, Kouneva said, because of her many affairs and the death of her young daughter, which stopped her, too, from composing. "Why do women stop?" she asked. "Because of the life distractions. That's a lost cre-ative legacy to me." Kouneva said she is on a journey now, that she is more of a feminist thinker than she was before. "I feel motivated to write my own music because other women composers in the past did not. And that's a loss."[51]

Kouneva's composition *Claire Vick's Sketchbook* (the liner notes refer to Clara Wieck Schumann), described as "period romantic drama," consists of four moments of orchestral music in a Romantic style with titles that seem to be designed to represent Clara Schumann's states of mind: "Claire Vick's Longing"; "Claire Vick's Regrets"; "Claire Vick's Haunted Heart," which in-cludes a piano solo, since Clara Schumann was an accomplished pianist; and "Claire Vick's Thwarted Hopes." The accompanying notes include a photo of Schumann and describe the four movements as "a speculative pastiche of Clara Schumann's orchestral work (as *if* a lost sketchbook of her work has been discovered)."[52] But the notes begin with a quotation from Schumann, who, according to Kouneva, denounced composition by saying it was not a profession for women. "Naturally," writes Kouneva, "I disagree."[53]

Conclusions

The fields of the production of music for film, television, and beyond have always been a man's world, mainly because of the patriarchal conception of artistic creativity and the quotidian pressures of demanding hours that presume either an unmarried composer or one with a spouse to manage the household and children. But the generation of musicians—male and female—born in the 1970s and after has been working to make the business both less antithetical to having a home life and family and more tolerant of women and people of color. It was striking to me that, when I circulated my interlocutors' quotations for comments or edits, many of the men changed what they had said to employ inclusive pronouns. Anne-Kathrin Dern, in reviewing her quotes from our 2018 interview, said a lot of things had changed in the four years since, largely because of "the #MeToo movement and Time's Up movement going on" and because agents and studios are "making more of an effort (and putting more female executives in charge)."[54] Even a few years ago, some of my interviewees mentioned #MeToo, which helped accelerate the process of making the businesses more inclusive, especially while a notorious sexual harasser was occupying the White House, and the number of men who want to be more equal partners with their spouses has grown. The Alliance for Women Film Composers continues to flourish. Pinar Toprak has become the first woman composer to score a big-budget, superhero film, *Captain Marvel* (2019; see Savas 2019). Another woman, Hildur Guðnadóttir, won the Academy Award for Best Music (Original Score) for *Joker* in 2020; she is one of very few women ever to be nominated and one of only three to win. And there are more and more role models as well as more and more people serving as mentors. But change is slow.

NEOLIBERALIZATION AS (SELF-) EXPLOITATION

Having written a book about music and today's capitalism (Taylor 2016), I don't think it's necessary here to rehash the vast and growing literature on the subject of today's capitalism. The work I have found to be the most useful is that which is historical, and historicized, refraining from making proclamations about how everything has changed and, instead, attempting to discern just what is actually different from the past and what continues from the past, if sometimes in different forms.[1]

Neoliberal capitalism, as Pierre Bourdieu (1998, 34) once succinctly pointed out, is little different from what the earliest capitalists advocated. Specfically: Free markets unfettered from governmental interference, the appropriation of everything into the logic of the market, the transformation of all forms of value into economic value, the conversion of people with human characteristics into possessors of "human capital," with which they compete against each other in the marketplace. The results have been spectacularly successful for those at the top of the economic ladder, with income inequality at levels not seen in generations. Economic precariousness, once largely confined to those at the bottom of the economic ladder and those voluntarily entering risky professions like the arts, has become normal for increasing numbers of workers, some of whom toil in what is colloquially known as the "gig economy." In short, neoliberal capitalism is characterized by the expansion of the values of the market into every arena of life. "Neoliberal rationality," Wendy Brown (2005, 39–40) writes, "while foregrounding the market, is not only or even primarily focused on the economy; it involves extending and disseminating market values to all institutions and social action, even as the market itself remains a distinctive player."

Neoliberal capitalism is not simply a historical advancement on—or return of—a previous capitalism, but is the result of concerted efforts by conservative intellectuals, including economists (see Foucault 2008 and Stedman Jones 2012), who were aided by the rise of digital technologies in the 1980s, which played a major role in making the world more globally interconnected; *globalization* became a buzzword to describe the late twentieth and early twenty-first centuries (see Bourdieu 2003, 74–75).

While the cultural businesses have been with us for generations (if one includes publishing), the rise of neoliberal capitalism has introduced changes that are less evident to the casual observer as well as shifts that are more overt (some of these have been discussed in previous chapters). This final chapter before the conclusion considers the more noticeable neoliberal turns in film and television music production: the ubiquity of digital technologies as well as changes in the social relations of production among composers that affect how they are paid.

There are other things one could say about neoliberalization and this business, in particular, the trend of media companies being acquired by massive multinational corporations, which has had the effect of threatening the creative freedom and autonomy of so-called creative workers with the rise of bottom-line-motivated businesspeople. Older musicians are best positioned to understand this transition. The veteran Earle Hagen (1919–2008), perhaps most famous for having written the whistling theme to *The Andy Griffith Show* (1960–68), said in 1997,

> The people who guided the entertainment business came from the entertainment business, they had people who took care of bottom line, who had the budget, who had to advise them on budgets. But their main function was the creation of entertainment. And they knew what they were doing. And today you have a lot of people who are more concerned with the bottom line than they are the end result. And what happens is you wind up with the upside-downness of it. In protecting the bottom line, you lose the entertainment value. . . . I think it should be the people in the entertainment business who should provide entertainment. And people who take care of the bottom line should provide the bottom line—there's room for both, but you put the wrong people in control of entertainment and you're changing it to a bottom-line industry. And I think that's what's happened.[2]

But most the people in these pages experienced such trends only indirectly, mainly in the tightening of budgets and time pressures, as I will discuss.

I understand neoliberalism (as I did in Taylor 2016) as a set of policies and practices that, combined with the rise of digital technologies—which have themselves facilitated an increasingly globally connected world—have dramatically altered the work and private lives of virtually everyone. Here, however, I am particularly concerned with how neoliberal capitalism has helped shape people's self-conceptions and conduct. As we know from Marx, changes in productive forces inevitably lead to changes in the relations of production, as we have already seen with these workers' laboring lives.

I have been relying on Michel Foucault to theorize the conduct of the workers in these pages but here want to shift to an update and extension of his work by philosopher Byung-Chul Han (2017, 79), who argues that neoliberal capitalism represents a shift from the industrial capitalism theorized by Foucault, in which power acted on the body, to a capitalism that acts on the mind—from biopolitics to "psychopolitics," which Han defines late in his book as "a technology of domination that stabilizes and perpetuates the prevailing system by means of psychological programming and steering." We already know from Max Weber (and Clifford Geertz and Foucault and many others) how structures and patterns of power can infiltrate people's thoughts and actions, but Han wants to move from a Foucauldian conception of "discipline" to a more extreme form: People no longer simply discipline themselves; they exploit themselves (he also argues that they surveil themselves through social media and big data, but I will not pursue that here). Power in neoliberal capitalism is not confrontational, but smart: it cajoles, it insinuates, it cozies up, it lures people into self-exploitation. "The neoliberal technology of power does not prohibit, protect or repress; instead, it prospects, permits and projects," Han writes (38).[3]

There is more to Han's argument, but I am most concerned with his point about self-exploitation and want to pursue that. Han (2017, 3) builds his argument on the idea of freedom—which David Harvey (1985) had pointed out is a key trope in neoliberalism—that is, that neoliberalism exploits people's conceptions of their own freedom to deliver them into slavery: "Everything that belongs to practices and expressive forms of liberty—emotion, play and communication—comes to be exploited." The endless project of self-fashioning and self-optimizing in today's society, which gives subjects a sense of freedom, is in fact subjugating them. This is a much more efficient form of exploitation than what Han terms "allo-exploitation," exploitation from without. Today, he says, neoliberal capitalism turns workers into entrepreneurs; "everyone is an *auto-exploiting labourer in his or her own enterprise*. People are now master and slave in one" (5). And because of the efficiency of smart power, people don't even know they have been subjugated to it. "A significantly more efficient technology of power makes sure that people subordinate themselves to power relations *on their own*" (14). Foucault's argument about the neoliberal subject who is an entrepreneur of himself (2008; see also Dilts 2011) "engages in auto-exploitation willingly—and even passionately" (Han 2017, 28).

Han seems to think that neoliberal capitalism has succeeded industrial capitalism (and therefore the disciplining effect of power), but I would say that the latter is still residual, to recall Raymond Williams (1977). Film and television production is not industrial, I have been arguing, but artisanal, though workers have internalized the disciplining effects of power present from industrial capitalism, as I have also been arguing. Nonetheless, the ideologies of neoliberalism have infiltrated this world in that many workers are now self-exploiting, as Han characterizes all workers (all people, really) in neoliberal capitalism.

This chapter examines the effects of neoliberal capitalism as it affects the workers presented in these pages, particularly in terms of imperatives to work harder—to self-exploit; the effects of digital technologies; and changes in pay structures that encourage entrepreneurialism but also self-exploitation, a system that handsomely rewards a very few while everyone else increasingly struggles.

Digital Days (and Nights)

Perhaps nothing has done more to neoliberalize the cultural businesses than the introduction of digital technologies in the production, recording, and distribution of music. These technologies led to new efficiencies, but—as I have said many times in these pages—they have also resulted in the acceleration of work schedules and incessant demands for last-minute changes of composers and everyone else, which, composers believe, has negative effects on the quality of music being produced. For these musicians, as for the rest of us, digital technologies have ushered in unparalleled benefits, which come at a high cost of demands for ever-greater productivity, ever-greater availability, all as we watch the value of our labor enrich those at the top of the economic ladder. All this is legible within a classical Marxian framework: Those who own the means of production (or in this case, those who can act as rentiers, the owners of copyrights—studios—and their managers—studio executives and producers) have been ceaseless in their efforts to exploit their workers, with ever-greater efficiency, to the extent that workers willingly exploit themselves.

Technology in these fields is no different from in any other domain: it has been a powerful means by which workers have been forced into working under conditions of neoliberal capitalism (see Taylor 2016), especially by compelling people to accomplish more in less time, as discussed in chapter 2. Technology is both a cause and effect of neoliberalization in general as well as in these fields: People work harder and longer (though there has been some pushback against this, as discussed in the previous chapter); work has speeded up; many live musicians have been replaced by digital technologies or by musicians in places where it is cheaper to record, high-bandwidth internet making it possible to share massive files; and more. Technology is also a traditionally male domain, one of the ways that the patriarchy is continually reconstituted, as we saw in chapter 6; this is no different in the cultural businesses (see Hesmondhalgh and Baker 2015). In earlier chapters I covered some of the technological changes that have occurred since my interlocutors began working in these businesses. This chapter will address some of the more recent changes as well as people's understandings of how these technological advancements have altered not just how composers and others do what they do, but how the music itself has changed.

My interviews reveal different attitudes between generations with respect to technology. Younger musicians don't know of a time without them. Some older composers who critique the sound of today's music do so because they think creativity has been curtailed by the new technologies, while many younger musicians think that these technologies permit more and/or newer forms of creativity. Older musicians are more ambivalent and critical since they have witnessed all the negative influences as well as the positive changes. For people who never knew the era of having more time to compose and higher budgets to hire more musicians, this isn't an issue.

These new technologies slowly entered the scene with early synthesizers such as the Moog in the 1960s, the transition to MIDI, and they have not stopped. I cover this earlier history in a manuscript that's in preparation (Taylor n.d.b), so here I will jump nearer the present. Composer Bruce Broughton, who got into the business in the 1960s, said that it wasn't until the 1990s with the rise of sampling, sound synthesis, and the ability to sync easily with picture, and the possibility of sharing files over the internet, that everything really changed, saying, "It opened the way for a lot of people to work in music and films who otherwise would never have gotten in." Broughton's last comment refers to the reality in the music business that early adopters of new technologies tend to be younger people in rock and other popular musics, which gave these musicians a way into the film and television businesses since older musicians were slower to make the transition (see also Taylor 2012). Broughton also told me that when he started, writing film scores was a process of "sheer imagination," whereas today it is a matter of "manipulating virtual instruments, composing software and computer programs." Broughton said, "When you're writing notes down on the page, there's no sound source to reference other than the piano or the guitar (if a referencing instrument is used at all), and you can use your imagination freely. But now that's pretty much gone."[4]

Music editor Kevin Crehan believes that he was able to enter the field in the early 1990s because he had an engineering degree and was able to understand the transition and explain it to others. A good deal of engineering knowledge was required in order to transition from recording sound on film to videotape, where problems of syncing audio and video were common, so that, he said, they were constantly "chasing time code" with the Pro Tools system.[5]

Digital music technologies were later used to replace live musicians, introduce efficiencies, and save money, but musicians are still valued for the sounds they can produce. Composers began to be hired not just for their knowledge of digital technologies, which has become pretty much universal, but for their skills in creating music that sounded like electronic popular musics. Producer J. J. Abrams said that he hired Michael Giacchino for his television series *Alias* (2001–6) because he thought Giacchino would fit in with himself and the other workers on the show and because "I was looking for someone who was equally effective at writing for an orchestra and with synthesizers" (quoted in Krogh 2002b; see also Bond 2003a).

Changes in Labor Processes

Interviewees who have lived through the shift to digital technologies told me it has changed the way they work. Composer Bruce Broughton said that he formerly composed entirely at the piano and still does, mostly. But if it's low-budget project, he'll compose a lot on the synthesizer: "I'll make it up right there. I won't even write it down—just play it with my tracks and then mix it down when it's finished."[6]

Digital technologies have changed people's working methods and workflows. Composer Christopher Wong said that because he is classically trained, he knows how to compose with pencil and paper, but he nonetheless employs a good deal of computer technology. Wong also said that the ability to write music down is less important now that composers can completely bypass notating anything. As we have seen in other discussions, a composer can simply generate a MIDI mockup on their computer and then turn over the file to an orchestrator who can use the MIDI file to produce a notated score and parts and who will understand what the composer is trying to do with the various instruments represented in the MIDI mockup. The orchestrator will correct and improve the orchestrated score and transfer it to the copyist to print out for live musicians to play.[7]

This doesn't always work that well for the instrumentalists. Composer Bruce Broughton said that, today, "the playing musicians are used to being abused (a tough word, but I'll stand by it) by the quality of music and notation that they often have to read and the way in which they have to perform and record it. Copyists today often have to act as 'post-orchestrators' when they listen to a composer's mockups and have to devise parts and scores based upon the input ability of either the composer or orchestrator, neither of whom has the musical skill to do either job adequately." Broughton said it is also common that copyists must prepare scores that have been constructed to sound a certain way for a recording rather than a performance: "one that is going to be recorded section by section over a period of sessions" (striping) instead of "all at once, with the entire orchestral ensemble playing together in the same room."[8]

Digital technologies made it easier to work on more than one project simultaneously. Composer John Nordstrom said that, before digital, if a composer had their mixer set up in a certain way, they couldn't work on anything else "because you already had all your reverbs, EQs and levels perfectly set, everything was analog." If you were working on a particular show, you had a sort of template, with strings coming through a couple channels with a certain level of reverb and so forth. Nordstrom said, "You had to take a picture—and there were no digital cameras back then—and take a lot of notes to try to remember, 'How did I have this set up?'" Nordstrom said he had to turn down jobs sometimes because he was working on an episodic television show that was going to require a week, and there was no way he could do something else that would necessitate resetting all his equipment and finish both jobs on time. "Today," he said, "you can go from hip-hop to orchestra in one click. Just open a file in Pro Tools and Logic, and a thousand mix details that you worked on are perfectly set and ready to go."[9]

But, of course, filmmakers know how much more efficient composers can be now, so they have become accustomed to demanding changes at the last minute, as we have seen, which creates tensions throughout the entire process. Composers today no longer produce a score or audio file without a good deal of input from directors and producers; according to contractor Dan Savant, they need to be able to answer their bosses' technical queries and suggestions for creative edits. Savant thinks that composers today can't be just composers. "They have to be great communicators and mediators themselves to do their work."[10]

Composers for television can be so pressed for time that they never receive the final edit of the program, which means that it is up to the music editor to make the final changes to the music to make it fit to picture. The music editor receives stems from the composer and that's all. After listening to music editor Andrés Locsey describe his work, I told him that it seemed to me that the job of the music editor has become more important in the digital era because so many last-minute changes can be requested and the composer can't simply change the score or compose something new on the spot (the composer isn't generally at the dubbing stage, anyway). Locsey agreed, saying, "Yes, you can't go back to Bratislava and record again, you know," adding that there are always a good deal of last-minute fixes.[11] He estimated that the YouTube show *Cobra Kai* usually needs twenty fixes at the final dubbing. "The composer can do big changes to the music before it is recorded if they receive notes, but once we get to the dub stage those changes can only be done by the music editor via audio editing and are typically less big changes." Also, on the dubbing stage, even when his employees, composers Zach Robinson and Leo Birenberg, are present and they have a suggestion, it is Locsey who carries it out "because I'm the only one that can do anything at that moment. Because it's all in audio; it's all in stems. The mixers have it on the board, already on the system."[12] The rise of these digital technologies has thus brought with it the elevation of the music editor and has altered the relations of production.

Some people I interviewed believe that today's composers aren't as experienced as in the past, not having worked their way up (as composers' assistants, orchestrators, arrangers, composers of additional music). Music contractor Dan Savant said that, in the old days, when a problem occurred in any stage of the music production process, the composer would usually know how to deal with it, working alongside the music supervisor, who was usually head of music for the studio involved. "But today," Savant said, "a music supervisor's job is to work with the director to choose known recorded songs to license for certain scenes." But back in the 1950s through the 1970s, he said, "the music supervisor, or the head of music for the studio would usually know orchestration and conducting and even had composition abilities."[13]

DOWNSIZING/OUTSOURCING

The adoption of digital technologies has made it possible to write a score without any live musicians or only a few.[14] Composer Ben Decter talked about this transition, which was well underway when he entered the business in the mid-1990s working for Mike Post. In that era, Post would often hire one live musician for each episode, whereas many musicians used to come in twice a day, five days a week, for Post's sessions. Decter remembers studio musicians leaving Los Angeles because of the lack of work, telling me of a great Los Angeles–based studio guitarist who had moved to Nashville (one of the three major centers for studio musicians and recording, along with Los Angeles and New York City). Decter told me, "We were watching people who were on the front lines feeling that change. And it was because of people like me and the technology that we were using, which was starting to get really sophisticated."[15]

Today, combinations of electronics with live musicians are fairly common. Bruce Broughton told me of a recent project with a budget for four musicians, not enough to record in a studio. So, Broughton recorded them at his home studio, one at a time. "I started with the guitar, added a clarinet, a cello, and finally a fiddle player. That was my orchestra, four musicians, and it sounded great—literally a homemade job, something that would never have been done forty-five years ago." Broughton said he has worked on shows where there is a lot of synthesized music but "just enough live musicians to make it sound real, with a sense of a real performance and real humanity."

For composers, it's important to have live musicians whenever possible. As Broughton said memorably in chapter 2, "It's the human personality that makes all the difference. You can't get that off of a sampler, so if you get a real person to perform, it just makes the score bloom. If I do it on a synthesizer (and I have done my fair share of purely synthesized scores), it's emotionally flat. It sucks."[16] Composers agree that some sounds just can't be synthesized or duplicated with samples. Christopher Wong told me in 2012 that he rarely enjoyed a budget that permits him to hire a live musician but that once in a while he will try to hire one anyway. He talked about a film in which "we needed some big-band, Frank Sinatra–sounding cues with all the screamy, first trumpet stuff, and you can't do that on MIDI; it's just impossible to make it sound right; you need a real trumpet player to pull that off."[17] In our more recent interview, he said the situation still varies a good deal based on budget. "Sometimes," he said, "I'll be lucky, and all the instruments on the score will be live. But sometimes you get just a bit of money to work with, and you prioritize parts of the recording to be live while other parts are MIDI—whatever the best way to spend the money is in getting the recording to sound as real as possible." About fifteen years ago, Wong told me, MIDI strings sounded more realistic than brass and winds, so, "if you had to choose, you would keep the fake strings and record some live winds and brass to put in the mix." Since then, he says, "the MIDI developers have been more successful in improving the winds and brass, while the strings haven't gotten that much more realistic, and so now the strings are the weak point in a MIDI mix; today if I had to choose, I usually record live strings and keep the MIDI brass and winds or maybe replace just two or three of the woodwinds along with the strings."[18]

With the introduction of more and more technology, and more and more sophisticated technology, music workers who are not just good at music are necessary in the production of film and television music. The music copyist I interviewed made an interesting point about the growth of technology and the sound of live musicians:

> For motion pictures it gets very risky to put millions and millions of dollars into a film and trust electronics to bring home the emotion that you're trying to get people to feel. It's very risky to do that. So, most films, where they're spending $30, $40, $50 or $100 million, they want to hear real strings, just really pulling at the heartstrings, and they want to hear real French horns—when it gets on to the high seas in *Pirates of the Caribbean*, you have sixteen French horns. I mean they want to make absolutely sure you get the feel for the high seas. Music is not one of the places where you want to skimp too much.[19]

Unlike most of the people whose work is discussed in these pages, however, this copyist said he enjoys the luxury of working on big-budget films.

Performers, too, prefer working with others, live. Some feel as though the absence of energy that comes from playing with others has made the process of playing along with music that has already been recorded less enjoyable. Bassist Carol Kaye told me that the people recording today are at a disadvantage because they're not playing in a band. "They're trying to overdub one by one by one and for feeling," she said. "That's the worst thing you can do because you've got the feeling of one person only, not the feeling of fifty people playing together." She described the films of the 1950s into the 1970s as having had "the greatest music ever" because "you have huge bands that were playing together. You had the feelings of everybody playing together. We felt that, and it felt great."[20]

It is perhaps instrumentalists who feel the decline in budgets the most, as their numbers are visibly diminishing. Trumpet player Jeff Bunnell told me that all the current problems in the business come down to money. Composers want the job, so they'll take less money:

So now they turn around and say, "I can't have a sixty-piece orchestra, so I'll have twenty-eight." And then pretty soon, "I can't have twenty-eight, but I'm going to have nine." And pretty soon they say, "I'm going to do it all in my home studio, and I'm going to have a guitar player come to my house every other week because there are a few cues for guitar, and I don't play guitar." So now it's one guy only every other week, and the producers seem fine with that. And that's a frustrating thing. They don't seem to care; they just want to save the money.[21]

For Bunnell and other instrumentalists, the amount of money spent on a big-budget film, and how little of it is devoted to the music budget, is also frustrating, as fewer and fewer musicians are employed in Los Angeles and more scores are recorded overseas. A film that makes hundreds of millions of dollars, yet, he wondered, an extra $250,000 couldn't have been spent on the music? Bunnell said, "I suppose if I had an employee who said, 'I can save you a quarter of a million dollars,' I'd say, "Great, how do we do that?' 'Well, we don't record in LA; we go to Prague. And the music won't be as good, but hopefully no one will notice, and we'll make $100 million dollars, and you'll save $250,000.'" Bunnell thinks the standards of recorded music have been lowered by recording abroad, with people "caring more about the money and less about the product."[22]

The American Federation of Musicians (AFM) ensures that those who do manage to get gigs are well paid, though this has also had the effect of driving some recording abroad. Composer Anne-Kathrin Dern expressed some frustration with the union because of the high costs of the royalties that projects must pay to the union, which on big productions could run into the millions.[23] (The Los Angeles AFM does, however, have a provision for low-budget rates; it can be found at www.afm47.org.) Dern said that the up-front costs in London and Los Angeles are about the same but that the union costs raise the price in Los Angeles. (According to Kraft 2013a, costs are somewhat lower in London and lower still in Seattle.) A trade press article from 2013 tallied some numbers. The main issue is secondary market repayments, which is to say, residuals paid out once a film is released into the secondary markets as a DVD or shown on cable, television, or a streaming service. In London and elsewhere, these payments don't have to be issued; musicians are paid a fee up front, and that is all. This article offered some figures of then-recent hit films: *Pirates of the Caribbean* (2003) was recorded in Los Angeles, and secondary market repayments of nearly $3 million needed to be made (Kraft 2013b, 8). Dern also said that older studios, such as Disney, Paramount, Warner, Universal, and Fox, are still recording in Los Angeles for the sake of tradition, but the newer studios are not signing contacts with the union.[24]

The outsourcing of the jobs of instrumental musicians has affected not only musicians, but everyone who works with them: recording engineers, studio personnel, and others. Mixer Michael Stern told me that when he first moved to Los Angeles in 1990, there were six major scoring stages and that they were always busy. At the time of our interview, he said there were three, which sit empty most of the time, and so musicians, engineers, and music editors were suffering.[25]

WORKING AT HOME

One major advantage of these new digital technologies is that it is now possible for composers to not just work at home (as they had in the past, with pencil, paper, and piano); now they can produce a high-quality mockup, even record live musicians, all without leaving home. Film or video recordings don't have to be moved around physically anymore, since broadband internet makes it easy to exchange files. All this, of course, means that people can work all the time.

The big breakthrough in terms of affordability and compactness was with the rise of Alesis Digital Audio Tape in the early 1990s. "For the first time in history," Michael Stern said, "you could have a 24-track recording studio in your bedroom for $10,000." But, he told me, this was the death knell for a lot of commercial recording studios where high-quality recordings were once made: "You had to go somewhere where they had these huge machines. An analog 24-track tape machine weighed hundreds of pounds, and they were the size of a Maytag dishwasher." But the new digital machines were much smaller and could be connected to one another. So, in the early to mid-1990s, he said, everything changed. "You've never seen an industry change so quickly. Recording studios went out of business."[26]

The next step, according to Stern, was the advent of what became Pro Tools, which also emerged in the early 1990s. Stern said he was "absolutely fascinated and thrilled by seeing these machines inside a computer, where you didn't have to cut tape. You could put audio in the computer and make nondestructive edits. The power of that was immediately apparent to me, and I decided that I needed to learn this technology." Stern said that the sound quality also continued to rise, so that it could approach, and then equal, the quality of analog recordings. When we talked in 2012, Stern said he didn't foresee major changes at that point.[27]

The rise of affordable home studios has changed everything. Terry Wollman, who is a guitarist, recording artist, music director, and more, told me, "The very fact that we are sitting and doing an interview in my recording studio is not something that would have happened twenty years ago. We would be sitting in my practice room, but not a world-class, fully automated recording studio that's set up to score to picture where I can write for film and television."[28] Wollman said it has become expected of musicians today to have a recording studio and to know how to be an engineer; otherwise, they can't find work.

Wollman also said that having one's own recording studio has become expected by the business for a couple of reasons. Since it's possible to make high-quality recordings at home, the people who are making budgets don't include recording studios anymore, on the assumption that people can do it at home. The other reason, of course, is speed. Wollman provided an illustrative anecdote:

> Years ago, I got a call from a music supervisor who said, "We need a classical piece of music for harp and piano," and I said, "Okay, great, when do you need it?" "Right now! Like, today. We already filmed the scene, and we need to replace a piece of music that was already filmed. We couldn't get clearance on this piece of music, but there's close-ups of

the hands of the musicians playing along to this music, so now we need to write a piece of music that visually fits what's going on because we can't re-film." And I said, "Okay." So, I watched a clip of the scene and composed a piece of music that fit the tempo, then asked what I thought was certainly a reasonable question: "What's the budget and timeline so I can go to a studio and hire a harpist and a pianist?" And they said, "Oh, no, there's no time or money; you need to just do this." And I asked, "I can't hire a harpist?" To which they replied, "Can't you just do it on the synthesizer?" "I suppose, yeah, with samples, absolutely." So, I had to write a traditional classical piece of music and have the technical skills to be able to put it in at the time of videotape, get it to sync, engineer it, and then play the parts.[29]

Today's musicians don't necessarily know how to do everything they once did, including reading and writing music, but they have learned new skills in the digital realm.

Changes in the Music

Many composers and other music workers I interviewed discussed how the nature of film and television music has changed with the rise of digital technologies, though some of their comments are as much about broader shifts in the business that have affected music production.

Some composers also criticized what they characterized as the homogenization of sound. David Schwartz told me he thinks that television music isn't as subtle as it could be, partly because there are fewer back-and-forth conversations with showrunners and because the amount of music used in television is rising.[30] Composer Ben Decter expressed the same opinion. Increasingly homogenized sound is on the rise due in part to the prevalence of what is known as library music or production music (prerecorded all-purpose music that isn't specially composed for a particular film, television program, or advertisement). This music, which has been available for decades (see Taylor 2012), is losing some of its stigma, and more and more well-known composers are writing for libraries. Some think that this is having a negative effect. Decter said, "There's been an interesting tension with the phenomenon of library music." Decter believes that it is a big business and that the quality of the music in the libraries is exceptionally high. It's not made to order for a particular film, episode, or commercial, so "you don't get what you get from a score, which is a body of music that cohesively helps tie things together and helps tell the story on screen." But library music is frequently used, often because it's cheaper than hiring a composer; for a commercial, producers might pay $150 for a library track instead of perhaps tens of thousands for a piece of original music. There are a number of films and episodes that employ library music extensively. Decter told me of losing a job because of it. "I once had that experience when competing for a commercial. They said, 'Oh, it's down to the last couple submissions; it could be you.' But then the call came: 'We decided to go with a library track.'"[31] Some of the library music companies boast of hosting music by established composers.[32]

In addition to causing what some interviewees thought was a decline of subtlety in television music, digital technologies have increased demand for music on television. David Schwartz told me, "There has also been a move toward a lot—a lot—of music. And I think there's a fear that if the music stops, people are going to switch the channels, a fear that seems to come from the networks on down." But Schwartz thinks that a break in the music allows the drama to be built up.[33]

Several composers discussed a golden age of film music composition when filmmakers gave composers a good deal of latitude. Deborah Lurie told me there aren't many filmmakers today who would leave empty spaces or have faith that their composer's music would help carry the film, saying, "The trust Alfred Hitchcock gave Bernard Herrmann to carry such a large part of his films was extraordinary. Or Spielberg with John Williams." Today, Lurie said, "I think a lot of film music is utilitarian. It does a job, and filmmaking seems to tell stories in a faster, more frenetic way with more cuts, as if the audience has a shorter attention span and needs more stimulus in any given sequence. That makes it tougher for composers to write true themes rather than fragments and short motifs." Lurie said she is exploring other sorts of composition work, that she's less interested in writing for film, because the way films are made has changed. The kind of microsurgery on films that digital technologies have made possible can often deny viewers the "sense that a score is being born over a time or the idea that there could be themes and development and a beginning, middle, and end." Real storytelling in a musical score is much more challenging now, she said: "With digital production, anything is possible and changeable at the drop of a hat, so they try every which way to play each moment, like having a music editor put up forty pieces of music to see which one works best, so you can imagine a composer trying to write a cohesive score when moments are so heavily scrutinized and tinkered with in isolation like that." And then the producers' and directors' reactions are along the lines of, "'Well, this used to be orchestral here; now let's try jazz.' And like, after scoring a scene a few times, you might hear—'Oh you didn't get the call? That scene's a song now; don't worry about it.'" Lurie talked about her own experiences writing music with Danny Elfman:

> He would write these masterful pieces of music, and I'd be sitting in the back of his studio practically moved to tears, thinking that what he had written was amazing, and the director would say something like, "That's good . . . but we recut the scene. Now this happens over there," blah, blah, blah. And I would be thinking, "What? No!" And my job was often to shift the cue around, writing like little bridges as masking tape, reconstructing it like a puzzle to fit the picture changes. I had to put this beautiful thing back together as best you can. It was like I was gluing up a beautiful vase or something.[34]

Lurie thinks that one of the reasons why streaming shows and television are of such high quality is because the schedules don't permit such micromanaging.

Crushing schedules, the use of the same software, fewer classically trained composers in the business, bosses who micromanage—all are reasons for older composers' perceptions that film and television music has declined and become homogenous. But there's another reason. One composer, who got into the business in the 1980s, talked about how the directives came down from producers and directors, starting perhaps as early as the 1990s but certainly in this century, for composers not to use a melody. "They didn't want it. It's too corny or it tips off the audience. They don't want any emotion. They just want ambiance. So really what they want is wallpaper." This composer thought this was in part simply a result of changing trends, that producers and directors desire to do something different, and they try to avoid music that sounds like their father's or grandfather's. "So, they say, 'Well, that's corny to have a melody.' They don't want to lead the audience on. And so, they just really want you to just tread water and be ambient."[35] It's striking that, in the same era when many academics were busy discussing postmodernism in cultural production and its characteristics, such as the "waning of affect" famously theorized by Fredric Jameson (1984), people in authority in cultural production were in fact deliberately engineering it.

Getting Paid

While working in these fields has historically been precarious for everyone, this precariousness was not introduced by the rise of neoliberal capitalism. But it has certainly intensified, necessitating a new term—*precarity*—to label the instability of people's work lives in these fields, given the glut of musicians who want to enter this business, the uncertainty about the future of broadcast networks and cable with the rise of streaming services, the different way that musicians are paid by streaming services, the declining amount of money paid for music, and still other developments.

In some ways, all this seems paradoxical: There is more content being produced (more cable channels, more streaming services); there are more and more managers, not just because there is more content being produced but also because of the managerialization and bureaucratization of these fields of cultural production; and schools such as the Berklee College of Music are producing more and more and more graduates. But at the same time, more money is going to the top, which is also more populated than in the past. There are thus multiple pressures that keep music and other budget items down (though budgets overall seem to be going up, at least on streaming platforms; see Katz 2019 and Ryan and Littleton 2017) and that keep money out of musicians' pockets.

Finding work and getting paid enough to make a living were recurring issues for all the musicians in this study, something that came up in our conversations without me having to ask. Most agree that it is harder and harder to make a living, while there are a few musicians who are paid extremely well. Less money is being spent on music, and the money saved increasingly moves to the people at the top of the production chain, as composer David Schwartz pointed out, observing that it was essentially the same thing that was happening in the US more generally: "The money is going to the top—it's going to the people who are above the line, the movie stars, and the big producers and the directors. We can get into the whole politics of the country; it's not that different than what else is happening."[36] Music editor Craig Pettigrew said the same thing: "The money they're saving is going into a producer's pocket. The producers aren't getting poor. They're making the same kind of money. It's unfortunate."[37] The rise in income inequality is not just occurring in music production but is business-wide (see Laporte 2018). This is just one of many changes that have occurred in the business in the past few decades though certainly the most consequential for composers. Veteran composer Bruce Broughton told me in 2013, "I started in 1967, forty-six years ago. Because I was a part of staff at CBS, I knew what we paid composers; I knew what the deals were in television. I know what the deals are now. I've seen the deals change."[38] Today's television composer makes about the same or only a little more in inflation-unadjusted dollars than in the era when Broughton began his career (Borum 2015a, xvii), which is to say that, in real dollars, most are paid a small fraction of what they once were, still receiving $2,000–$3,000 per hourlong episode.[39] Broughton said that in the time he has been in the business, he has seen the deals and working conditions worsen.[40]

The overall decrease in funding in the past ten years has been a major change in the business. Producer Harvey Myman told me that producers can no longer hire someone to write a title song, for example. If a show did have a title song, Myman said, it would be removed when the show went into syndication so that royalties wouldn't have to be paid. Part of the reason for this, he said, is that with streaming, licenses have to be secured not just for the US but for the world, which is prohibitively expensive.[41]

The difficulties for composers are myriad, as I have discussed, and also in part because of the demise of their union, and because of the rise of digital technologies, which has had multiple effects, as we have seen. In addition, there are fewer episodes per season on network television, and a streaming series season might consist of only ten to fifteen episodes, or even fewer, which means less work. Networks are more reluctant to be patient to let a show with poor ratings attempt to find an audience over time, so a series might be canceled after thirteen episodes, whereas in the past it would probably have been allowed more time to find an audience. And, finally, the advent of streaming has introduced different mechanisms by which composers get paid.

Paying Composers

Pay varies considerably from film (where musicians do not even get paid, or paid very much, for student or young filmmakers' work) to a television or streaming series or a video game. Top composers can make up to $2 million for a film, though the average film composer makes about $50,000 annually (Gleeson 2018), so there is a good deal of variability within every medium. Today's composers also compete with cheaper, prerecorded library music; they also compete with preexisting songs chosen by music supervisors that are increasingly finding their way into television programs, films, and streaming episodes. Some of these songs can costs tens or even hundreds of thousands of dollars to license, which makes for less money that can be spent on composers for original music and live musicians to record it.

There are two ways that composers are paid, the fee-based deal and what is known as the package deal. Today, the former is for big-budget films; the latter, for everything else. Composers can say that they only agree to a fee-based deals in which they receive a creative fee, and thereby enter into discussions about the budget, which determines the size of the orchestra and the number of days of recording. Robert Kraft, president of Fox Music from 1994 to 2012, told me that, in film, "If you have a Marvel film, you wouldn't give Ludwig Göransson or Alan Silvestri a package: 'Here's $3 million; we'll see you at the finish line.' It doesn't behoove anybody. It's not an integrated working relationship with a composer on that much music and money."[42]

THE PACKAGE DEAL

But the main way that most composers in this study are paid today is through the package deal. This is the common practice of awarding the composer for either television or film a lump sum, out of which they pay not only themselves, but any live musicians they might use, their orchestrator or arranger if they employ one, their scoring mixer, and still other music workers they might need. Before the package deal, the studio would cover such costs. The composer would hire whomever and send the bill to the studio.

The package deal was common practice in independent films after World War II; it was less common in television in this era but was in use. Earle Hagen (1919–2008) claims in his autobiography to have been the first recipient of such a deal in television, for *The Andy Griffith Show* around 1960, calling it a "flat package" (Hagen 2000).[43] The major studios weren't paying for music that way back then, though composer Stu Phillips recalled that there was some talk of major composers making package deals with the studios.[44] Everyone once made a good deal of money before the package deal because they could bill the studio for a lot of things they didn't necessarily have to bill for. Score mixer Phil McGowan told me that if people owned their own equipment, they could bill the studio for renting that equipment as well as for the actual mixing. And the studio would pay it.[45]

For a time, according to Stephan Eicke, this was a good deal for composers, who realized that they could record their orchestral score in Eastern Europe, employ some synthesized or sampled music, and keep the cost of the production of the score down in order to maximize their fee. But the studios soon learned about this trick, and budgets began to decline. Eicke (2019, 35) writes that composers have had to become adept at estimating the cost of producing their scores at home, at anticipating the number of musicians needed, recording time, edits, and so on. It is possible for composers to renegotiate the deal, but it is difficult.

By the turn of this century, various industry professionals estimated that virtually all television deals were packages, as were 80 percent of independent films; studio deals were about 30 percent packages (Barth 2002, 4). In the past fifteen years or so, according to McGowan, pretty much everything is a package deal, with rare exceptions, since package deals relieve studios of a good deal of administrative work—by passing it on to the composer. Studios give the composer anywhere from $20,000, or less if it's an independent film, up to $1 million or $2 million, but McGowan thinks a usual budget is at least $100,000, which doesn't give the composer much wiggle room because recording live musicians in an orchestra could cost tens of thousands of dollars in a single day, and would be half the budget. Since the composer is paying for everything, they are "expected to keep their budget reined in because whatever is left over after paying everybody is their fee."[46]

The package deal as the norm in most film and television started to take off in the early 1970s and was further propelled after a strike by members of the American Federation of Musicians (AFM) in 1980–81 over residuals (royalties) in the reuse of television films. AFM president Victor Fuentealba said in a statement, "There is a long-standing, obvious and illogical inequity whereby musicians receive no reuse payment when TV films on which they have worked are rerun on TV, while producers make such payments to actors, directors and writers" (Grein 1980). This strike was overshadowed by a strike of the Screen Actors Guild (SAG) and the American Federation of Television and Radio Artists (AFTRA), which the musicians joined in solidarity; Fuentealba complained about "playing second fiddle" (Tusher 1980, 84), and the musicians' strike dragged on. The AFM finally settled early in 1981, not having gained much; the scales increased 9 percent per year for the next three years, and the pension increased from 8 to 9 percent. The reuse issue wasn't altered from what was in their existing contract; video and pay TV would have to be negotiated in the future.

And, indeed, according to Alan Elliott, a composer and producer (who knows some of this history from the inside because his father, Jack, was a major television and film composer), the leading music agents Michael Gorfaine and Sam Schwartz, along with Mike Post, undercut the strike by embracing the package deal. According to Elliott, after the shift toward the package deal, music budgets were cut at least in half, and all expenses were paid by the composer, who got to keep what wasn't spent producing the score.[47] This means that composers were less likely to work with anyone else—including live musicians—unless it was absolutely necessary, and it also became more important for them to be able to work at home with their own equipment so that they wouldn't have to rent recording studios and pay recording engineers.

I asked Post about the package deal, and he said he was one of the first to use it, and thought that Earle Hagen was indeed the first who had secured such a deal. Post says he negotiated a package deal very early on. Producer Stephen J. Cannell (1941–2010), whom Post describes as his best friend, left Universal Studios in 1979 to form his own production company, Stephen J. Cannell Productions; Post characterizes this as Cannell becoming "the deficit financer himself." Post said that when Cannell saw the budget for *The Rockford Files* and how little Post and his composing partner Pete Carpenter were being paid (he recalled the entire music budget as being $27,500 per episode), Cannell asked Post what he wanted. Post explained that the back end was good, so he didn't need anything more, but Cannell insisted. So, Post said, he consulted with Carpenter and then suggested to Cannell that he package the music budget. Cannell, he said, balked, worrying that his friend would lose money. Post responded, "No, I'm going to get rich. You watch. The same way that you're becoming the deficit financer for the film—that's what I want to do with the music." Cannell agreed since it wouldn't cost any more money. Post said he also convinced Cannell to give him half the publishing rights, which he did.[48]

The establishment of the package deal system was facilitated also by the rise of digital technologies; if more and more composers were making more and more music with fewer and fewer live musicians, it was easier for studios to charge composers with taking care of everything themselves. Digital technologies also played a role in the saturation of the field of television and film music, which meant that increasing numbers of people were trying to enter the business and could do so with only their home studios, and they were willing to charge little or nothing in order to gain a foothold. The package deal system gave them a way undercut the competition (see Adams 1999).

Composers today seem ambivalent, at best, about the package deal; a survey from 2010 reported that 78 percent of composers would prefer to do away with it and create a payment scheme separate from the cost of production and that just over 72 percent said they wanted a union (see the *Film Music Magazine Composer Unionization Survey* 2010).[49] David Schwartz told me that it's difficult these days to earn as much as he did as when he started writing for television in the early 1990s. Part of the reason is that the scale has gone up for union musicians, whose rate has doubled in this period. He doesn't mind paying it, but it is a cost.[50] Other workers in the industry said much the same thing about earning less (see Barth 2002).

It's important to understand the package deal system as yet another way to cut costs employed by those espousing neoliberal policies and ideologies. The rise to common usage of the package deal system occurred when the federal government was changing the way it funded many programs. What were known as "categorical" grants to cover specific items were increasingly consolidated into larger "block grants," which were seen as more flexible ways to disburse federal funds to state and local governments. Consolidation and the use of block grants begin in the post–World War II era and were largely nonpartisan, but in the Reagan era, block grants became highly partisan and ideological (Conlan 1984, 260). Earlier block grants were at a level of funding that was higher than that of the programs they replaced through consolidation; Reagan used block grants to cut spending, at levels of 25 percent in fiscal year 1982 (261). Timothy J. Conlan (1984, 269), a scholar of policy and government, argues that whereas block grants began as a management strategy for making program administration simpler and permitting local adaptations, under Reagan, block grants became part of the apparatus of conservatism in reducing government spending.

Whether or not the package deal has resulted in smaller budgets, everyone I spoke to agrees that budgets aren't what they used to be, perhaps especially in television. A 2013 trade press article reported that several years prior, "a handful" of programs had budgets of more than $100,000 per episode, but the author wrote that he thought only two shows (*Glee* and *Grey's Anatomy*) would reach that amount (Gallo 2013, 27). As David Schwartz told me, "The budgets have been shrinking and shrinking and shrinking. And they've been deducting stuff from our packages. For example, before they used to pay us if we did vocals, but now they take it back from us. It's getting harder and harder."[51] Ben Decter, a successful television and documentary film composer who worked with Mike Post early in his career, also observed that budgets are going down. Decter told me in 2012 that he thought budgets then were half of what they were fifteen or twenty years prior.[52]

And composer Cindy O'Connor said that since she got into the business in the early 1990s, when she started working as an assistant to composer

Mark Isham, "Budgets have gotten tiny." Not everything was a package deal when she started, she said. Composers received a writing fee as well as a budget for production and for the orchestra. Now, she said, the writing fee is pretty much gone, composers receive a lump sum, and composers must decide how much they want to spend and retain for their fee. She said that for composers early in their careers, "a lot of the time we just put the whole budget into live players or getting a really good mixer or a fabulous new sample library." Sometimes, she said, they would take a calculated risk in the hopes that the project would take off and that they could recoup their expenses through the back end (residuals) or that this project would lead to a bigger project. But, she said, "It is kind of sad—as somebody who observed what the big budgets used to be—that so often they're tiny and composers are opting to just invest the whole thing into a great-sounding score."[53] As composer Matt Hutchinson put it: "I feel like I work harder for the same money that I used to."[54]

Composers are well aware of the increased pressure the package deal puts on them to cut costs in order to try to be able to earn anything. Ryan Shore told me that he understands why package deals are popular, since it can be simpler for producers to say, "'Here's our budget for the score,'" instead of delving into all the details of how much various aspects cost in the production of a score. This, Shore said, therefore allows the composer to produce the score and make decisions about how best to achieve the final music. He said, "You want your clients to be extremely happy, and you want your music to sound fantastic, and you want to do everything you can to best serve all aspects of the project." In the end, Shore thinks the package system succeeds because composers really want to do their very best work.[55] They end up exploiting themselves.

A 1999 article exposes some of the negotiations that go on behind the scenes in the film world. For an ABC film called *Rear Window* (1998, a TV movie remake of the 1954 Hitchcock classic), the composer was offered a package of $50,000 out of an overall budget of $8 million. The producers wanted a "fully symphonic" sound, but the composer, David Shire, could only hire nineteen musicians at most, and that while spending $10,000 of his personal funds. His plan was to do what was common in television music, employ live strings forward in the mix and enrich them with synthesized sounds. Shire thought he needed a twenty-six-person ensemble for this, and that included putting his own fee into hiring the musicians. Shire's mention of his financial difficulties to other composers resulted in terminated conversations with his bosses. But Shire was able to get the ear of one of the show's stars, Christopher Reeve, who asked not the producers, but the network to cover the extra $25,000 that Shire thought was necessary. That didn't work, either, until Reeve threatened to withhold publicity for the film. At the last minute, ABC finally released the funds (Adams 1999).

The decline in budgets and the rise of the package deal constitute two of the main reasons why more and more composers work in teams. An individual composer might not be able to make enough money to survive from a single television series, so they accept more jobs, hire composers to write additional music, and hope eventually to come out ahead. Otherwise, Joey Newman told me, being a composer doesn't make sense financially and this practice is the only way to have a life and a family.[56]

Further in the supply chain, recording engineer and mixer Michael Stern said that he preferred to be paid by the studio rather than the composer "because it's more beneficial to the scoring mixer in terms of getting IATSE [International Alliance of Theatrical Stage Employees] union health benefits, pension, welfare benefits." And, he said, it's better for the composer since, of course, it's not coming out of the composer's package. But many budgets these days are packages, he said, and so composers must pay. Stern said that, sometimes, because it costs so much to record a large-scale film score, composers become investors themselves, which means that "they go way over the budget they're given and end up paying to record their own score." Stern said this frequently happens, but, "It is sometimes worth it to them as an investment in their career; hopefully they will make up the money on back-end royalties and cement their relationship with film studios and directors."[57] This happens in games as well. Michael Giacchino said that in scoring *The Lost World*, to record with a live orchestra was prohibitively expensive in Los Angeles, so they went to Seattle, where they were still $17,000 over budget. "So," Giacchino said, "I ended up putting in everything I was getting paid to cover the extra costs. I figured it was a great opportunity and a chance to show what I could do, and who knows? It could lead to something else"—namely, *Alias*. This series, as it turns out, was a hit television program for ABC from 2001 to 2006 (see Krogh 2002a, 34), and, later, in 2010, Giacchino won an Academy Award for his score to *Up*. This kind of trajectory is rare, of course, but the allure of it frequently compels composers to use their personal funds in order to be able to write and record the scores they want. They exploit themselves, passionately.

Robert Kraft told me that, from his perspective, the only difficulty with a package deal is when the money in the package is gone "and the director says, 'I want changes,' because that becomes the question of, who pays for the changes? The composer says, 'I've delivered what you asked me for, and you want another day of recording, and you want to add an orchestral date that wasn't in my package deal. Well, we've got to find some more money, or you have to, or you have to accept what I've sent.'"[58]

The package deal has not only had the effect of reducing budgets; it has turned composers into managers (see Barth 2002). Theodor Adorno (1991, 122) said of management in the cultural businesses that it "is not simply imposed upon the supposedly productive human being from without. It multiplies within this person himself." Composers' de-skilling in some musical matters (which one could characterize broadly as "analog"—knowing how to write for an orchestra, conduct a score, and more) has been replaced by the necessity of managing everything in the music supply chain. Film composer Jeremy Borum (2015b) writes that composers were formerly one person in the music supply chain, their main tasks being writing music, attending recording sessions, and little more. Today, he said, composers are "responsible for every step of the music team's process. . . . The support network, which used to be built-in, has evaporated" (1). Composers are no longer music specialists; they must do everything, possessing qualities of artistry, craft, and business. "We are not composers," Borum writes, "we're the CEOs of small music businesses and we're responsible for every aspect of music production" (1).

The package deal system, emerging in this neoliberal moment, is also a case of the devolution of authority and processes of "responsibilization" that are part of this ideology, this "political rationality," as Wendy Brown calls it, elaborating on the concept from Foucault. According to Brown (2015, 129), "contemporary neoliberal governance operates through isolating and entrepreneurializing responsible units and individuals, through devolving authority, decision making, and the implementation of policies and norms of conduct. These are the processes that make individuals and other small units in workplaces responsible for themselves while binding them to the powers and project of the whole." Composers have been managerialized and responsibilized.

Composers I have spoken to recognize this shift. Joey Newman described himself as a kind of middle manager in between the producers and the people he hires to produce his music. No one is trained to be a manager, he said, or to manage a business—they're trained to be artists. Newman thinks that the people who do well financially in the business are those who are good at business, people who know how to "sell the product"—themselves as brands. Newman told me, "I'm the product; I'm the brand," and he thinks that developing a skill set on business strategies and marketing is a plus for film and television composers today.[59] Composers learn how to be managers because they must.

Turning composers into managers is a form of control, a way to bureaucratize the production of music. And bureaucratization, as we know from David Graeber (2015)—and personal experience—stifles creativity and the imagination (see also Adorno 1991; Davis and Scase 2000; Ryan 1992). The managerialization of the music supply chain is part of the bureaucratization of everyday life, a kind of managerialism we are all increasingly subject to, and actors in.

TELEVISION, FILM, AND THE BACK END

Now let's get into more specifics. Even in this era of the package deal, composers' pay varies considerably. From where composers sit, it can be difficult to understand. Ben Decter told me, "I find the pay quite random. In my experience, the most writing and the longest time I've put in for the least amount of money is for documentary films."[60] Although advertising pays well, mostly in terms of the amount of money received for the amount of music written, in Decter's view, television pays the best, for two reasons: One, if all goes well, composers will work on multiple episodes, not a single film or commercial; second, royalties. In terms of commercials made in the United States, composers receive royalties as a musician (if they perform), not as a composer (see Taylor 2012). US television shows, however, air all over the world. "One of the things I get a kick out of when the quarterly statements come is to see money from Slovenia and Turkey and Israel and Greece and Sweden, and it's for stuff I've written as recently as six months ago and as long ago as *Silk Stalkings*, twenty years ago. Everything I've ever written, apparently, stays out in the broadcast world and plays somewhere. I could not support my family without such long-term payments."[61]

Royalties are clearly important to composers, and several interviewees mentioned them. They're usually referred to as the "back end," money earned after receiving the initial payment for the film or show has been made; some think of royalties as a kind of informal retirement plan.[62] Matt Hutchinson told me that residuals (royalties) are a major concern because they can make up a substantial part of a composer's income. "If you've got a show, and it lasted thirteen episodes and then it's canceled and you wonder what you're going to live off of the next year, well, the back end helps you get through those periods where you're looking for that next thing."[63]

Music editor Craig Pettigrew said he knows people who survive on those payments, people over fifty who aren't getting called to do recording sessions anymore.[64]

A big issue for music editors (as opposed to composers) is that their pension plan is directly funded by residuals (payments aren't disbursed directly to individuals), which means it's not being fed by streaming. Andrés Locsey told me that his union is seeking an agreement with producers. "Something's got to change," he said, "both for the composers and for us."[65]

As budgets have declined, the pay for most of the people interviewed for this book, especially those who work in small and/or independent films, is nothing like what composers in television, streaming, and big-budget films can earn. Christopher Wong, who mostly writes music for films produced in Vietnam based on connections made with student directors at UCLA, told me that his pay isn't remotely like the famous composers John Williams, Hans Zimmer, Danny Elfman, or Michael Giacchino, who can make $1–2 million per picture, but, he added, "there are thousands of guys like me who don't get paid nearly as much as those guys do, and we're making a normal living in LA, trying to pay our rent like everyone else. But we're still part of the industry; we're making films that people go out to see in theaters or watch on Netflix." Wong said that Netflix has a lot of "product" that viewers might never have heard of, films and episodes that boast no stars, but, nonetheless, "something like over a hundred people worked on making this movie that you've never heard of." And, he said, there are hundreds of movies and episodes like that on Netflix or being issued on DVD that viewers don't realize are being made by hundreds of people, people who are "just trying to make a living like anyone working at a university or at a bank. We don't make big money; we're not famous because we are working musicians."[66]

With, sometimes, several composers writing music, it is important to keep track of who wrote what. Deborah Lurie explained that the back end is generated from the cue sheet, a list of all the pieces off music in the film or episode and who wrote them. If there is a composer who writes additional music, that composer and the main composer will split the amount in one way or another.[67] Composers must sign a certificate of authorship, a contract with the studio, verifying that they wrote the cue(s) as represented on the cue sheet. Another composer told me that there is a good deal of gossip concerning composers and their additional music composers. Sometimes these composers have only a verbal agreement. One hears endless stories, this composer said, like "'Oh, I hear that person went back on his cue sheet deal.'" This composer said that certificates of authorship are also relevant when it comes time for awards: "If all sorts of other names are all over the cue sheet, then people wonder, 'Hmm, is this Oscar-worthy?' So, then sometimes you get composers being stingy about their cue sheet because it looks bad."[68]

STREAMING AND THE FRONT END

Increased precarity in a precarious field has become a fact of life: Not only are there fewer jobs for performing musicians; there are also fewer jobs that pay well for composers. And, most recently, streaming has introduced even more uncertainty and economic instability. Music editor Andrés Locsey said that in the world of streaming, he isn't necessarily hired to work on a twenty-four-program season as on a network. Locsey said that if you won a network job, you were set for a year's work. The advent of streaming has potentially brought more work, but a streaming "season" might be only six or ten episodes, so "you get two months' worth of work," which might be nonunion.[69]

Also, the pay scheme for streaming programs is different from that of broadcast or cable television. Recording engineer and mixer Phil McGowan said that because streaming services don't share their viewing data, the American Society of Composers, Authors and Publishers (ASCAP) and Broadcast Music, Inc. (BMI), the performing rights organizations that secure royalty payments for their rights-holder members, don't know how many people are viewing and therefore can't request royalties for their members. McGowan said that royalties are going away because everything that is seen after a theatrical release is now viewed via streaming, not television. A composer might receive a cash bonus from a streaming service if a program is successful, but it pales in comparison, McGowan said, to what composers would receive in the form of royalties.[70]

But, with streaming, a composer might be paid more up front (producer Harvey Myman told me they might receive 125 percent of what they would get for a network series).[71] Hutchinson said that streaming payments were not great in the beginning but have gotten better, and he thinks that in order to do well with a streaming show, the program needs to be a smash, but there are many shows that are hardly watched. He told me, "I think everybody is just hoping that they hit that diamond in the rough, lightning in the bottle, that they're going to have the big hit show and that that's going to catapult them." But he recognizes that that doesn't happen for everyone, which means "there's going to be a lot more people for whom it's more of a grind, I think. You're just going to have to do more shows and more shows to keep income coming in."[72]

Cindy O'Connor wrote the music for the ABC television drama series *Once Upon a Time* with Mark Isham from 2011 to 2018 and talked about the difference between then and now. "*Once Upon a Time* ran for seven years, and then the idea would be that it would get picked up in syndication, and it would run every night on some random channel, and you'd make a bazillion dollars." But today, she said, programs will air and then just stream: "Streaming is the new reruns, and it pays so much less than the old reruns."[73]

I received varying reports from composers about streaming services and royalties. Ryan Shore said that composers receive residuals from streaming services, which is often negotiated by performing rights organizations.[74] That is still true as of this writing. Deborah Lurie said, "Royalties have completely changed since the streaming days. The older systems behind theatrically released films and broadcast television were substantially more favorable for composers. Streaming has completely changed the game in so many ways, and one of them is definitely regarding money. Many composers are currently speaking out about it and trying to change the system."[75]

Cindy O'Connor said that even though streaming pays more up front, the fact that there are no royalties means it is important to claim the writer's share of any composition. She has heard that some of the streaming services are attempting to take the writer's share of royalties in exchange for more of an up-front fee (this is true; see Kranhold 2019). Normally, she said, the composer keeps the writer's share and whoever is employing her retains the publisher's share. She said that some streaming services "are trying to push giving you a little more up front if you just sign over your writer's share. It just seems like a deal with the devil from everything we were taught coming up: Don't ever give away the writer's share, no! Because you'll have that forever and that's your retirement." O'Connor said composers now must try to guess how long the project might last and then decide whether to take the money up front as a short-term gamble. In her view, "The fact that these deals are being made at all sets a bad precedent for everybody."[76]

Video games, like streaming episodes and films, pay up front, but there are no royalties. Games seem to pay better, with separate budgets for composers and production (see Muddiman 2019). Fees are based on how commercial the game is and how many people are expected to buy it. Penka

Kouneva told me that the production companies she works for do pay well and that her fee is negotiable, not set. She said she has worked with smaller companies that paid less and would accept lesser pay if she wanted the job. "The game studios pay a fee for the music per minute; there's no royalties at all except for some rare situations, like game cues being used in trailers or being aired on TV." Having left television in 2007, Kouneva told me, "Now I seek to return to scoring television. Scoring TV helps generate higher composer royalties."[77]

Composer Bruce Broughton witnessed the dissolution of the composers' union, one of the many unions challenged or busted starting with the neoliberal era, with Ronald Reagan's busting of the air traffic controllers' union in 1981, a signal moment. The busting of the Composers and Lyricists Guild of America was the result of a lawsuit brought by the union against the producers in which the composers were demanding to be able to own the publishing rights to their music (as discussed in chapter 3), a request that producers ignored. Members of the Guild went on strike in 1971 over this issue but were put off and, so, engaged a lawyer to mount an antitrust action against studios, television networks, and producers. This suit gained a good deal of attention and had some success (CBS came to an agreement with composers and lyricists), but the suit was dismissed by a judge in 1974, a decision that was overturned in 1975, which should have sent the case to trial. But the studios delayed, hoping to drain the coffers of members of the Guild involved in the suit. A settlement was reached in 1979 granting limited rights to composers and lyricists but was difficult to exploit given its legal complexities. The Guild then attempted to negotiate a contract, and the studios stalled again. Broughton assumed the presidency of the Guild in the early 1980s and tried to reinvigorate it, but the draining of finances had crippled the Guild and in June 1982 it was no more.[78]

Older composers lamented the demise of their union. "Twice," Bruce Broughton told me, "I was part of a group that tried to reorganize a union, to no avail."[79] Broughton and composers continue to feel the need for a union (see Burlingame 1997 and Robb 1998), and there have been subsequent attempts to unionize composers, particularly in 2009–11, when a drive to create the Association of Media Composers and Lyricists (AMCL) was spearheaded by Alan Elliott, Broughton, James Di Pasquale (who had assisted in creating the Society of Composers and Lyricists in 1983), and Alf

Clausen (Bond 2010). This proposed union was to join with the Teamsters to form a collective bargaining unit. But negotiations with studios and the Alliance of Motion Picture and Television Producers (AMPTP) did not result in an agreement, the AMPTP refusing to recognize the AMCL. The producers still viewed composers as independent contractors, as the National Labor Relations Board had ruled in the 1980s, a status that does not permit such workers to organize (see Burlingame 2010). A major demand seemed to have been health care; Broughton, the AMCL organizing committee chairman, said, "It's still a fairness issue," since all of the other creative workers in the industry enjoyed basic health care benefits (Burlingame 2011).

Joey Newman said he believed it would be difficult to re-form the union since not all the composers agreed about what they wanted. Part of the problem, he said, is the existence of agents. "It's going to be hard to unionize when agencies have such a big say in it all. They want to be able to have the freedom to do as much for their clients as possible, which can differ from client to client. A set standard may affect their business model." So instead of relying on a union to get paid, Newman, like all other composers, must count on performing rights organizations, such as ASCAP and BMI, to monitor performances of his music to provide a critical supplemental income. He views streaming platforms, as well as video game companies, as being part of a software culture rather than a cultural production world, so their attitude toward intellectual property is different. The problem, he told me, "is that a place like Netflix was a software-based ecosystem; they're software developers, not filmmakers, so they say, 'We own your stuff because that's what we do as a company. You provide it, we pay for it, and then we own it.'" But that's not how it works in his world, Newman said, where composers normally are permitted to own the writer's share of their product for which they receive residuals. Newman thinks this is why people have a hard time agreeing on how to pay and get paid. He thinks that the television network model is still the best since it provides royalties that arrive sooner and can last longer.[80]

A trade press article from 2013 provided a useful flowchart showing how money comes in and is paid out to composers; it omits streaming, which does not make payments to performing rights organizations (see figure 7.1).

Recently, following the conclusion of interviews for this book, Joey Newman told me that the situation with streaming services and royalties has improved somewhat. Streaming companies have hired more executives from film and television who have been hired into more familiar studio-system

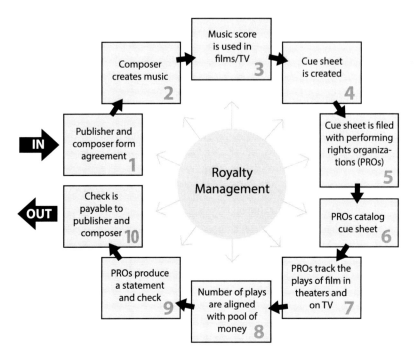

7.1. Royalty payments flowchart (adapted from Simon 2013).

jobs. Newman thinks that royalties from streaming have slowly gotten somewhat better but are still not at the level of network television. Also, he said, ASCAP and BMI have become more aware of the payment discrepancy between network television and streaming services. But composers are still frustrated that streaming services do not disclose how many streams a film or episode receives, unlike in television, where Nielsen ratings track viewers. Composers have no way of knowing if their film or show is on a streaming service, which affects ratings.[81]

Paying Everyone Else

Now let me look at how music workers after the composer are paid. Most, of course, are part of the package deal given to composers, so they feel the restrictions of smaller budgets every bit as much as the composers. Composers who require live musicians frequently engage a music contractor, who is in charge of finding musicians who play particular instruments.

Contractor Dan Savant told me how the money works from his perspective. Budgets vary greatly, as we have seen. A recent film he worked on had a budget of $450,000 for five days of recording, an amount that included the musicians, studio, recording engineer, orchestration, music copying, everyone. He was told that the maximum for music was $400,000, so he massaged the budget down to four days of recording with fewer musicians. Right after that, Savant received a call from someone who wanted a similar score (same number of musicians, roughly the same number of minutes of music) for another film, so he quoted the $450,000 figure, assuming he would be told that the budget was lower. The client had a fit, Savant said, so he inquired about their budget, which turned out to be $150,000. Savant said that the $450,000 figure did not include the artistic fee for the composer but that the $150,000 figure had to include that fee. This precipitated a discussion about hiring union versus nonunion musicians (the latter being cheaper). Savant is supportive of the union, so trying to keep jobs in the union while pleasing his client takes a lot of negotiation and compromise. And he feels he has to try to talk filmmakers out of recording abroad to save money, arguing that the performance standards aren't as high.[82]

For some workers, there is a fairly set fee, though this is negotiable. Orchestrator David Krystal said that people in his field are paid by the page (which is based on the tempo of the music), that $80 is standard in Los Angeles, per the union, but that this figure can go up or down depending on the budget or if it is a television program, which pays less. Before the orchestration is complete, orchestrators give an estimate of the number of pages. Krystal said the more established people can command a higher price, and some composer clients will insist on hiring their favorite orchestrator.[83]

The problem composers face of people willing to work for little or no pay exists for music editors as well, though, unlike the composers, who no longer have a union, music editors are unionized. Nonetheless, a good deal of nonunion work is being done. "I've done nonunion work where they will say, 'This is the budget; take it or leave it,'" David Craig Pettigrew told me. "And sometimes you take it, sometimes you leave it." Pettigrew understands how a young composer can be taken advantage of to write a score for little or nothing, but they can't do that with music editors due to their union; instead, they tell the composer they can't afford to hire a music editor and so the composer will have to do that task as well.

A useful and comprehensive trade press article by Richard Kraft from 2013 details the sorts of costs involved in recording in Los Angeles compared to in London and Seattle, and it is clear that the main difference concerns these back-end expenses. Kraft (2013a) begins by noting that, according to the American Federation of Musicians (AFM), the number of films recorded using their members dropped 43 percent from 2003 to 2012. The costs of the recording process alone are quite divergent, hugely different: Recording in Los Angeles, in Kraft's hypothetical, costs 31 percent more than in London but more than twice as much as in Seattle. Los Angeles does have some things going for it, mainly, travel expenses; those members of the production crew who would need to travel to London or Seattle can remain in Los Angeles. This means that recording in Los Angeles costs about the same as in London but is almost twice as much as in Seattle. Kraft (2013a, 8) thinks that Los Angeles is thus reasonably competitive on up-front costs (musicians, contracting, conductor, librarian, studio rental, cartage, music prep, travel, and mixing) under conditions where there is a lot of travel and "high orchestration rates" outside of Los Angeles.

The real difference is the back end, which Kraft also calculates. In London and Seattle, there are "buyouts" in which musicians are not paid for future uses of their recording, unlike in Los Angeles, where the back end is paid (as on a soundtrack album and other licensed uses as well as on DVDs, television, cable, or streaming airings); in Kraft's hypothetical, this can be as much as $1.8 million (Kraft 2013a, 8). Add the back end to the up front and, even subtracting travel costs for Los Angeles recordings, the differences are substantial: Recording in Los Angeles can cost as much as $2.1 million as compared to a maximum of about $331,000 in London and $246,000 in Seattle (Kraft 2013a, 9).

Conclusions

The decline in budgets, in part through the block grant strategy of providing less while expecting (nonunionized) composers to do more, the transformation of composers into managers, and the outsourcing of instrumentalists' jobs all speak to the neoliberalization of these fields of cultural production since the 1970s. The composers interviewed for this book told me that their work now requires more effort and is more stressful, especially if they go over budget, in which case they must make up the difference out of their own pockets (see Muddiman 2019).

The neoliberalization of these businesses is perhaps nowhere better demonstrated than in the fact of increased competition. Although there may be more jobs as a result of the boom in streaming services, such services don't necessarily pay as well, and there is no guarantee of a back end as in network television. And almost everyone is willing to work for nothing, or very little, in order to get a foot in the door. But the rise of teams of composers supervised by a brand-name composer has also meant that a few composers are still doing extremely well. David Schwartz's point about how more and more of the money in film and television is going to the top is as accurate as when he made it, though "the top" also includes a few star composers and instrumentalists. As composer Anne-Kathrin Dern said in her critique of the Los Angeles chapter of the American Federation of Musicians, the union protects the top two hundred players while everyone else struggles.[84]

"THOUSANDS OF GUYS LIKE ME"

One of the goals of this book has been simply to show what these largely unknown music workers do. I have, for the most part, deliberately stayed away from the most famous composers (not that I would have had access to most of them anyway) because I am interested in the work of these everyday musicians. What do these "thousands of guys like me," as composer Christopher Wong referred to himself in the previous chapter, actually do?[1] What are the roles of the other people in these businesses? This alone, I hope, is a salutary contribution of *Working Musicians*.

I think no interview summed up the current state of affairs better than that with an LA-based composer, which captures all of the decisions made about money in today's world of film and television production.[2] The composer spoke of attending a recording session for *Mad Men*, where he heard that the composer (David Carbonara) had lost money during the first year of the show because they weren't recording anything with union musicians and he had to cover the cost of his orchestrations. And instead of paying for a thirty-piece orchestra, the producers had him triple-track a ten-piece orchestra (hiring ten people to play three times)—even though *Mad Men* was a huge hit. According to a *Los Angeles Times* article, Carbonara received $7,000–$13,000 per episode, but because it was a package deal, he didn't make enough to support his family (Verrier 2009). The producers evidently felt that their money was better spent elsewhere "I read last week they spent $250,000 to license a Beatles song on one episode," the composer told me. "They'll spend a quarter of a million dollars for one song but don't think, 'Why not have a forty-piece orchestra for our original score?'"

This composer said it's the same in the world of advertising:

They'll drop six figures routinely for a pop song to use in advertising, but the budgets for composed music in advertising are rarely great anymore. You get those calls nowadays—this is something new in the past couple of years. They'll say things like, "Oh, there's no demo budget, but if you have some ideas for the spot, we'd love to hear them." What? They don't want to spend. I don't know how much that is routine or if I have just run into those particular producers, but these are the same people you see fly in and stay at Shutters on the Beach [an extremely expensive hotel]. So, you say, "Really? You're not even paying demo fees? You have four people flown in here to mix a thirty-second commercial when we could just email you the thing and you could give us notes." I guess it's a value judgment.[3]

Profligacy at the top, parsimony everywhere else.

The current uncertainty about the future of broadcast television, cable, and streaming is another stressor for today's musicians. Everyone is sure that the current model—proliferating streaming services that listeners pay for individually—won't last, but no one is sure which streaming services will emerge on top, when cable channels will cease or cease to be offered by particular providers, or what will happen with the old broadcast networks. Worries over the loss of the back end, even with a more lucrative front end, further increase precarity, and anxieties.

To address these and other issues considered in this book, I have sought to construct a theoretical framework that gets to larger questions about how group production in these fields of cultural production operates in today's neoliberal capitalism, endeavoring, after Max Horkheimer and Theodor Adorno, to learn what the cultural businesses can tell us about our capitalism and how it relies on existing structures of patriarchy. These workers are engaged in cultural production—sometimes emanating from their own heads (with input from bosses), as is the case for composers—and sometimes working in much more technical ways as part of a supply chain, which means a good deal of working alone in a windowless room.

We already knew that capitalism is endlessly adaptable; as a social form, it could hardly be otherwise. What is striking, however, is the extent to which periods of stasis can last for quite some time, but then a small trigger can alter any form of production. Triggers can be technological, as with the rise of digital technologies; structural, as in the way that the advent of package deals to composers turned some composers into capitalist entrepreneur-managers of teams of composers; they can be social, registering shifts in the social world as with the entrance of more women into these fields and the desire of many long-term participants to find a better work-life balance than the business has countenanced in the past. Some triggers can have complex effects, as with digital technologies, since they have also made it possible for people to enter the business without having spent many thousands of dollars on equipment and formal training, thus facilitating working at home. And new technologies can transform forms of cultural (or other) production that were once capitalist into artisanal forms, as with photography and painting and, more recently, digital photography vis-à-vis film photography.[4]

Nineteenth-century conceptions of creativity as a faculty of men akin to nature itself persist in the cultural businesses, but composers' creative freedom is subordinated to that of the directors and producers, and whatever is culturally thought to be feminine about those permitted to be considered as creative (such qualities as moodiness, impetuousness) is removed as music moves through its supply chain, which introduces refinements and rationalizations. Composers' work is viewed as a kind of natural resource that is accumulated by dispossession, composers having been paid a fee but largely forbidden from owning the copyrights of their music, which has been a major issue for decades and was the main reason the composers' union, the Composers and Lyricists Guild of America, sued the Producers Guild of America, only to witness the demise of the union in 1982 after a bitter decade-long struggle.

Once the composer's labor is acquired, their music enters one of two supply chains: the first, analog (from composer to orchestrator to copyist to contractor to performer to recording engineer); the second, a digital supply chain that also starts with the composer and moves to a scoring mixer and music editor. These chains intersect with the product of the recording engineer's labor, which also goes to a mixer and music editor. Value is created at every step, as we know from the indispensable work of Anna Tsing (2015 especially).

This accretion of value is mainly a question of fitting the music to picture or, rather, fitting it to the idea of the picture that directors and producers articulate to those before them in the supply chain. It is they who are permitted, in this complex system of the management of creative freedom, to decide what use-value is, with the ultimate goal, of course, of realizing surplus-value for studios or networks or game manufacturers. It may be, as Horkheimer and Adorno said, that the capitalist owners of cultural businesses are more intent on realizing exchange-value than anything else, but as we know from Marx, use-value and exchange-value must be viewed dialectically: One doesn't exist without the other. In focusing on the production of use-value in this book, I have not been tacitly assuming that exchange-value is less important than use-value in an attempt to swing the pendulum away from Horkheimer and Adorno. I have focused on a relatively small supply chain that produces use-values for bosses and, they hope, viewers.

Group production complicates identifying, articulating, and advocating for particular workers' conceptions of use-values in every project. This can be a cause of immense frustration for music workers, especially composers, who frequently must deal with producers and directors who don't know musical terminology, or whose grasp of it is tenuous, or whose possession of some musical knowledge is more an impediment to communication than a facilitator. It is through composers' encounters with their bosses, bosses' encounters with studio music workers, and still others that use-values are carved out, compromised, agreed upon.

But use-values aren't produced without labor, in this case, the labor of many musicians with high levels of skill and expertise. So let me conclude, at last, with a final iteration about what these musicians emphasized over and over, whether or not I asked: They just want to be able to make a living doing their work, a desire that is increasingly difficult to realize as music budgets continue to shrink while the proliferating bosses profit.

There is no easy way to reform a system that depends on the dreams of young musicians hoping for fame and fortune who are willing to exploit themselves. I think I thus might prefer to turn my attention toward what many of these musicians are already doing, finding and making value in Tsing's "pericapitalist" places from where capitalism has come and gone, or never deigned to visit (2015). I would listen to Jan Stevens's ethereal and seductive music he wrote to accompany yoga practice, Joey Newman's killer rock band with his father as the lead singer, Stu Phillips's orchestrations of Sergei Rachmaninoff's piano etudes and preludes he produces just for fun, Sharon Farber's and Christopher Wong's concert music, Penka Kouneva's orchestral compositions in the name of bygone women composers who never had a chance. Neoliberal capitalists have no interest in these profit-less endeavors—this music is silent to them.

Introduction

1   See also the chapter "Culture Industry Reconsidered" in Adorno 1991.

2   Ben Decter lecture at UCLA, March 13, 2017.

3   There is now an abundant literature about the precarity of workers in the arts fields, including classical music (see Ritchey 2019), though more visibly to most people in the realm of popular music (see, for just a few examples, Hesmondhalgh and Baker 2011; Sakakeeny 2015; and Umney and Kretsos 2015).

4   Gergely Hubai (2012) has compiled many of these stories in a book examining the phenomenon of the replacement score.

5   See Negus and Pickering 2004 for a discussion of creativity and commerce in the media industries.

6   For studies of the music itself, see Burlingame 1996; Deaville 2011; and Rodman 2010 on television; Cooke 2008; Prendergast 1992; and Wierzbicki 2009 on film; and Cheng 2014 and Miller 2012 on games.

7   Bruce Broughton interview by the author, Los Angeles, July 31, 2013.

8   Christopher Wong interview by the author, Los Angeles, July 20, 2012.

9   The Internet Movie Database lists eleven credited orchestrators for *King Kong*, plus one more uncredited.

10   A trade press article (Rodd 2011) offers advice on how to build one's own studio.

11   For useful studies of music in other global film industries, see, among others, Booth 2008; Morcom 2007; and Slobin 2008.

Chapter 1. Group Production, the Collective Laborer, Supply Chains, and Fields

1   Thanks are due to Anna Morcom for recommending the Prasad book.

2   Paul Dwyer rehearses the writings of those who have argued for different historical modes of media production (Christopherson and Storper 1986; Storper and Christopherson 1987, 1989; Storper 1989, 1993), an earlier one that was more Fordist and a more recent one that is more flexible (Caldwell 2008). Dwyer offers a critique of those authors who view film and television production as a form of Fordist production (including Staiger in Bordwell, Staiger,

and Thompson 1985) through a comparison with actual Fordist production, a Ford factory in Michigan, concluding that the sort of standardization possible in industrial manufacturing is not the same sort achieved in media production. According to Dwyer (2015, 992), industrial standardization results in "absolute and measurable uniform parts and products," whereas Bordwell, Staiger, and Thompson as well as Storper and Christopherson employ "standardization" in media production "to describe subjective, stylistic similarities among unique products." In this, of course, they follow Horkheimer and Adorno, whose indictment of the culture industry rests in large part on the assumption that all of its products are standardized, the same. Dwyer points out that, since in film production the end product is unique and not standard, there was no possibility of creating an assembly line mode of production. Dwyer explores other ways of characterizing media production, the theory of "flexible specialization" (Piore and Sabel 1984) and of post-Fordism (Murray 1987). Both theories assumed a market saturation of like products, necessitating abandoning the manufacture of standardized products through reliance on flexible production systems.

3   For a rare writing on a musician, see Bourdieu 2001.

4   On television, see Newcomb and Alley 1983; on film, see Caldwell 2008 and Ortner 2013.

5   See, at least, Duménil and Lévy 2003 and 2018 for recent treatments and Ehrenreich and Ehrenreich 1979 for a classic one.

6   I will discuss the demise of the Composers and Lyricists Guild of America at greater length in Taylor n.d.b.

7   Oren Hadar interview by the author, Los Angeles, August 24, 2017.

8   The trade press occasionally offers advice about networking, e.g., Kimpel 2006.

9   See Anderson 2014 for a discussion of social capital among popular musicians in the recording business.

10   Ben Decter interview by the author, Los Angeles, July 2, 2012.

11   Zach Robinson interview by the author, Los Angeles, October 3, 2017.

12   Joey Newman interview by the author, Los Angeles, July 31, 2017.

13   Alan Meyerson interview by the author, Santa Monica, CA, September 21, 2017.

14   Michael Stern interview by the author, Calabasas, CA, August 24, 2012.

15   "Flora" interview by the author, Santa Monica, CA, July 19, 2012.

16   Andrés Locsey interview by the author, Highland Park, CA, July 7, 2018.

17   Tom Calderaro interview by the author, Los Angeles, November 12, 2012.

18   Miriam Mayer, interview by the author, Calabasas, CA, July 12, 2019.

19   Calderaro interview 2012.

20   Jan Stevens interview by the author, Los Angeles, August 29, 2011. Persistence and the maintenance of one's network are points emphasized in some of the how-to guides for composers, such as Rona 2000.

21   Robinson interview 2017.

22   Edward Trybek interview by the author, Pasadena, CA, October 16, 2018.

23   Kurt Farquhar telephone interview by the author, March 19, 2020.

24   Trybek interview 2018.

25   Craig Pettigrew interview by the author, Studio City, CA, August 27, 2012.

26   Ryan Shore interview by the author, Burbank, CA, August 23, 2017.

27   Stevens interview 2011.

28   Matt Hutchinson interview by the author, Los Angeles, July 6, 2018.

29   Mayer interview 2019.

30   Phil McGowan interview by the author, Beverly Hills, CA, August 21, 2018.

31   Hutchinson interview 2018.

32   Newman interview 2017.

33   Hutchinson interview 2018.

34   Deborah Lurie interview by the author, Studio City, CA, October 18, 2018.

35   Kamran Pasha interview by the author, Los Angeles, July 10, 2019.

36   Pasha interview 2019; see Crucchiola 2019 for a breakdown of the issues.

Chapter 2. Creativity

1   Michael L. Siciliano (2021) raises somewhat similar questions though writes from the perspective of the sociology of work, which is not my orientation here.

2   See *Paul Simon: Born at the Right Time* (1993), directed by Susan Lacy and Susan Steinberg.

3   See also Sherry B. Ortner's classic "Is Female to Male as Nature Is to Culture?," collected in Ortner 1996.

4   See Born 2005b for a different treatment of the distribution of creative agency.

5   Harvey Myman interview by the author, Los Angeles, September 19, 2019.

6   Kamran Pasha interview by the author, Los Angeles, July 10, 2019.

7   Alf Clausen interview by Adrienne Faillace, Television Academy Interviews, November 25, 2014, https://interviews.televisionacademy.com.

8   Pasha interview 2019.

9   Pasha interview 2019.

10   Miriam Mayer interview by the author, Calabasas, CA, July 12, 2019.

11   Sharon Farber interview by the author, Granada Hills, CA, July 30, 2012.

12   Matt Hutchinson interview by the author, Los Angeles, July 6, 2018.

13   Mike Post telephone interview by the author, October 12, 2021.

14   Post telephone interview 2021.

15   David Schwartz interview by the author, Pacific Palisades, CA, July 31, 2012. Upon reviewing his interview quotations for this book, Schwartz said that he might have said some things differently compared to his initial interview.

16 Schwartz interview 2012.

17 Hutchinson interview 2018.

18 Joey Newman interview by the author, Los Angeles, July 31, 2017.

19 Ben Decter lecture at UCLA, March 13, 2017.

20 Decter lecture at UCLA 2017.

21 Anne-Kathrin Dern interview by the author, Marina del Rey, CA, October 9, 2018.

22 Schwartz interview 2012.

23 John Nordstrom interview by the author, Santa Monica, CA, June 11, 2012.

24 Christopher Wong interview by the author, Los Angeles, July 20, 2012.

25 Kurt Farquhar telephone interview by the author, March 19, 2020.

26 Hutchinson interview 2018.

27 Ryan Shore interview by the author, Burbank, CA, August 23, 2017.

28 Dern interview 2018.

29 Bruce Broughton interview by the author, Los Angeles, July 31, 2013.

30 Lalo Schifrin interview by the author, Beverly Hills, CA, October 17, 2017.

31 See *Score: A Film Music Documentary* (2016), directed by Matt Schrader.

32 Tom Calderaro interview by the author, Los Angeles, November 12, 2012.

33 Wong interview 2012.

34 Calderaro interview 2012.

35 Craig Pettigrew interview by the author, Studio City, CA, August 27, 2012.

36 "Barry" interview by the author, Burbank, CA, August 6, 2012.

37 Kevin Crehan Zoom interview by the author, November 26, 2021.

38 Crehan interview 2021.

39 Newman interview 2017.

40 Cindy O'Connor interview by the author, Long Beach, CA, October 28, 2018.

41 Penka Kouneva interview by the author, Encino, CA, November 12, 2018.

42 Broughton interview 2013.

43 Schwartz interview 2012.

44 Farber interview 2012.

45 Calderaro interview 2012.

46 Calderaro interview 2012.

47 Edward Trybek interview by the author, Pasadena, CA, October 16, 2018.

48 Trybek interview 2018.

49 Alan Meyerson interview by the author, Santa Monica, CA, September 21, 2017.

50 Dan Savant interview by the author, Glendale, CA, September 6, 2012.

51 Phil McGowan interview by the author, Beverly Hills, CA, August 21, 2018.

52 McGowan interview 2018.

53 McGowan interview 2018.

54 Meyerson interview 2017.

55 Oren Hadar interview by the author, Los Angeles, August 24, 2017.

56 Andrés Locsey interview by the author, Highland Park, CA, July 7, 2018.

57   Calderaro interview 2012.

58   "Flora" interview by the author, Santa Monica, CA, July 19, 2012.

59   Newman interview 2017.

60   Newman interview 2017.

61   See Wierzbicki 2019 for a study of film music composers who have crossed over into the concert hall.

62   Farber interview 2012.

63   Wong interview 2012.

64   Kouneva interview 2018.

65   Stu Phillips interview by the author, Los Angeles, September 16, 2013.

Chapter 3. Composers' Labor

1   Randy Newman R. U. Nelson Lecture, UCLA, March 24, 2021 (Zoom).

2   Genre typecasting goes back at least a few decades; see Ainis 1989.

3   Robert Kraft telephone interview by the author, September 19, 2019.

4   Kraft interview 2019.

5   Kraft interview 2019.

6   Lee Holdridge interview by the author, Los Angeles, August 31, 2021.

7   These skills are listed on the Berklee website. https://www.berklee.edu/film-scoring/bachelor-of-music-in-film-scoring.

8   "Flora" interview by the author, Santa Monica, CA, July 19, 2012.

9   Andrés Locsey interview by the author, Highland Park, CA, July 7, 2018.

10   Ryan Shore interview by the author, Burbank, CA, August 23, 2017.

11   Kurt Farquhar telephone interview by the author, March 19, 2020.

12   Jan Stevens interview by the author, Los Angeles, August 29, 2011.

13   Penka Kouneva interview by the author, Encino, CA, November 12, 2018.

14   Stevens interview 2011.

15   Kraft interview 2019.

16   Kraft interview 2019.

17   Kevin Crehan Zoom interview by the author, November 26, 2021.

18   Ben Decter interview by the author, Los Angeles, July 2, 2012.

19   John Debney interview by Jon Burlingame, August 1, 2017. https://interviews.televisionacademy.com.

20   Stevens interview 2011.

21   Alan Elliott lecture at UCLA, May 29, 2013.

22   For more on Post's working methods, see Fink 1998 and Barth 2011.

23   Decter interview 2012.

24   Mike Post telephone interview by the author, October 12, 2021.

25   Debney interview by Burlingame 2017.

26   Decter interview 2012. For an account of working with Post by someone who predates Decter, see Barth 2015.

27   Post interview 2021.

28   "Flora" interview 2012.

29   Joey Newman telephone interview by the author, July 2, 2020.

30   Tom Calderaro interview by the author, Los Angeles, November 12, 2012.

31   Calderaro interview 2012.

32   Deborah Lurie interview by the author, Studio City, CA, October 18, 2018.

33   Calderaro interview 2012.

34   Lurie interview 2018.

35   Newman interview 2020.

36   Joey Newman interview by the author, Los Angeles, July 31, 2017.

37   Zach Robinson interview by the author, Los Angeles, October 3, 2017.

38   Robinson interview 2017.

39   "Shawn" interview by the author, 2017. A 2017 issue of *The Score*, a publica-
     tion of the Society of Composers and Lyricists, includes an editorial by the
     society's president criticizing, obliquely, the exploitation of composers
     (Irwin 2017).

40   Robinson interview 2017.

41   Robinson interview 2017.

42   Alex Hackford Skype interview by the author, October 6, 2017.

43   Hackford interview 2017.

44   Shore interview 2017.

45   Kouneva interview 2018.

46   Kouneva interview 2018.

47   Lurie interview 2018.

48   Lurie interview 2018.

49   Matt Hutchinson interview by the author, Los Angeles, July 6, 2018.

50   Everyone I spoke to discussed this as a recent trend, but it was already un-
     derway in the 1970s, part of a strategy of studios making deals with music
     publishers and record labels; see Skiles 1976 and, especially, Smith 1998.

51   Shore interview 2017.

52   Hutchinson 2018. For more on composing for advertising, see Taylor 2012.

53   Kraft interview 2019.

54   Alan Meyerson interview by the author, Santa Monica, CA, September 21,
     2017.

55   "Flora" interview 2012.

56   "Flora" interview 2012.

57   David Krystal interview by the author, Los Angeles, September 17, 2018.

58   Edward Trybek interview by the author, Pasadena, CA, October 16, 2018.

59   Calderaro interview 2012.

60   Hutchinson interview 2018.

61   Shore interview 2017.

62   Robinson interview 2017.

63   Trent Reznor telephone interview by the author, April 23, 2020.

64 Reznor interview 2020.

65 Kurt Farquhar telephone interview by the author, March 19, 2020. For more on the paucity of African Americans and women in film and television, see Vaughn 1990.

66 Farquhar interview 2020.

67 Farquhar interview 2020.

68 Farquhar interview 2020.

69 Farquhar interview 2020.

70 Farquhar interview 2020.

71 Newman interview 2017.

72 Stu Phillips interview by the author, Los Angeles, September 16, 2013.

73 Newman interview 2017.

74 Newman interview 2017.

75 Decter interview 2012.

76 Farquhar interview 2020. Reality series on network channels pay well because they generate royalties (see Matthews 2015); for a discussion of reality television music, see Bond 2004.

77 Farquhar interview 2020.

Chapter 4. The Music Supply Chain after the Composer

1   David Krystal interview by the author, Los Angeles, September 17, 2018.

2   Edward Trybek interview by the author, Pasadena, CA, October 16, 2018.

3   Trybek's team, known as Tutti Music Partners, is profiled in Romanelli 2020.

4   Trybek interview 2018.

5   Krystal interview 2018.

6   Andrés Locsey interview by the author, Highland Park, CA, July 7, 2018.

7   Trybek interview 2018.

8   Alf Clausen interview by Adrienne Faillace, Television Academy Interviews, November 25, 2014, https://interviews.televisionacademy.com.

9   "Barry" interview by the author, Burbank, CA, August 6, 2012; see also Borum 2017.

10 "Barry" interview 2012.

11 Dan Savant interview by the author, Glendale, CA, September 6, 2012.

12 Jeff Bunnell interview by the author, Woodland Hills, CA, June 28, 2012.

13 Bunnell interview 2012.

14 It's hard to convey what playing "musically" means to nonmusicians, but it is the term musicians employ to describe playing or singing that is not mechanical, playing or singing that is expressive but in keeping with whatever style the music being performed is in and showing understanding of that style, performing in a way that doesn't draw attention to the performer,

but attempts to honor the composer's conception of the work to the best abilities and knowledge of the performer. There is a good deal of space for individual conceptions of musicality; thus, music lovers frequently disagree over whether or not a particular musician or performance is musical.

15 Bunnell interview 2012.
16 Carol Kaye telephone interview by the author, October 17, 2018.
17 Terry Wollman interview by the author, Los Angeles, June 8, 2012.
18 Christopher Wong personal communication with the author, March 20, 2022.
19 Alan Meyerson interview by the author, Santa Monica, CA, September 21, 2017.
20 Oren Hadar interview by the author, Los Angeles, August 24, 2017.
21 Kevin Crehan Zoom interview by the author, November 26, 2021.
22 Meyerson interview 2017.
23 Hadar interview 2017.
24 Hadar interview 2017.
25 Savant interview 2012.
26 Hadar interview 2017.
27 Hadar interview 2017.
28 Hadar interview 2017.
29 Locsey interview 2018.
30 Locsey interview 2018.
31 Craig Pettigrew interview by the author, Studio City, CA, August 27, 2012.
32 Pettigrew interview 2012.
33 Crehan interview 2021.
34 Locsey interview 2018.
35 Locsey interview 2018.
36 Pettigrew interview 2012.

Chapter 5. Challenges

1   Joey Newman telephone interview by the author, July 2, 2020.
2   Miriam Mayer interview by the author, Calabasas, CA, July 12, 2019.
3   Penka Kouneva interview by the author, Encino, CA, November 12, 2018.
4   Joey Newman interview by the author, Los Angeles, July 31, 2017.
5   John Nordstrom interview by the author, Santa Monica, CA, June 11, 2012.
6   Newman interview 2017.
7   Ryan Shore interview by the author, Burbank, CA, August 23, 2017.
8   "Adam" interview by the author, 2017.
9   Shore interview 2017.
10 Shore interview 2017.
11 Zach Robinson interview by the author, Los Angeles, October 3, 2017.

12   Newman interview 2020.

13   Kouneva interview 2018.

14   Tom Calderaro interview by the author, Los Angeles, November 12, 2012.
      The film was probably *Mission: Impossible* (1996), which is discussed by
      Gergely Hubai (2012), who says it was the director, Brian De Palma, who
      didn't approve of the music, believing that Cruise wouldn't like it. Hubai
      says that Cruise's then-wife, Nicole Kidman, recommended Danny Elfman
      as a replacement for Alan Silvestri.

15   Matt Hutchinson interview by the author, Los Angeles, July 6, 2018.

16   Jan Stevens interview by the author, Los Angeles, August 29, 2011.

17   David Schwartz interview by the author, Pacific Palisades, CA, July 31, 2012.

18   Deborah Lurie Zoom interview by the author, March 17, 2022.

19   Phil McGowan interview by the author, Beverly Hills, CA, August 21, 2018.

20   Andrés Locsey interview by the author, Highland Park, CA, July 7, 2018.

21   Locsey interview 2018.

22   Oren Hadar interview by the author, Los Angeles, August 24, 2017.

23   Alan Meyerson interview by the author, Santa Monica, CA, September 21,
      2017.

24   Meyerson interview 2017.

25   Hutchinson interview 2018.

26   Mike Post telephone interview by the author, October 12, 2021.

27   Post interview 2021.

28   Hutchinson interview 2018.

29   Mayer interview 2019.

30   Stevens interview 2011.

31   Newman interview 2017.

32   Meyerson interview 2017.

33   Lurie Zoom interview 2022.

34   Deborah Lurie interview by the author, Studio City, CA, October 18, 2018.

35   Robert Kraft telephone interview by author, September 19, 2019.

36   Kraft interview 2019.

37   Stevens interview 2011.

38   Schwartz interview 2012.

39   Schwartz interview 2012.

Chapter 6. It's a Man's, Man's, Man's, Man's World

1   Penka Kouneva interview by the author, Encino, CA, November12, 2018.

2   "Renée" interview by the author, 2108; see also Greiving 2009.

3   Nan Schwartz interview by the author, Los Angeles, September 17, 2021.

4   Zach Robinson interview by the author, Los Angeles, October 3, 2017.

5   John Nordstrom interview by the author, Santa Monica, CA, June 11, 2012.

6   Matt Hutchinson interview by the author, Los Angeles, July 6, 2018.

7   Hutchinson interview 2018.

8   Jan Stevens interview by the author, Los Angeles, August 29, 2011.

9   Tom Calderaro interview by the author, Los Angeles, November 12, 2012.

10 Michael Stern interview by the author, Calabasas, CA, August 24, 2012.

11 Alan Meyerson interview by the author, Santa Monica, CA, September 21, 2017.

12 Ryan Shore interview by the author, Burbank, CA, August 23, 2017.

13 Anne-Kathrin Dern interview by the author, Marina del Rey, CA, October 9, 2018.

14 Joey Newman interview by the author, Los Angeles, July 31, 2017.

15 Newman interview 2017. Newman and other composers discuss parenting and working in Kowal 2014; see also Borum 2011.

16 Robinson interview 2017.

17 Oren Hadar interview by the author, Los Angeles, August 24, 2017.

18 Shore interview 2017.

19 Edward Trybek interview by the author, Pasadena, CA, October 16, 2018.

20 Dern interview 2018.

21 Andrés Locsey interview by the author, Highland Park, CA, July 7, 2018.

22 Kouneva interview 2018.

23 Alf Clausen interview by Adrienne Faillace, Television Academy Interviews, November 25, 2014, https://interviews.televisionacademy.com.

24 Sharon Farber interview by the author, Granada Hills, CA, July 30, 2012.

25 Farber interview 2012.

26 Shore interview 2017.

27 Joey Newman interview 2017.

28 Michael Stern interview by the author, Calabasas, CA, August 24, 2012.

29 Miriam Mayer interview by the author, Calabasas, CA, July 12, 2019.

30 Dern interview 2018.

31 For an appreciation of Walker by other women composers, see Dunn et al. 2007.

32 Cindy O'Connor interview by the author, Long Beach, CA, October 28, 2018.

33 Nan Schwartz interview by the author, Los Angeles, September 17, 2021.

34 Farber interview 2012.

35 "Renée" interview, 2018.

36 Sharon Farber personal communication with the author, April 22, 2022.

37 Farber interview 2012.

38 Mayer interview 2019.

39 Mayer interview 2019.

40 Dern interview 2018.

41 Farber interview 2012.

42 Farber interview 2012.

43 Dern interview 2018.

44   Dern interview 2018.

45   Dern interview 2018.

46   Dern interview 2018.

47   Farber interview 2012.

48   Farber interview 2012.

49   Dern interview 2018.

50   "Renée" interview 2018.

51   Kouneva interview 2018.

52   Penka Kouneva, *The Rebirth of Id* (Los Angeles: Varèse Sarabande, 2017), UPC
      03020675508 4.

53   Kouneva, *Rebirth of Id*, liner notes.

54   Anne-Kathrin Dern, personal communication with the author, May 11, 2022.

Chapter 7. Neoliberalization as (Self-)Exploitation

1   In addition to the scholarship already cited, see Boltanski and Chiapello
      2005; Bourdieu 1998, 2003; Brown 2005, 2015; Duménil and Lévy 2004,
      2011, 2018; Foucault 2008; Harvey 2005; Piketty 2014, 2020; Sanyal 2013;
      Sennett 2006; Stedman Jones 2012; and Streeck 2020, among others.

2   Earle Hagen interview by Jon Burlingame, Television Academy Interviews,
      November 17, 1997, https://interviews.televisionacademy.com.

3   For more on exploitation in media industries, see Hesmondhalgh 2017.

4   Bruce Broughton interview by the author, Los Angeles, July 31, 2013.

5   Kevin Crehan Zoom interview by the author, November 26, 2021.

6   Broughton interview 2013.

7   Christopher Wong interview by the author, Los Angeles, July 20, 2012.

8   Broughton interview 2013.

9   John Nordstrom interview by the author, Santa Monica, CA, June 11, 2012.

10   Dan Savant interview by the author, Glendale, CA, September 6, 2012.

11   Andrés Locsey interview by the author, Highland Park, CA, July 7, 2018. For
      more on recording in Bratislava, see Garcia 2004.

12   Locsey interview 2018.

13   Savant interview 2012.

14   I consider the American Federation of Musicians' reactions to new digital
      technologies in Taylor n.d.b.

15   Ben Decter interview by the author, Los Angeles, July 2, 2012.

16   Broughton interview 2013.

17   Wong interview 2012.

18   Christopher Wong personal communication with the author, March 20, 2022.

19   "Barry" interview by the author, Burbank, CA, August 6, 2012.

20   Carol Kaye telephone interview by the author, October 17, 2018.

21   Jeff Bunnell interview by the author, Woodland Hills, CA, June 28, 2012.

22   Bunnell interview 2012.
23   Anne-Kathrin Dern, interview by the author, Marina del Rey, CA, October 9,
      2018.
24   Dern interview 2018.
25   Michael Stern interview by the author, Calabasas, CA, August 24, 2012.
26   Stern interview 2012.
27   Stern interview 2012.
28   Terry Wollman interview by the author, Los Angeles, June 8, 2012.
29   Wollman interview 2012.
30   David Schwartz interview by the author, Pacific Palisades, CA, July 31, 2012.
31   Decter interview 2012.
32   For more on production music, see Grey 2015.
33   Schwartz interview 2012.
34   Deborah Lurie interview by the author, Studio City, CA, October 18, 2018.
35   "Drew" interview by the author, 2021.
36   Schwartz interview 2012.
37   Craig Pettigrew interview by the author, Studio City, CA, August 27, 2012.
38   Broughton interview 2013. Broughton told Jeremy Borum that the fee
      when he was at CBS (1967–77) was $2,000 per one-hour episode and that
      the other studios could pay as much as $2,500 per one-hour episode; in-
      dependent studios would be around $1,800 (Borum 2015a, xvii). In 1967
      dollars, $2,000 would be worth over $15,000 today.
39   Broughton recently told me that, since our 2013 interview, it's less clear how
      people are paid today, except that it's mostly done as a complete package deal.
      Bruce Broughton personal communication with the author, March 15, 2022.
40   Broughton interview 2013.
41   Harvey Myman interview by the author, Los Angeles, September 19, 2019.
42   Robert Kraft, telephone interview by the author, September 19, 2019.
43   See also Earle Hagen interview by Jon Burlingame, November 17, 1997,
      https://interviews.televisionacademy.com; and "The Good, the Bad and the
      Ugly of Film Music Packaging" (2000).
44   Stu Phillips interview by the author, Los Angeles, September 16, 2013.
45   Phil McGowan interview by the author, Beverly Hills, CA, August 21, 2018.
46   McGowan interview 2018.
47   Alan Elliott lecture at UCLA, May 29, 2013; for more on the strike, see Bond 2010.
48   Mike Post telephone interview by the author, October 12, 2021.
49   This survey was conducted by *Film Music Magazine* and is now available
      here: https://www.yumpu.com/en/document/read/20838469/film-music
      -magazine-2010-composer-unionization-survey. The Film Institute's
      website announcing the survey results is here: https://filmmusicinstitute
      .com/fmm-survey-shows-strong-support-for-unionization-benefits-and
      -workplace-improvements-questions-about-teamsters/.
50   Schwartz interview 2012.

51   Schwartz interview 2012.

52   Decter interview 2012.

53   Cindy O'Connor interview by the author, Long Beach, CA, October 28, 2018.

54   Matt Hutchinson interview by the author, Los Angeles, July 6, 2018.

55   Ryan Shore interview by the author, Burbank, CA, August 23, 2017.

56   Joey Newman telephone interview by the author, July 2, 2020.

57   Stern interview 2012.

58   Kraft interview 2019.

59   Newman interview 2020.

60   Decter interview 2012.

61   Decter interview 2012.

62   For a good overview of how residuals work, see Sazer 2013.

63   Hutchinson interview 2018.

64   Pettigrew interview 2012.

65   Locsey interview 2018.

66   Wong interview 2012.

67   Lurie interview 2018.

68   "Renée" interview by the author, 2018.

69   Locsey interview 2018.

70   McGowan interview 2018.

71   Myman interview 2019.

72   Hutchinson interview 2018.

73   O'Connor interview 2018.

74   Shore interview 2017.

75   Deborah Lurie Zoom interview by the author, March 17, 2022.

76   O'Connor interview 2018.

77   Penka Kouneva interview by the author, Encino, CA, November 12, 2018.

78   This brief history is from Burlingame 2010. The Guild later re-formed as the Society of Composers and Lyricists but lacked the Guild's bargaining powers.

79   Broughton interview 2013; see Bond 2010.

80   Joey Newman interview by the author, Los Angeles, July 31, 2017.

81   Joey Newman personal communication with the author, April 22, 2022.

82   Savant interview 2012.

83   David Krystal interview by the author, Los Angeles, September 17, 2018.

84   Dern interview 2018.

Chapter 8. "Thousands of Guys like Me"

1   Christopher Wong interview by the author, Los Angeles, July 20, 2012.

2   "Hugh" interview by the author, 2012.

3   "Josh" interview by the author, 2012.

4   Thanks are due to my photographer cousin-in-law Jon Ortner for this last point.

Adams, Doug. 1999. "Sneaking a Peek at a Package Deal." *Film Score Monthly*, February, 15.

Adorno, Theodor. 1991. *The Culture Industry: Selected Essays on Mass Culture*. Edited by J. M. Bernstein. New York: Routledge.

Ainis, Jeffrey. 1989. "Film, TV and Music: Is It Love or Money?" *Hollywood Reporter*, August 29, S-5.

Alberti, Bob. 2003. *Up the Ladder and Over the Top: Memoirs of a Hollywood Studio Musician*. N.p.: Bob Alberti.

Anderson, Tim J. 2013. "From Background Music to Above-the-Line Actor: The Rise of the Music Supervisor in Converging Televisual Environments." *Journal of Popular Music Studies* 25, no. 3: 371–88.

Anderson, Tim J. 2014. *Popular Music in a Digital Music Economy: Problems and Practices for an Emerging Service Industry*. New York: Routledge.

Banks, Mark. 2010. "Craft Labour and Creative Industries." *International Journal of Cultural Policy* 16, no. 3: 305–21.

Barron, Frank. 1968. *Creativity and Personal Freedom*. Princeton, NJ: D. Van Nostrand.

Barth, Lori. 2002. "Package Deals: The Great Debate." *Score*, Fall, 1.

Barth, Lori. 2004. "Under the Gun." *Score*, Spring, 5–6.

Barth, Lori. 2007. "Alexandre Desplat: A Composer with No Boundaries." *Score*, Summer, 14–17.

Barth, Lori. 2011. "Up Close and Personal with Mike Post." *Score*, Summer, 17.

Barth, Lori. 2015. "Danny Lux: A Journey Forward." *Score*, Winter, 12–15.

Barth, Lori. 2017. "The Importance of the Music Contractor." *Score*, Winter, 1.

Battersby, Christine. 1989. *Gender and Genius: Towards a Feminist Aesthetics*. Bloomington: Indiana University Press.

Becker, Gary. (1964) 1994. *Human Capital: A Theoretical and Empirical Analysis with Special Reference to Education*. Chicago: University of Chicago Press.

Becker, Howard S. 1982. *Art Worlds*. Berkeley: University of California Press.

Bellis, Richard. 2006. *The Emerging Film Composer: An Introduction to the People, Problems and Psychology of the Film Music Business*. N.p.: Richard Bellis.

Benjamin, Walter. 1968. "The Work of Art in the Age of Mechanical Reproduction." In *Illuminations*, edited by Hannah Arendt, translated by Harry Zohn, 217–51. New York: Schocken.

Bernstein, Charles. 2019. "Rock Stars and Film Composers." *Score*, Spring, 7–8.

Boltanski, Luc, and Eve Chiapello. 2005. *The New Spirit of Capitalism*. Translated by David Elliott. New York: Verso.

Bond, Jeff. 2003a. "'Alias': Michael Giacchino." *Film Score Monthly*, July, 24–25.

Bond, Jeff. 2003b. "'Taken' with Her Music: Prolific Television Composer Laura Karpman Tackles Sci-Fi, Including an Online Videogame." *Film Score Monthly*, July, 30–31.

Bond, Jeff. 2004. "Getting Real." *Film Score Monthly*, July, 18–23.

Bond, Jeff. 2010. "Fight Club." *Hollywood Reporter*, January 12, 7–9.

Bonefeld, Werner. 2001. "The Permanence of Primitive Accumulation: Commodity Fetishism and Social Constitution." *Commoner*, issue 2 (September). https://thecommoner.org/back-issues/issue-02-september-2001/.

Booth, Gregory. 2008. *Behind the Curtain: Making Music in Mumbai's Film Studios*. New York: Oxford University Press.

Bordwell, David, Janet Staiger, and Kristin Thompson. 1985. *The Classical Hollywood Cinema: Film Style and Mode of Production to 1960*. New York: Columbia University Press.

Born, Georgina. 2005a. "On Musical Mediation: Ontology, Technology and Creativity." *Twentieth-Century Music* 2, no. 1: 7–36.

Born, Georgina. 2005b. *Uncertain Vision: Birt, Dyke and the Reinvention of the BBC*. New York: Vintage.

Borum, Jeremy. 2011. "A Question of Balance." *Score*, Spring, 1.

Borum, Jeremy. 2015a. *Guerrilla Film Scoring: Practical Advice from Hollywood Composers*. Lanham, MD: Rowman and Littlefield.

Borum, Jeremy. 2015b. "Team Building in an Indie World." *Score*, Winter, 1.

Borum, Jeremy. 2016. "Scoring the Next Gig." *Score*, Summer, 1.

Borum, Jeremy. 2017. "Sheet Music: The Map to Your Score." *Score*, Spring, 1.

Bourdieu, Pierre. 1984. *Distinction: A Social Critique of the Judgement of Taste*. Translated by Richard Nice. Cambridge, MA: Harvard University Press.

Bourdieu, Pierre. 1986. "The Forms of Capital." In *Handbook for Theory and Research for the Sociology of Education*, edited by John G. Richardson, 46–58. New York: Greenwood.

Bourdieu, Pierre. 1989. "Social Space and Symbolic Power." *Sociological Theory* 7, no. 1: 14–25.

Bourdieu, Pierre. 1990. *The Logic of Practice*. Translated by Richard Nice. Stanford, CA: Stanford University Press.

Bourdieu, Pierre. 1993. *The Field of Cultural Production*. Edited by Randal Johnson. New York: Columbia University Press.

Bourdieu, Pierre. 1995. *The Rules of Art: Genesis and Structure of the Literary Field*. Translated by Susan Emanuel. Stanford, CA: Stanford University Press.

Bourdieu, Pierre. 1998. *Acts of Resistance: Against the Tyranny of the Market*. Translated by Richard Nice. New York: Free Press.

Bourdieu, Pierre. 2001. "Bref impromptu sur Beethoven, artiste entrepreneur." *Sociétés et Représentations* 1, no. 11: 13–18.

Bourdieu, Pierre. 2003. *Firing Back: Against the Tyranny of the Market 2*. Translated by Loïc Wacquant. New York: New Press.

Braverman, Harry. 1998. *Labor and Monopoly Capital: The Degradation of Work in the Twentieth Century*. New York: Monthly Review Press.

Brown, Wendy. 2005. *Edgework: Critical Essays on Knowledge and Politics*. Princeton, NJ: Princeton University Press.

Brown, Wendy. 2015. *Undoing the Demos: Neoliberalism's Stealth Revolution*. New York: Zone.

Burlingame, Jon. 1996. *TV's Biggest Hits: The Story of Television Themes from "Dragnet" to "Friends."* New York: Schirmer.

Burlingame, Jon. 1997. "Composers Sing Non-Union Blues." *Variety*, October 15. https://variety.com/1997/film/news/composers-sing-non-union-blues -1116678320/.

Burlingame, Jon. 2010. "SCL's History: From SCA to CLGA to SCL." https://thescl .com/mission-and-history/.

Burlingame, Jon. 2011. "Composers Give Up Unionization Bid." *Variety*, July 22. https://variety.com/2011/music/markets-festivals/composers-give-up -unionization-bid-1118040305/.

Caldwell, John Thornton. 2008. *Production Culture: Industrial Reflexivity and Critical Practice in Film/Television*. Durham, NC: Duke University Press.

Caldwell, John T., M. J. Clarke, Erin Hill, and Eric Vanstrom. 2013. "Distributed Creativity in Film and Television: Three Case Studies of Networked Production Labor." In *The International Encyclopedia of Media Studies*, edited by Angharad N. Valdivia. Volume II, *Media Production*, edited by Vicki Mayer, 396–419. Malden, MA: Wiley-Blackwell.

Carter, Cynthia, Linda Steiner, and Lisa McLaughlin, eds. 2014. *The Routledge Companion to Media and Gender*. New York: Routledge.

Caves, Richard E. 2000. *Creative Industries: Contracts between Art and Commerce*. Cambridge, MA: Harvard University Press.

Cheng, William. 2014. *Sound Play: Video Games and the Musical Imagination*. New York: Oxford University Press.

"Chris Lennertz: Interview by Will Shivers." 1995. *Film Score Monthly*, September, 9–11.

Christopherson, Susan, and Michael Storper. 1986. "The City as Studio; The World as Back Lot: The Impact of Vertical Disintegration on the Location of the Motion Picture Industry." *Environment and Planning D: Society and Space* 4, no. 3: 305–20.

"Chuck Cirino, Peter Rotter: The Art and Craftiness of Scoring Low Budget Films." 1994. *Film Score Monthly*, August, 8–10.

Coleman, Todd. 1993. "Scoring a Job." *Hollywood Reporter*, June 18, S-10.

Conlan, Timothy J. 1984. "The Politics of Federal Block Grants: From Nixon to Reagan." *Political Science Quarterly* 99, no. 2: 247–70.

Cooke, Mervyn. 2008. *A History of Film Music*. Cambridge: Cambridge University Press.

Crisafulli, Chuck. 2000. "Conducting Experiments." *Hollywood Reporter*, May 26, s-3.

Crisafulli, Chuck. 2008. "Passing the Baton." *Hollywood Reporter*, January, 3.

Crucciola, Jordan. 2019. "The Hollywood Fight That's Tearing Apart Writers and Agents, Explained." *Vulture*, April 18. https://www.vulture.com/article/wga -hollywood-agents-packaging-explained.html.

Davis, Howard, and Richard Scase. 2000. *Managing Creativity: The Dynamics of Work and Organization*. Philadelphia: Open University Press.

Davis, Richard. 2010. *Complete Guide to Film Scoring: The Art and Business of Writing Music for Movies and TV*. 2nd ed. Boston: Berklee Press.

de Angelis, Massimo. 2001. "Marx and Primitive Accumulation: The Continuous Character of Capital's 'Enclosures.'" *Commoner*, issue 2 (September). https:// thecommoner.org/back-issues/issue-02-september-2001/.

de Angelis, Massimo. 2004. "Separating the Doing and the Deed: Capital and the Continuous Character of Enclosures." *Historical Materialism* 12, no. 2: 57–87.

de Angelis, Massimo. 2007. *The Beginning of History: Value Struggles and Global Capital*. London: Pluto.

Deaville, James, ed. 2011. *Music in Television: Channels of Listening*. New York: Routledge.

Dilts, Andrew. 2011. "From 'Entrepreneur of the Self' to 'Care of the Self': Neo-liberal Governmentality and Foucault's Ethics." *Foucault Studies* 12 (October): 130–46.

Donham, Donald L. 2015. "Modes of Production." *International Encyclopedia of the Social and Behavioral Sciences*. 2nd ed., vol. 15, 714–17. https://doi.org/10.1016 /B978-0-08-097086-8.12110-5.

Duménil, Gérard, and Dominique Lévy. 2003. "Production and Management: Marx's Dual Theory of Labor." In *Value and the World Economy Today: Production, Finance and Globalization*, edited by Richard Westra and Alan Zuege, 137–57. New York: Palgrave Macmillan.

Duménil, Gérard, and Dominique Lévy. 2004. *Capital Resurgent: Roots of the Neo-liberal Revolution*. Translated by Derek Jeffers. Cambridge, MA: Harvard University Press.

Duménil, Gérard, and Dominique Lévy. 2011. *The Crisis of Neoliberalism*. Cambridge, MA: Harvard University Press.

Duménil, Gérard, and Dominique Lévy. 2018. *Managerial Capitalism: Ownership, Management and the Coming New Mode of Production*. London: Pluto.

Dunn, Laura, Laura Karpman, Lolita Ritmanis, and Miriam Cutler. 2007. "Influence of an Icon." *Score*, Fall, 5–7.

Dwyer, Paul. 2015. "Theorizing Media Production: The Poverty of Political Economy." *Media, Culture and Society* 37, no. 7: 988–1004.

Ehrenreich, John, and Barbara Ehrenreich. 1979. "The Professional-Managerial Class." *Radical America* 11, no. 2: 7–31.

Eicke, Stephan. 2019. *The Struggle behind the Soundtrack: Inside the Discordant New World of Film Scoring*. Jefferson, NC: McFarland.

Ekman, Mattias. 2012. "Understanding Accumulation: The Relevance of Marx's Theory of Primitive Accumulation in Media and Communication Studies." *tripleC* 10, no. 2: 156–70.

Eskow, Gary. 2002. "Small Screen, Big Music: TV Composers on Writing under Pressure." *Mix*, April, 94–96.

Faulkner, Robert R. (1971) 2013. *Hollywood Studio Musicians: Their Work and Careers in the Recording Industry*. New Brunswick, NJ: Aldine Transaction.

Faulkner, Robert R. 1983. *Music on Demand: Composers and Careers in the Hollywood Film Industry*. New Brunswick, NJ: Transaction.

Feld, Steven. 1984. "Communication, Music, and Speech about Music." *Yearbook for Traditional Music* 16: 1–18.

Fink, Edward J. 1998. "Episodic's Music Man: Mike Post." *Journal of Popular Film and Television* 25, no. 4: 155–60.

Fitzgerald, Scott W. 2012. *Corporations and Cultural Industries: Time Warner, Bertelsmann, and News Corporation*. Lanham, MD: Rowman and Littlefield.

Fitzgerald, Scott W. 2015. "The Structure of the Cultural Industries: Global Corporations to SMEs." In *The Routledge Companion to the Cultural Industries*, edited by Kate Oakley and Justin O'Connor, 70–85. New York: Routledge.

Florida, Richard. 2002. *The Rise of the Creative Class and How It's Transforming Work, Leisure, Community and Everyday Life*. New York: Basic.

Foliart, Dan. 2011. "Musical Sustainability." *Score*, Summer, 3.

Follows, Stephen. 2020. "How Many People Work on a Movie?" Stephenfollows .com. April 6. https://stephenfollows.com/how-many-people-work-on-a -movie/.

Foucault, Michel. 1982. "Afterword: The Subject and Power." In *Michel Foucault: Beyond Structuralism and Hermeneutics*, edited by Hubert L. Dreyfus and Paul Rabinow, 208–26. Chicago: University of Chicago Press.

Foucault, Michel. 1984. "What Is an Author?" In *The Foucault Reader*, edited by Paul Rabinow, 101–20. New York: Pantheon.

Foucault, Michel. 2008. *The Birth of Biopolitics: Lectures at the Collège de France, 1978–1979*. Edited by Michel Sennelart. Translated by Graham Burchell. Basingstoke, UK: Palgrave Macmillan.

Fuchs, Christian. 2010. "Labor in Informational Capitalism and on the Internet." *Information Society: An International Journal* 26, no. 3: 179–96.

Fuchs, Christian. 2012. "Dallas Smythe Today: The Audience Commodity, the Digital Labour Debate, Marxist Political Economy and Critical Theory; Prolegomena to a Digital Labour Theory of Value." *tripleC* 10, no. 2: 692–740.

Gallo, Phil. 1997. "Keeping Score: New Ways in Film Music." *Variety*, November 3–9, 21–22.

Gallo, Phil. 2013. "TV Tunes: 10 Things the Music Industry Needs to Know about the Fall Season." *Billboard*, September 21, 26–27.

Garcia, Teresa. 2004. "Keeping Time." *Film Score Monthly*, November/December, 27–28.

Garnham, Nicholas. 1979. "Contribution to a Political Economy of Mass-Communication." *Media, Culture, and Society* 1, no. 2: 123–46.

Geertz, Clifford. 1973. *The Interpretation of Cultures*. New York: Basic.

Gleeson, Patrick. 2018. "How Much Money Does the Average Film Scorer Make?" *Chron*, June 29. https://work.chron.com/much-money-average-film-scorer-make-15385.html.

Goldwasser, Dan. 2000. "Shirley Walker's Musical Destination." *Soundtrack.net*, May 25. https://www.soundtrack.net/content/article/?id=55.

"The Good, the Bad and the Ugly of Film Music Packaging: Based on a Conversation with Stan Milander." 2000. *Score*, Fall, 5.

Graeber, David. 2006. "Turning Modes of Production Inside Out; or, Why Capitalism Is a Transformation of Slavery." *Critique of Anthropology* 26, no. 1: 61–85. https://doi.org/10.1177/0308275X06061484.

Graeber, David. 2013. "It Is Value That Brings Universes into Being." *Hau: Journal of Ethnographic Theory* 3, no. 2: 219–43.

Graeber, David. 2015. *The Utopia of Rules: On Technology, Stupidity, and the Secret Joys of Bureaucracy*. Brooklyn: Melville House.

Grein, Paul. 1980. "L.A. Studios Hurt by AFM Film-TV Strike." *Billboard*, August 9, 3.

Greiving, Tim. 2009. "This One Goes to 9." *Film Score Monthly Online*, September. https://www.filmscoremonthly.com/fsmonline/story.cfm?maID=2125&issueID=55.

Greiving, Tim. 2011a. "I Married a Film Composer, Vol. 1." *Film Score Monthly Online*, February. https://www.filmscoremonthly.com/fsmonline/story.cfm?maID=2942&issueID=72.

Greiving, Tim. 2011b. "I Married a Film Composer, Vol. 2." *Film Score Monthly Online*, April, https://www.filmscoremonthly.com/fsmonline/story.cfm?maID=3029.

Grey, Benôit. 2015. "Production Music Industry Shares Common Cause with Music Creators." *Score*, Spring, 1.

Hagen, Earle. 2000. *Memoirs of a Famous Composer Nobody Ever Heard Of*. N.p.: Earle Hagen.

Han, Byung-Chul. 2017. *Psychopolitics: Neoliberalism and New Technologies of Power*. Translated by Erik Butler. New York: Verso.

Hardt, Michael, and Antonio Negri. 2000. *Empire*. Cambridge, MA: Harvard University Press.

Hardt, Michael, and Antonio Negri. 2004. *Multitude: War and Democracy in the Age of Empire*. New York: Penguin.

Hartley, John, ed. 2005. *Creative Industries*. Malden, MA: Blackwell.

Harvey, David. 2005. *A Brief History of Neoliberalism*. New York: Oxford University Press.

Harvey, David. 2007. "Neoliberalism as Creative Destruction." *Annals of the American Academy of Political and Social Science* 610, no. 1: 22–44.

Harvey, David. 2010. *A Companion to Marx's Capital*. New York: Verso.

Hearn, Greg, Simon Roodhouse, and Julie Blakey. 2007. "From Value Chain to Value Creating Ecology: Implications for Creative Industries Development Policy." *International Journal of Cultural Policy* 13, no. 4: 419–36.

Heine, Eric. 2020a. "Film Composers Who Rock, Part 1." *Film Score Monthly Online*, February. https://www.filmscoremonthly.com/fsmonline/story.cfm?maID =7161&issueID=181.

Heine, Eric. 2020b. "Film Composers Who Rock, Part 2." *Film Score Monthly Online*, March. https://www.filmscoremonthly.com/fsmonline/story.cfm?maID =7194.

Hesmondhalgh, David. 2006. "Bourdieu, the Media and Cultural Production." *Media, Culture and Society* 28, no. 2: 211–31.

Hesmondhalgh, David. 2017. "Exploitation and Media Labor." In *The Routledge Companion to Media and Labor*, edited by Richard Maxwell, 30–39. New York: Routledge.

Hesmondhalgh, David. 2019. *The Cultural Industries*. 4th ed. Thousand Oaks, CA: SAGE.

Hesmondhalgh, David, and Sarah Baker. 2011. *Creative Labour: Media Work in Three Cultural Industries*. London: Routledge.

Hesmondhalgh, David, and Sarah Baker. 2015. "Sex, Gender and Work Segregation in the Cultural Industries." *Sociological Review* 63 (May, suppl. 1): 23–36.

Horkheimer, Max, and Theodor Adorno. 2002. *Dialectic of Enlightenment: Philosophical Fragments*. Edited by Gunzelin Schmid Noerr. Translated by Edmund Jephcott. Stanford, CA: Stanford University Press.

Hubai, Gergely. 2012. *Torn Music: Rejected Film Scores, a Selected History*. Los Angeles: Silman-James.

Hunt, Darnell, and Ana-Christina Ramón. 2021. *Hollywood Diversity Report 2021: Pandemic in Progress*. Los Angeles: UCLA College of Social Sciences.

Irwin, Ashley. 2017. "The Best of Times, the Worst of Times." *Score*, Winter, 3–4.

Jameson, Fredric. 1984. "Postmodernism, or the Cultural Logic of Late Capitalism." *New Left Review* 1, no. 146 (July/August): 53–92.

Jones, Candace, Mark Lorenzen, and Jonathan Sapsed, eds. 2015. *The Oxford Handbook of Creative Industries*. New York: Oxford University Press.

Jung, C. G. (1966) 1981. *Two Essays on Analytical Psychology*. 2nd ed. Translated by R. F. C. Hull. London: Routledge.

Kaplan, Jon. 2019. "Elfman off the Leash." *Film Score Monthly Online*, April. https://www.filmscoremonthly.com/fsmonline/story.cfm?maID =6843&issueID=172.

Katz, Brandon. 2019. "How Much Does It Cost to Fight in the Streaming Wars?" *Observer*, October 23. https://observer.com/2019/10/netflix-disney-apple -amazon-hbo-max-peacock-content-budgets/.

Keeble, David, and Richard Cavanagh. 2008. "Concepts in Value Chain Analysis and Their Utility in Understanding Cultural Industries." In *Compendium of Research Papers from the International Forum on the Creative Economy*, edited by the Conference Board of Canada, 161–70. Ottawa: Conference Board of Canada.

Kimpel, Dan. 2006. "Networking Nuances." *Score*, Summer, 1.

Kowal, Lynn F. 2014. "Tiny Feet and the Often-Tired Road to Musical Excellence." *Score*, Spring, 5.

Kraft, Richard. 2013a. "The Bottom Line: Is Los Angeles Competitive?" *Score*, Spring, 1.

Kraft, Richard. 2013b. "Ending the Exodus from Recording in L.A." *Score*, Winter, 7.

Kranhold, Kathryn. 2019. "TV and Film Composers Say Netflix, Other Streaming Services Insist on Buying Out Their Music Rights." *Hollywood Reporter*, December 11. https://www.hollywoodreporter.com/news/tv-film-composers -say-netflix-streaming-services-insist-buying-music-rights-1261940.

Krogh, John. 2002a. "Behind the Scenes of ABC's 'Alias': Composer Michael Giacchino Blends Orchestral Music and Electronics for One of the Hottest Shows on TV." *Keyboard*, July, 32.

Krogh, John. 2002b. "Q and A with 'Alias' Creator J. J. Abrams." *Keyboard*, July, 38.

Lampel, Joseph, and Jamal Shamsie. 2003. "Capabilities in Motion: New Organizational Forms and the Reshaping of the Hollywood Movie Industry." *Journal of Management Studies* 40, no. 8: 41–56.

Laporte, Nicole. 2018. "The Death of Hollywood's Middle Class." *Fast Company*, October 25. https://www.fastcompany.com/90250828/the-death-of -hollywoods-middle-class.

Larson, Randall D. 1998. "Shirley Walker." *Soundtrack*. https://cnmsarchive .wordpress.com/2013/09/13/shirley-walker/.

Lauzen, Martha M. 2022. "The Celluloid Ceiling in a Pandemic Year: Employment of Women on the Top U.S. Films of 2021." https://womenintvfilm.sdsu.edu /wp-content/uploads/2022/01/2021-Celluloid-Ceiling-Report.pdf.

Lewandowski, Natalie. 2010. "Understanding Creative Roles in Entertainment: The Music Supervisor as Case Study." *Journal of Media and Cultural Studies* 24, no. 6: 865–75.

Loraine, Breena. 2020. "'Hollywood's New Power Players': Music Supervisors and the Post-2010 Culture of Music Supervision and Sync." PhD diss., Department of Musicology, University of California, Los Angeles.

MacLean, Paul Andrew. 1993a. "A Conversation with Michael Lang, Session Keyboardist." *Film Score Monthly*, February/March, 25–26.

MacLean, Paul Andrew. 1993b. "A Conversation by Paul Andrew MacLean with Elmer Bernstein." *Film Score Monthly*, August/September, 14–15.

Mann, Michael. 2015. "How Do Directors Pick Composers to Score Their Films?" *Slate*, February 9. https://slate.com/human-interest/2015/02/michael-mann -how-do-directors-pick-composers-to-score-their-movies.html.

Marchese, David. 2020. "John Cusack Never Understood His Cusackness." *New York Times*, September 14. https://www.nytimes.com/interactive/2020/09/14 /magazine/john-cusack-interview.html?searchResultPosition=1.

Marx, Karl. 1990. *Capital: A Critique of Political Economy*. Vol. 1. Translated by Ben Fowkes. London: Penguin.

Marx, Karl. 1991. *Capital: A Critique of Political Economy*. Vol. 3. Translated by David Fernbach. London: Penguin.

Marx, Karl. n.d. *Theories of Surplus Value*. Part 1. Translated by Emile Burnes. Edited by S. Ryazanskaya. Moscow: Foreign Languages Publishing House.

Marx, Karl, and Friedrich Engels. 1970. *The German Ideology*. Edited by C. J. Arthur. New York: International.

Matthews, Christopher M. 2015. "When Things Get Real on TV, Music Pays Real Well." *Wall Street Journal*, July 28. https://www.wsj.com/articles/hot-gig -in-hollywood-composing-background-music-for-the-bachelorette -1438036366.

Maxwell, Richard, ed. 2001. *Culture Works: The Political Economy of Culture*. Minneapolis: University of Minnesota Press.

Mayer, Vicki. 2011. *Below the Line: Producers and Production Studies in the New Television Economy*. Durham, NC: Duke University Press.

Mayer, Vicki, Miranda J. Banks, and John Thornton Caldwell, eds. 2009. *Production Studies: Cultural Studies of Media Industries*. New York: Routledge.

McRobbie, Angela. 2016. *Be Creative: Making a Living in the New Culture Industries*. Malden, MA: Polity.

Meehan, Eileen R., and Ellen Riordan, eds. 2002. *Sex and Money: Feminism and Political Economy in the Media*. Minneapolis: University of Minnesota Press.

Meillassoux, Claude. 1981. *Maidens, Meal and Money: Capitalism and the Domestic Community*. New York: Cambridge University Press.

Miège, Bernard. 1989. *The Capitalization of Cultural Production*. New York: International.

Milestone, Katie. 2015. "Gender and the Cultural Industries." In *The Routledge Companion to the Cultural Industries*, edited by Kate Oakley and Justin O'Connor, 501–11. London: Routledge.

Miller, Kiri. 2012. *Playing Along: Digital Games, YouTube, and Virtual Performance*. New York: Oxford University Press.

Mollin, Fred. 1992. "Scoring for Television." *Film Score Monthly*, September, 15–16.

Morcom, Anna. 2007. *Hindi Film Songs and the Cinema*. Burlington, VT: Ashgate.

Mould, Oli. 2018. *Against Creativity*. London: Verso.

Muddiman, Hélène. 2019. "Scoring for Live Musicians in Los Angeles." *Score*, Fall, 32–36.

Murray, Fergus. 1987. "Flexible Specialization in the 'Third Italy.'" *Capital and Class* 11, no. 3: 84–95.

Negus, Keith, and Michael Pickering. 2004. *Creativity, Communication and Cultural Value*. Thousand Oaks, CA: SAGE.

Nelson, Camilla. 2010. "The Invention of Creativity: The Emergence of a Discourse." *Cultural Studies Review* 16, no. 2: 49–74.

Newcomb, Horace, and Robert S. Alley. 1983. *The Producer's Medium: Conversations with Creators of American TV*. New York: Oxford University Press.

Nietzsche, Friedrich. (1886) 1966. *Beyond Good and Evil*. Translated by Walter Kaufmann. New York: Vintage.

Nietzsche, Friedrich. (1883–88) 1968. *The Will to Power*. Edited by Walter Kaufmann. Translated by Walter Kaufmann and R. J. Hollingdale. New York: Vintage.

Nietzsche, Friedrich. 1974. *The Gay Science*. 2nd ed. Translated by Walter Kaufmann. New York: Vintage.

Nixon, Sean. 2003. *Advertising Cultures: Gender, Commerce, Creativity*. Thousand Oaks, CA: SAGE.

Norris, Chris. 2017. "Declaration of Independence: The Hemi Q and A with Steven Soderbergh." *Hemispheres*, August, 46–51.

Oakley, Katie, and Justin O'Connor, eds. 2015. *The Routledge Companion to the Cultural Industries*. London: Routledge.

Ortner, Sherry B. 1996. *Making Gender: The Politics and Erotics of Culture*. Boston: Beacon Press.

Ortner, Sherry B. 2013. *Not Hollywood: Independent Film at the Twilight of the American Dream*. Durham, NC: Duke University Press.

Ortner, Sherry B. 2016. "Dark Anthropology and Its Others: Theory since the Eighties." *Hau: Journal of Ethnographic Theory* 6, no. 1: 47–73.

Parker, Rozsika, and Griselda Pollock. 2013. *Old Mistresses: Women, Art and Ideology*. New York: I. B. Tauris.

Piketty, Thomas. 2014. *Capital in the Twenty-First Century*. Translated by Arthur Goldhammer. Cambridge, MA: Harvard University Press.

Piketty, Thomas. 2020. *Capital and Ideology*. Translated by Arthur Goldhammer. Cambridge, MA: Harvard University Press.

Piore, Michael J., and Charles F. Sabel. 1984. *The Second Industrial Divide: Possibilities for Prosperity*. New York: Basic.

Prasad, M. Madhava. 1998. *Ideology of the Hindi Film: A Historical Construction*. New Delhi: Oxford University Press.

Prendergast, Roy M. 1992. *Film Music: A Neglected Art*. New York: W. W. Norton.

Rainbird, Mark. 2004. "Demand and Supply Chains: The Value Catalyst." *International Journal of Physical Distribution and Logistics Management* 34, nos. 3–4: 230–50.

"Randy Newman." 1994. *Film Score Monthly*, May, 10–13.

Reckwitz, Andreas. 2017. *The Invention of Creativity: Modern Society and the Culture of the New*. Translated by Steven Black. Malden, MA: Polity.

Rhodes, S. Mark. 2004. "Keeping up with the Bluths: David Schwartz Talks about Composing for Television." *Film Score Monthly*, November, 10–12.

Ritchey, Marianna. 2019. *Composing Capital: Classical Music in the Neoliberal Era*. Chicago: University of Chicago Press.

Robb, David. 1998. "Composers Say They're Paupers in Royalty Game." *Hollywood Reporter*, September 18–20, 1.

Rodd, John. 2011. "Against a California Sky: Building a Studio from the Ground Up." *Score*, Summer, 1.

Rodman, Ronald. 2010. *Tuning In: American Narrative Television Music*. New York: Oxford University Press.

Romanelli, Kristen. 2014. "Band of Sisters." *Film Score Monthly Online*, August. https://www.filmscoremonthly.com/fsmonline/story.cfm?maID =4804&issueID=116.

Romanelli, Kristen. 2020. "Tutti: Orchestrating Together." *Film Score Monthly Online*, March. https://www.filmscoremonthly.com/fsmonline/story.cfm ?maID=7215&issueID=182.

Rona, Jeff. 2000. *The Reel World: Scoring for Pictures*. San Francisco: Miller Freeman.

Rose, Elizabeth. 2014. "Women's Work: Film, TV and Game Composers." *Score*, Summer, 5–8.

Rosenberg, Nathan. 1963. "Capital Goods, Technology, and Economic Growth." *Oxford Economic Papers* 15, no. 3: 217–27.

Ryan, Bill. 1992. *Making Capital from Culture: The Corporate Form of Capitalist Cultural Production*. New York: Walter de Gruyter.

Ryan, Maureen, and Cynthia Littleton. 2017. "TV Series Budgets Hit the Breaking Point as Costs Skyrocket in Peak TV Era." *Variety*, September 26. https://variety.com/2017/tv/news/tv-series-budgets-costs-rising-peak-tv -1202570158/.

Sakakeeny, Matt. 2015. "Playing for Work: Music as a Form of Labor in New Orleans." *Oxford Handbooks Online*. https://doi.org./10.1093/oxfordhb /9780199935321.013.23.

Sanyal, Kalyan. 2013. *Rethinking Capitalist Development: Primitive Accumulation, Governmentality and Post-Colonial Capitalism*. New York: Routledge.

Savas, Kaya. 2018a. "Germaine Franco: Becoming Part of the Story." *Score*, Fall, 12.

Savas, Kaya. 2018b. "TV Pilots Then and Now: How the Pilot-Scoring Process Is Shaping the Future of TV." *Score*, Summer, 1.

Savas, Kaya. 2019. "The Marvelous Pinar Toprak." *Score*, Spring, 14–19.

Sazer, Marc. 2013. "Residuals and Royalties for Musicians and Others." *International Musician*, March, 5.

Schelle, Michael. 1999. *The Score: Interviews with Film Composers*. Los Angeles: Silman-James.

Schrader, Matt, and Trevor Thompson. 2017. *Score: A Film Music Documentary—The Interviews*. Los Angeles: Epicleff Media.

Schultz, Theodore. 1959. "Investment in Man: An Economist's View." *Social Science Review* 33, no. 2: 109–17.

Schultz, Theodore. 1972. "Human Capital: Policy Issues and Research Opportunities." In *Human Resources*, vol. 6 of *Economic Research: Retrospect and Prospect*. New York: National Bureau of Economic Research.

Seeger, Charles. 1977. *Studies in Musicology, 1935–1975*. Berkeley: University of California Press.

Sennett, Richard. 2006. *The Culture of the New Capitalism*. New Haven, CT: Yale University Press.

Siciliano, Michael L. 2021. *Creative Control: The Ambivalence of Work in the Culture Industries*. New York: Columbia University Press.

Simon, Marty. 2013. "An Action Guide to Royalty Management." *Score*, Winter, 1.

Skiles, Marlin. 1976. *Music Scoring for TV and Motion Pictures*. Blue Ridge Summit, PA: Tab.

Slobin, Mark, ed. 2008. *Global Soundtracks: Worlds of Film Music*. Middletown, CT: Wesleyan University Press.

Smith, Jeff. 1998. *The Sounds of Commerce: Marketing Popular Film Music*. New York: Columbia University Press.

Smith, Jeff. 2001. "Taking Music Supervisors Seriously." In *Cinesonic: Experience the Soundtrack*, edited by Philip Brophy, 124–46. North Ryde NSW, Australia: Southwest.

Smythe, Dallas W. 1977. "Communications: Blindspot of Western Marxism." *Canadian Journal of Political and Social Theory* 1, no. 3: 1–27.

Solie, Ruth. 1980. "The Living Work: Organicism and Musical Analysis." *19th-Century Music* 4, no. 2: 147–56.

Stahl, Matt. 2011. "From Seven Years to 360 Degrees: Primitive Accumulation, Recording Contracts, and the Means of Making a (Musical) Living." *tripleC* 9, no. 2: 668–88.

Stedman Jones, Daniel. 2012. *Masters of the Universe: Hayek, Friedman, and the Birth of Neoliberal Politics*. Princeton, NJ: Princeton University Press.

Storper, Michael. 1989. "The Transition to Flexible Specialisation in the US Film Industry: External Economies, the Division of Labour, and the Crossing of Industrial Divides." *Cambridge Journal of Economics* 13, no. 3: 273–305.

Storper, Michael. 1993. "Flexible Specialisation in Hollywood: A Response to Aksoy and Robins." *Cambridge Journal of Economics* 17, no. 4: 479–84.

Storper, Michael, and Susan Christopherson. 1987. "Flexible Specialization and Regional Industrial Agglomerations: The Case of the U.S. Motion Picture Industry." *Annals of the Association of American Geographers* 77, no. 1: 104–17.

Storper, Michael, and Susan Christopherson. 1989. "The Effects of Flexible Specialization on Industrial Politics and the Labor Market: The Motion Picture Industry." *Industrial and Labor Relations Review* 42, no. 3: 331–47.

Streeck, Wolfgang. 2020. *How Will Capitalism End? Essays on a Failing System*. New York: Verso.

Takis, John. 2006. "A Woman of Many Capes, Part 1." *Film Score Monthly Online*, October. https://www.filmscoremonthly.com/fsmonline/story.cfm?maid=534.

Taylor, Timothy D. 1997. *Global Pop: World Music, World Markets*. New York: Routledge.

Taylor, Timothy D. 2001. *Strange Sounds: Music, Technology and Culture*. New York: Routledge.

Taylor, Timothy D. 2007. *Beyond Exoticism: Western Music and the World*. Durham, NC: Duke University Press.

Taylor, Timothy D. 2012. *The Sounds of Capitalism: Advertising, Music, and the Conquest of Culture*. Chicago: University of Chicago Press.

Taylor, Timothy D. 2016. *Music and Capitalism: A History of the Present*. Chicago: University of Chicago Press.

Taylor, Timothy D. 2017. *Music in the World: Selected Essays*. Chicago: University of Chicago Press.

Taylor, Timothy D. 2020. "Maintenance and Destruction of an East Side Los Angeles Indie Rock Scene." In *The Oxford Handbook of Economic Ethnomusicology*, edited by Anna Morcom and Timothy D. Taylor. New York: Oxford University Press. https://www.oxfordhandbooks.com/view/10.1093/oxfordhb/9780190859633.001.0001/oxfordhb-9780190859633-e-27.

Taylor, Timothy D. n.d.a. *Producing Value, Valuing Production: Selected Essays*. In preparation.

Taylor, Timothy D. n.d.b. *In the Factory of Fine Arts: Music in Television from the 1940s to the 1980s*. In preparation.

Terkel, Studs. 1974. *Working: People Talk about What They Do All Day and How They Feel about What They Do*. New York: Ballantine.

Thomas, Hillary. 2007. "Filmmakers Reveal Their Opinions of Working with Composers." *Score*, Winter, 1.

Trakin, Roy. 1990. "TV Music Hits a High Note." *Hollywood Reporter*, August, S-10–S-12.

Tsing, Anna. 2009. "Supply Chains and the Human Condition." *Rethinking Marxism: A Journal of Economics, Culture and Society* 21, no. 2: 148–76.

Tsing, Anna. 2013. "Sorting out Commodities: How Capitalist Value Is Made through Gifts." *Hau: Journal of Ethnographic Theory* 3, no 1: 21–43.

Tsing, Anna Lowenhaupt. 2015. *The Mushroom at the End of the World: On the Possibility of Life in Capitalist Ruins*. Princeton, NJ: Princeton University Press.

Turner, Terence, 1979. "Anthropology and the Politics of Indigenous Peoples' Struggles." *Cambridge Journal of Anthropology* 5, no. 1: 1–43.

Tusher, Will. 1980. "Dramatic Turn in Strike Talks; Actors Caucus." *Variety*, September 3, 1.

Umney, Charles, and Lefteris Kretsos. 2015. "'That's the Experience': Passion, Work Precarity, and Life Transitions among London Jazz Musicians." *Work and Occupations* 42, no. 3: 313–34.

Vaughn, Christopher. 1990. "Film and Television Music . . . in the Minority Key. . . ." *Hollywood Reporter*, August, S-25–S-26.

Verrier, Richard. 2009. "Composers, Lyricists Make a Union Pitch." *Los Angeles Times*, November 8, B1.

Wacquant, Loïc. 2013. "Symbolic Power and Group-Making: On Pierre Bourdieu's Reframing of Class." *Journal of Classical Sociology* 13, no. 2: 274–91.

Wacquant, Loïc, and Aksu Akçaoğlu. 2017. "Practice and Symbolic Power in Bourdieu: The View from Berkeley." *Journal of Classical Sociology* 17, no. 1: 55–69.

Waldman, Alan. 1996. "Music for a Song." 1996. *Hollywood Reporter*, January 13, 35.

"Walker on Walker." 2007. *Film Score Monthly Online*, https://www.filmscoremonthly
.com/daily/article.cfm?articleID=5709.

Wasko, Janet. 2003. *How Hollywood Works*. Thousand Oaks, CA: SAGE.

Wasko, Janet, Graham Murdock, and Helena Sousa, eds. 2011. *The Handbook of
Political Economy of Communications*. Malden, MA: Wiley-Blackwell.

Weber, Max. (1905) 2001. *The Protestant Ethic and the Spirit of Capitalism*. Translated
by Talcott Parsons. New York: Routledge.

Wierzbicki, James. 2009. *Film Music: A History*. New York: Routledge.

Wierzbicki, James, ed. 2019. *Double Lives: Film Composers in the Concert Hall*.
New York: Routledge, 2019.

Williams, Raymond. 1977. *Marxism and Literature*. New York: Oxford University
Press.

Williams, Raymond. 1981. *Culture*. London: Fontana.

Williams, Raymond. 1983. *Keywords*. London: Fontana.

Zimmerman, Kevin. 1989. "Film, TV and Jingle Composers Know the Score."
Variety, August 2, 32.

Zimmerman, Kevin. 1991. "Filmers Pay Fiddlers for High-Strung Scores." *Variety*,
March 18, 10.

block grants by government, package deal pay
structure compared to, 198
Bochco, Steven, 150
Bold and the Beautiful, The (television series), 63
Bonefeld, Werner, 85
Borner, Gustavo, 34
Bourdieu, Pierre: cultural production and re-
search of, 2–4, 6, 8, 14, 21–22, 29–30; habitus
concept of, 38; on new social personality of
the artist, 46; on social capital, 31–33, 36; on
symbolic capital, 41–46
Brahms, Johannes, 175
branding: by big-name composers, 101; game
music as, 104–5; nichification of composers
and, 106–7
Braverman, Harry, 3–4, 106
Broadcast Music, Inc. (BMI), 136, 204, 207
Broughton, Bruce, 8–9, 66, 71–72, 181–83, 185,
193–94, 206–7
Brown, Wendy, 37, 65, 177–78, 201
Bruckheimer, Jerry, 66
budget constraints: composers' creative freedom
and, 8, 17–18, 56–57, 62–63; creative freedom
and, 76–78; digital technology and, 71–72;
downsizing and outsourcing and, 185—188;
home studios as solution to, 167; orchestrators
and, 122–23; package deal pay structure and,
195–202; video game music production, 102.
See also money, creative freedom and role of
Bunnell, Jeff, 125–27, 187
bureaucracy: cultural production and, 25; in film
and television, 139–48
Burton, Tim, 169
buyouts, in recording business, 210

cable television: future uncertainty of, 213;
music production and, 8
Calderaro, Tom: on budget constraints, 77; on
collaboration, 225n14; on creative freedom,
72–73; on music production process, 99–100;
on orchestrators, 110, 121–22; on perseverance, 34–35; on time constraints, 66–67; on
time management and work-life balance, 160
Caldwell, John T., 3, 85
Cannell, Stephen J., 149–50, 197
Capital (Marx), 25, 87–88
capitalism: composers' labor in context of,
81–88; cultural production and, 213–15;
cultural studies and, 1–13; Han's discussion
of, 179–80; Marx's collective labor theory and,
25–29; music production and influence of, 16;

self-exploitation and, 177–80; team-based
music production and, 96–101; teamwork
ideology of, 65; use-value in, 86–88. *See also*
neoliberalization
Captain Marvel (film), 176
Carbonara, David, 211
career sustainability, for composers, 91–94
Carpenter, John, 168
Carpenter, Pete, 97–98, 197
Cassavetes, John, 77
Celluloid Ceiling (Lauzen), 156
certificate of authorship, 203
Charlie and the Chocolate Factory (film), 100
Cirino, Chuck, 78
Claire Vick's Sketchbook (Kouneva composition),
175–76
class divisions: creative class, 11; group production and, 24–25; music workers and role of,
2–3; precariat class, 10–11
Clausen, Alf, 35, 58–59, 68–69, 123–24, 165, 206–7
Cobra Kai (YouTube series), 136, 184
collaboration: of directors and composers,
59–66, 81, 83–84, 140–41, 143–46; of rock
bands and directors, 108–13; of showrunners
and composers, 64–66
collective labor, 14; fields of cultural production
and, 22, 29–46; group production and, 23–29;
supply chains and, 25–29; teamwork by
composers as, 64–65
Collins, Phil, 150
communication: about music and sound,
148–55; group production and, 138–39
composers: accumulation by dispossession of
work of, 84–88; authority strategies of, 142–43;
authorship attribution for, 203–4; big-budget
vs. small-budget workers, 9; bureaucratization and managerialism impact on, 139–48; as
capitalist entrepreneurs and managers, 96–101;
career sustainability for, 91–94; communication
problems of, 148–55; constraints on creative
freedom of, 59–66; creative function and
group production of, 56–59; creative outlets
for, 78–80; cultural studies of, 2–3; digital
technology impact on, 71–72, 180–92; directors'
collaboration with, 59–66, 81, 83–84, 140–41,
143–46; game music production by, 102–5;
group production and, 22; hiring process for,
88–105; labor of, 81–84; as managers, 201;
music editors and, 134–37; nichification of,
105–7; oversaturation of, 115–18; package deal
pay structure and, 96–97, 195–202; pay for,

194–95; pay for streaming productions, 204–5; as performers, 125; prestige hierarchies for, 70–71; publishing rights to films scores by, 9; self-exploitation by, 177–211; social capital for, 36, 38–40; symbolic capital for, 42–45; technology's impact on, 7–8; on television productions, 142–43; time constraints for, 66–70, 159–61; union proposals for, 206–8; women as, 167–76; work for hire agreements for, 85; work-life balance for, 161–66

Composers and Lyricists Guild of America (CLGA), 7–8, 28–29, 84, 206

concert music, composers' production of, 78–80

conduct: of performers, 126–29; power and, 37

conductors, 125–29

Conlan, Timothy J., 198

conscious management, cultural production and, 24–25

coolness: nichification of music and, 106–7; pop and rock music prestige and, 107–13; symbolic capital and, 45–46

copyists, 68, 123–24, 186–87

copyright ownership: composers' surrender of, 84–88; producers' right to, 82

craftspeople, industrial management of, 20

creative freedom: composers' constraints and, 59–66; digital technology and, 71–72; media variations and, 70–71; money and power and, 76–78; music editing, 76; for music workers, 72–78; orchestrators, 72–74; outsourcing impact on, 128–29; recording engineers and mixers, 74–76; research on, 9–10; time constraints on, 66–70

creative function: cultural businesses and, 4–5; group production and, 56–59

Creative Industries (Hartley), 11–12

creative outlets for composers, 78–80

creative personality, 5

creativity: accumulation by dispossession of, 84–88; cultural businesses and role of, 4, 10–13, 20–23; discourses on, 9–10, 48–50; gender and, 50, 54–56, 214–15; labor and, 50–52; naturalization of, 52–54; primitive accumulation as harvesting of, 85; Romantic conception of, 14, 52–53; time pressures as stimulus to, 67–69; triumphalism school of, 11–12

credibility, networking and role of, 34

credits in cultural production, as symbolic capital, 41–42

Crehan, Kevin, 69, 94, 130–31, 136, 182

Cruise, Tom, 225n14

cue sheets, for music composition, 203–4

cultural capital, hiring process for composers and, 88–91

cultural production: art vs. commerce dichotomy in, 22–23; author function in, 49–50; capitalism and, 213–15; communication in, 148–55; French literature and, 30; gender and, 15; neoliberalization and, 193–94; power and, 37; recent changes in, 105–18; social capital and, 32–40; supply chains and, 27–29; writing/printing divide in, 139

Culture (Williams), 24–25

cultural businesses: British studies of, 5; commodity production in, 27–29; creative class and, 11; gender issues in, 55–56, 156–58; neoliberalization and, 177–80; policymakers' awareness of, 10; studies of, 1–13, 19–23

Cusack, John, 139

Daft Punk, 108

Davis, Richard, 85

De Angelis, Massimo, 85

Debney, John, 97–98

Decter, Ben: on creative freedom, 62; on digital technology, 117, 185; on pay structure for composers, 97–98, 198, 202; on production process, 94–95; on social hierarchies, 32–33

delegation of work, composers' reliance on, 68

De Palma, Brian, 225n14

Dern, Anne-Kathrin: on creative freedom, 62–63; on digital technology, 188; on teamwork, 65–66; on unionization, 211; on women composers, 171–76; on work-life balance, 161, 164, 166–67

de-skilling, 201; digital technology and, 106–7

Desplat, Alexandre, 61

Devlin Connection, The (television program), 169

digital technology and content: changes in music and, 190–92; copyists and, 123–24; creative freedom and impact of, 71–72; digital file production, 131–37; downsizing and outsourcing and, 185–88; globalization and, 179; impact on composers of, 114–15; labor processes and impact of, 182–85; music production and, 7–8, 15–16; neoliberalization and, 180–92; nichification of music and, 106–7; orchestrators' management of, 72–74, 122–23; package deal system and, 197; performers and, 128–29; pop and rock music and, 107–13; supply chains and production of, 27–29; time pressure on composers and, 82–83

gaming. *See* video gaming

Garner, James, 149–50

Geertz, Clifford, 16–18, 179

gender: creativity and, 50, 54–56; cultural production and, 15, 156–58; digital technology and, 181; work-life balance and, 161–66

Gender and Genius (Battersby), 52–55

genius, creativity and, 52–53

genres in cultural production: creative freedom and, 65–66; nichification of composers and, 105–7

German Ideology, The (Marx and Engels), 41

ghosting, in music production, 96, 99–101

Giacchino, Michael, 39, 182, 200, 203

gig economy, self-exploitation and, 177–80

Gorfaine, Michael, 196–97

governance, Foucault's concept of, 65

government, cultural businesses and, 10

government policy: block grants, 198; cultural businesses and, 10

Graceland (Simon album), 53–54

Graeber, David, 202

group production: authority and, 138–39; collective labor and, 23–29; communication and, 138–39, 148–55; creative function and, 56–59; diffusion of authority, 144–46; fields of, 22, 29–46; forms of capital and, 30–31; music workers and, 14–15; supply chain creation of value and, 28–29, 215. *See also* Williams, Raymond

Guðnadóttir, Hildur, 176

habitus, Bourdieu's field theory and, 30

Hackford, Alex, 102–3

Hadar, Oren, 28–29, 76, 130, 132–34, 147, 163

Hagen, Earle, 179, 195, 197

Han, Byung-Chul, 7, 179–80

harmony, musical effects of, 107

Harry Potter "industry," 10

Hartley, John, 11–12

Harvey, David, 82, 85, 87, 179

Hesmondhalgh, David, 5, 55

Hill Street Blues (television series), 97

hip-hop music, in film and television scores, 113–14

hipness: nichification of music and, 106–7; pop and rock music prestige and, 107–13; symbolic capital and, 45–46

hiring process: for composers, 88–105, 115–18; for music workers, 121; for performers, 127–28

Hitchcock, Alfred, 77

Hoblit, Greg, 150

Holdridge, Lee, 85

Hollywood Diversity Report (Hunt and Ramón), 3

Hollywood Studio Musicians: Their Work and Careers in the Recording Industry (Faulkner), 8–9

home studios: digital technology and, 188–90; music production in, 94–95; work-life balance and, 166–67

homogenization of sound, digital technology and, 190–92

Horkheimer, Max, 1–2, 6–7, 12, 19–20, 213, 218n2

Howard, James Newton, 9

Hubai, Gergely, 225n14

human capital, cultural businesses and, 10–11, 177

Hunt, Darnell, 3

Hurwitz, Mitch, 63, 155

Hutchinson, Matt: on collaboration, 143–44; on communication issues in production, 148–50; on creative freedom constraints, 60–62, 64–65; on hierarchy of prestige, 43–44; on musical skills, 110; on nichification in music production, 107; on package deal pay structure, 199; on royalty payments, 202; on time management and work-life balance, 159

independent contractors, music workers as, 103–4, 124–25, 208–9

indie rock, use in film and television of, 108

industry, as term for cultural businesses, 19–20

instrumentalists, 125–29, 183, 187, 211

International Alliance of Theatrical Stage Employees (IATSE), 200

"In the Air Tonight" (Collins song), 150

Isham, Mark, 169, 199, 205

Jackson, Henry, 103

Jameson, Fredric, 192

Jeffersons, The (television series), 113

Joker (film), 176

Jones, Quincy, 127–28

Jung, Carl, 55

Kant, Immanuel, creativity and epistemology of, 52

Karpman, Laura, 170, 173

Kaye, Carol, 127–28, 187

Kickstarter campaigns, composers' use of, 79

Kidman, Nicole, 225n14

King, Carole, 168

King Kong (2005 film), 9

music quality, digital technology and changes in, 190–92

music training, hiring process for composers and, 88–91

music workers: bureaucratization and managerialism and, 139–48; career sustainability for, 91–94; creative freedom for, 72–78; creativity for, 50, 119–21; cultural studies of, 1–13; pay schemes for, 208–10; self-exploitation by, 177–211; symbolic capital for, 43; time constraints for, 66–70; training of, 121; video game music production, 102–5; women as, 167–76; working conditions for, 14; work-life balance for, 161–66. *See also* specific music workers, e.g., orchestrators

Myman, Harvey, 58, 194, 204

National Labor Relations Board, 207

naturalization of creativity, 52–54

Negus, Keith, 48

Neighborhood, The (television series), 115

Nelson, Camilla, 48

neoliberal capitalism. *See* capitalism

neoliberalization: digital technology and, 180–92; income inequality and, 193–94; increased competition and, 210–11; package deal pay structure and, 195–202; as self-exploitation, 177–211

Netflix, 8, 110, 203, 207

networking relationships: cultural production and role of, 35–40; social capital and, 31–40

Newman, Alfred, 153

Newman, Joey: on authority and collaboration, 139–41, 151; on creative freedom constraints, 62, 64–65, 70, 77–78; on digital technology, 115–17; on ghosting, 99–100; on group production and collaboration, 44; on home studios, 166–67; music by, 215; on networking, 33; on package deal pay structure, 200–201; on streaming royalties, 207–8; on unionization, 206–7; on work-life balance, 161–62

Newman, Randy, 66, 113

Newman, Thomas, 93, 134

nichification in music production, 105–7

Nielsen ratings, 208

Nietzsche, Friedrich, 54

Nine Inch Nails, 111

nonlinearity, in video game music production, 102–5

Nordstrom, John, 63, 141, 158–59, 183–84

NYPD Blue (television series), 150

O'Connor, Cindy, 70, 169, 198–99, 205

Off the Map (television series), 94–95

Once Upon a Time (television series), 205

"Operation Homecoming: Writing the Wartime Experience" (PBS documentary), 32–33

orchestrators: rock band musicians and, 109–10; creative freedom for, 72–74; nichification of music and, 105–7; pay scheme for, 209; work of, 121–23

organic unity, creativity and, 53

outsourcing of music production, 13, 105, 128–29, 185–88, 195–96

overproduction of composers, in film and television, 115–18

ownership of cultural production: composers' surrender of, 82, 84–88, 181; Marx on, 41

Oxford Handbook of Creative Industries (Jones, Lorenzen, and Sapsed), 156

package deal pay structure, 96–97, 195–202; pitfalls of, 212

Parker, Rozsika, 5, 55–56

Pasha, Kamran, 45, 58

patriarchy, in cultural businesses, 4–5, 13, 213–15

pay schemes: composers' pay, 194–95, 204–8; digital technology impact on, 15–16; for music workers, 208–10; neoliberalization and, 193–209; overproduction of composers impact on, 115–18; package deal pay structure, 96–97, 195–202; royalty payment flowchart, 208; streaming and, 204–6; variations in, 202–4; video gaming, 205–6

performers, music workers as, 125–29; digital technology and, 187–88

performing rights, composers and, 204, 206–7

perseverance: hiring process for composers and, 88–91; as skill set, 116–18; social capital and, 35, 218n20

personality, social capital and, 39–40

Pettigrew, Craig, 40, 67–68, 135–36, 193, 203, 209

Petty, William, 87

Phillips, Stu, 80, 116, 215

Pickering, Michael, 48

pilot shows, music work on, 91–94

Pirates of the Caribbean (film), 188

political rationality, 201

Pollock, Griselda, 5, 55–56

pop music, in film and television, 107–13

popular music, importation into film and television of, 105–7

Portman, Rachel, 157

Post, Mike, 60–61, 96–98, 149–50, 185, 196–97

Powell, John, 169

power: creative freedom and, 76–78; social capital and, 37–40; social relations of production and, 119–20; symbolic capital and, 41

precariat class, 10–11, 217n3 (intro.)

Prendergast, Roy M., 85

prestige hierarchies: creative freedom and, 70–71; as symbolic capital, 41–46

primitive accumulation: composer's work as example of, 84–88; recorded music and, 86

Producers Guild of America, 214

production studies, 5; social relations of production, 119–20

Protestant Ethic and the Spirit of Capitalism, The (Weber), 96

Pro Tools recording software, 131, 163, 182, 184, 189

Rabin, Trevor, 66

race, music workers and role of, 2–3, 113–14

Rachmaninoff, Sergei, 80, 215

radio, group production in, 138–39

Ramón, Ana-Christina, 3

Reagan, Ronald, 198, 206

reality television, music production for, 117–18

Rear Window (television movie remake), 199–200

Rebirth of Id (Kouneva album), 175

Reckwitz, Andreas, 10–11

recording engineers: creative freedom for, 74–76; digital technology and, 182; downsizing and outsourcing and, 188; package deal pay structure and, 200; pay for streaming for, 204; work of, 129–31

recording sessions: collaboration in, 148; copyists and, 123–24; costs of, 209–10; mixing and, 132–34; musicians' share of profits from, 86; outsourcing of, 13, 105; performers and, 125–29

Reeve, Christopher, 200

relationships: power in, 37–40; as social capital, 32–40

Remote Control studio, 98–99

reproduction technologies: conscious management and, 25; group production and, 139

reputation, as symbolic capital, 42

residuals, musicians' strike over, 196

responsibilization ideology, 201

rewrites of music, television productions and, 95

Reznor, Trent, 111–12

Rhimes, Shonda, 94–95

Rise of the Creative Class, The (Florida), 11

Ritmanis, Lolita, 170, 172

Robertson, Mark, 34

Robinson, Zach, 33, 35, 100–101, 110–11, 136, 142–43, 157, 162–63, 184

Rockford Files, The (television series), 149–50, 197

rock music, in film and television, 107–13

Romantic movement, creativity and, 14, 52–53

Rosenberg, Nathan, 20–21

Ross, Atticus, 111–12

Rotter, Peter, 78

Routledge Companion to the Cultural Industries, The (Oakley and O'Connor), 156

royalties: for composers, 202–4; payment flow-chart, 208; for streaming products, 204–5, 207–8. *See also* performing rights, composers and

Samantha Who? (television series), 154

Savant, Dan, 74–75, 125, 131–32, 184–85, 209

Schenker, Heinrich, 53

Schifrin, Lalo, 9, 66, 79, 85

Schumann, Clara, 175

Schwartz, David: on communication issues, 148, 154–55; on creative freedom, 63; on group production, 145; on overproduction of composers, 115; on package deal pay structure, 193, 198; in pay for composers, 211; on television music production, 191; on temp music, 61, 71, 219n15

Schwartz, Nan, 157, 169–71

Schwartz, Sam, 196–97

scores: composers' production of, 121; mixing of, 75; orchestration of, 121–23; recording engineers and, 129–31

Scorsese, Martin, 77

Screen Actors Guild (SAG), 196

Scriabin, Alexander, 80

Scrubs (television series), 35, 92

Seattle, film music recording in, 210

secondary market repayments, 188

self-exploitation: digital technology and, 180–92; economic precarity and, 193–209; neoliberalization and, 177–211

Shakespeare, William, 10

Shamsie, Jamal, 20–21

Shire, David, 199–200

Shore, Howard, 42, 91, 103

Shore, Ryan: on authority and collaboration, 141–42; on contracting, 103–4; on creative freedom, 65; on credits, 42; on hiring process, 91; on music skills, 110; on nichification, 107–8; on package deal pay structure, 199; on work-life balance, 161, 163–64 showrunners: ageism and hiring of, 45; Black showrunners, 113–14; composers' collaboration with, 64–66, 145–46; creative authority of, 22; hiring of music workers by, 59; music production and duties of, 4, 94–95; temp music used by, 61–62

Silk Stalkings (television series), 98

Silverado (film), 8

Silvestri, Alan, 66, 225n14

Simon, Carly, 168

Simon, Paul, 53–54

Simpsons, The (television series), 35, 58–59, 68–69, 123–24

single-camera work, 114–15

Smythe, Dallas, 20

social capital: Bourdieu's field theory and, 31–40; development of, 100–101; group production and, 31; maintenance of, 36–40; of performers, 127–28; for women composers, 171–76

social hierarchies: creative freedom and, 76–78; Bourdieu's field theory and, 30; music production and, 4, 14; social capital and, 32–33

social relations of production, 119–20

Social Network, The (film), 111–12

Society of Composers and Lyricists (SCL), 206

Soderbergh, Steven, 56–58

Solie, Ruth, 53

Sony Computer Entertainment America, 102

Sorkin, Aaron, 111

Spielberg, Steven, 81

spotting sessions, 94–95

Stahl, Matt, 86

Staiger, Janet, 20

standardization: cultural production and, 20; mixer's role in, 133–34

Star Wars (film series), 107

state, capitalism and influence of, 10–11

stems (groups of audio tracks), 131–34

stems, creative freedom and use of, 74–76

Stephen J. Cannell Productions, 197

Stern, Michael, 33, 160, 167, 188–89, 200

Stevens, Jan, 215; on authority and collaboration, 151, 154; on gaming music production, 92–93; on perseverance, 35; on prestige and credits, 42; on production process, 95; on time management and work-life balance, 159–60

Stranger Things (Netflix series), 110

Strauss, Richard, 80

streaming services: future uncertainty of, 213; hiring for composers and, 91–94; impact on

composers of, 114–15; pay for composers in, 204–8; symbolic capital and impact of, 44–45

striping, by recording engineers, 130

Struggle behind the Soundtrack, The (Eicke), 9

suites of music, video game production, 103–5

supply chain: collective labor and, 27–29; composers' position in, 83–84; digital technology in music production and, 15–16; forms of capital and hierarchy of, 31; group production and, 23–29; labor processes in, 87–88; managerialization of music production and, 201–2; mixer and, 131–34; music production and, 3–7, 14, 16, 214–15; music workers in, 119–21; orchestrators' role in, 121–23; of production and labor processes, 94–95; recording engineers and, 129–31; use-value production and, 86–88; value work and, 55–56; work-life balance and, 161–66

sweetening, by recording engineers, 130–31

symbolic capital, 41–46

synthesized mockups, composers' use of, 95

Tasso, Torquato, 51–52

Taylorism, cultural production and, 21

team productions: in capitalist cultural businesses, 96–101; by composers, 82–84; by orchestrators, 122

teamwork, composers' use of, 64–65

television production: abstract labor in, 20–23; authority issues in, 141–43; bureaucratization and managerialism in, 139–48; communication issues during, 148–55; creative freedom in, 78; creative function and group production in, 57–59; digital technology and music changes in, 190–92; evolution of, 8; future uncertainty of, 213; group production in, 138–39; hiring for composers on, 91–94; live musicians for, 94–95; multi- and single-camera work in, 114–15; nichification of music in, 105; overproduction of composers in, 115–18; package deal pay for composers in, 195–96; pay for composers in, 194–95, 202–4; pop and rock music in, 107–13; popular music imports in, 105–7; prestige hierarchies in, 70; supply chains in, 83–84; time constraints on composers in, 68–69, 184–85; urban scoring style for music in, 113–14. *See also* cable television; episodic television, impact on music production of

temp music, film and television use of, 61–62, 93–94